THE MANAGEMENT OF ETHNIC SECESSIONIST CONFLICT

To my family

The Management of Ethnic Secessionist Conflict

The Big Neighbour Syndrome

ABEYSINGHE M. NAVARATNA-BANDARA

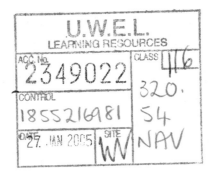
Dartmouth

Aldershot • Brookfield USA • Singapore • Sydney

Published by
Dartmouth Publishing Company Limited
Gower House
Croft Road
Aldershot
Hants GU11 3HR
England

Dartmouth Publishing Company
Old Post Road
Brookfield
Vermont 05036
USA

British Library Cataloguing in Publication Data
Navaratna-Bandara, Abeysinghe M.
    Management of Ethnic Secessionist
    Conflict:Big Neighbour Syndrome
    I. Title
    320.54

Library of Congress Cataloging-in-Publication Data
Navaratna-Bandara, Abeysinghe M., 1949–
    The management of ethnic secessionist conflict : the big neighbour
    syndrome / Abeysinghe M. Navaratna-Bandara.
        p.   cm.
    Includes bibliographical references and index.
    ISBN 1-85521-698-1 (HB)
    1. Ethnic groups–Political activity. 2. Minorities–Political
    activity. 3. Decentralization in government. 4. Self-
    determination, National. 5. Secession. I. Title.
    JF1061.N39   1995
    320.1'5–dc20   95-22888
                                                                    CIP

ISBN 1 85521 698 1

Printed and bound in Great Britain by Ipswich Book Co. Ltd., Ipswich, Suffolk

Contents

Abbreviations

ADF	Arab Deterrent Force
AIADMK	All India Anna Dravida Munnetra Kazhagam
BCL	Bougainville Copper Limited
BRA	Bougainville Revolutionary Army
DDC	District Development Councils
DMK	Dravida Munnetra Kazhagam
EOKA	Ethnike Organosis Kyprion Agouistion
EPRLF	Eelam People's Revolutionary Liberation Front
EROS	Eelam Revolutionary Organization of Students
ETA	Euzkadi Ta Askatasuna
JVP	Janatha Vimukthi Peramuna
IPKF	Indian Peace Keeping Force
LTTE	Liberation Tigers of Tamil Eelam
MNLF	Moro National Liberation Front
MNF	Mizo National Front
MST	Multinational Supervisory Team
OIC	Organization of Islamic Conference
PLOTE	People's Liberation Organization of Tamil Eelam
PNGDF	Papua New Guinea Defence Force
SAARC	South Asian Association for Regional Co-operation
SPLA	Sudanese People's Liberation Army
TMT	Turk Mukavemet Teskilati
TRNC	Turkish Republic of Northern Cyprus
TULF	Tamil United Liberation Front
UNP	United National Party

Preface

The book is a revised version of a doctoral thesis submitted to the University of York in 1992. It is a comparative survey of the role of a Big Neighbour state on the management of an ethnic secessionist conflict in several small states around the globe.

By integrating three concepts, namely, 'ethnic secessionism', 'devolution' and 'Big Neighbour', the study develops a model of the conditions under which devolution of government may be the preferred settlement of an ethnic secessionist conflict in a modern state subject to the influence of a larger neighbouring state - the Big Neighbour.

The analytic model is applied to five Big Neighbour situations around the world, namely India/East Pakistan, Turkey/Cyprus, Australia/Papua New Guinea, India/Sri Lanka, and Syria/Lebanon.

The actuators of Big Neighbour involvement are grouped into 'ethnic' and 'strategic' dimensions. The case studies show that although ethnic ties have political importance, the involvement of a Big Neighbour in the secessionist conflict is inevitable once the situation endangers its strategic interests.

The conditions under which 'devolution' or 'powersharing' rather than 'repression', 'secession', or 'annexation' becomes the preferred policy option of the Big Neighbour in the secessionist situation form the second element of the model.

The investigation shows that containment of the secessionist conflict through a devolutionary or other power-sharing settlement is normally preferred, because to maintain the territorial integrity of the secession-affected state is the least risky option for the Big Neighbour's own national interests.

The model identifies four roles that the Big Neighbour can adopt in its efforts to obtain a devolutionary settlement, namely, the 'pressure role', the 'big-stick role', the 'interventionist role', and the 'invitational role'; and also incorporates the roles of other external actors - other regional powers, the Great Powers, intergovernmental organizations, and non-governmental organizations. It was found that the vigorous involvement of a Big Neighbour state, playing one or more of these roles, can stabilize the conflict's external system and contain the conflicting parties in their internal environment, eventually to accept devolution or power-sharing as compromise settlement.

At the University of York I was fortunate in having Professor Andrew Dunsire as my supervisor. I have profited immeasurably from his generosity, and his many ideas and suggestions. I am greatly indebted to him for the knowledge and training I have acquired through this research.

Dr. Adrian Leftwich and Dr. Neil Carter served as members of my thesis committee. I appreciate their generosity in providing valuable advice and comments.

I am grateful to the Commonwealth Scholarship Commission in the United Kingdom for offering me a Commonwealth Academic Award for 1988-1991. This provided the necessary financial support for this study.

I owe special thanks to Professor Wiswa Warnapala, Professor Y. R. Amarasinghe, Professor R. A. L. H. Gunawardane, Sumanasiri Liynage and K. Selvaratnam (all of the University of Peradeniya, Sri Lanka) for their valuable advice and encouragement in the pursuit of this study and its publication. I must thank Amitha Bandara Andagala of the Computer Unit of the Faculty of Arts, University of Peradeniya, for his competent assistance in preparing the camera-ready-copy of the book.

I should like to thank Amanda Richardson and Ann Newell of Dartmouth for their competent editorial support and prompt attention to queries.

Last but not least, my wife Udula and children Mihithika, Arjuna and Anuja deserve special thanks for their patience and forbearance.

A.M. Navaratna-Bandara
Department of Political Science
University of Peradeniya
Peradeniya
Sri Lanka

1 The Conceptual Universe of the Study

Introduction

No political society is immune from social conflict. Sometimes social conflicts are related to the inherent ethnic composition of the human society in which the existing political authority finds its legitimacy. Such conflicts if not resolved or regulated in time, are capable of leading to protracted socio-political crises. At an early stage a few of them could be resolved by suppression. A majority of them cannot ever be resolved completely. Only containment, management or moderation can be expected (cf. Kabir 1985:88).

This study is about the regulation or management of crises oriented towards one such type of contemporary conflict; *ethnic secessionist conflicts in modern states*. We shall not attempt an overall coverage of the management of ethnic secessionist conflicts but aim to extend existing knowledge of one particular method of ethnic conflict management; *the devolution of government*.

No society, however, is politically an island. All countries have neighbours, and inhabit a network of international relations. Internal conflicts can spill over frontiers, and nearly always have an external dimension. The study focuses on this external dimension, and in particular, on the situation where a Big Neighbour may find it necessary to take a hand.

Before elaborating the details of the objectives, the scope, the methodology, the research problem and the working hypotheses of the study, we shall first clarify the conceptual background of these two key elements, 'ethnic secessionism' and 'devolution'.

'Ethnic' refers in this study to the links among a community of people who share one or more characteristics among the following; a common language, religion, culture or heritage, a common race or colour and a common historical origin or existence. These characteristics distinguish such a community from others, particularly within their shared political and physical environment.

According to Walker Connor 'the predominant modern states are multiethnic' (Connor 1972:320). In 1971 by analysing the ethnic composition of a total of 132 contemporary states he concluded that only 12 modern states can be considered free of ethnic conflict and in 53 states (40.2 percent) the population is divided into more than five significant groups (Connor 1972:320).

Today ethnicity by its own characteristics represents a powerful source of conflict in the modern state, which can sometimes outweigh the significance of other conventionally emphasized social conflicts, such as class and elite conflict. It has provided a sense of identity to minority and regional ethnic groups encouraging them to resist the processes of subordination, enforced by the larger political authority, the 'nation state' or the dominant ethnic group. An aspect of today's ethnic upheaval is the role played by these conflicts themselves in shaping ethnic identities and generating ethnic consensus among minority ethnic groups.

This 'ethnic nationalism' (Smith 1971:186-7, 215-27, also see Yun 1990) has displaced the conceptual foundation of the modern state, the 'nation state' concept; and has broadened conventional knowledge of the phenomenon of nationalism. Of diverse social conflicts which have been created by ethnic nationalism in our time, the most formidable one is 'ethnic secessionism', the object of our study.

Ethnic Secessionism

Secession' by its lexicographic meaning implies '…an action of seceding or fawmal withdrawing from an alliance, a federation, a political or religious organization' (*Shorter Oxford Dictionary*, Vol.2,1959:1825).

By ethnic secessionism we mean the seeking by an ethno-regional movement (cf. Esman 1985:439) with its own territorial homeland of formal withdrawal from a sovereign state to form its own nation state or to join with another already established state (cf. Seton-Watson 1975:1). This entails a few more qualifications.

Firstly, an ethnic secessionist movement is one declaring an exclusive homeland right to territory belonging to an existing state of which its people are members. Thus it is a movement which generates ethnic consensus in its community along geographical lines, on a territorial basis (cf. Knight 1982:523-4).

Secondly, as a geoethnic movement it further identifies a common historical habitation of their community in this homeland. In this meaning it is a movement seeking the revival of a political society which existed in their historical past or is imagined at present to have existed in the past (cf. Anderson 1987:15-16).

Thirdly, such an ethno-regional movement represents an inbuilt resistance to 'national integration', or to 'nation building', as envisaged by the existing state. Thus it is an agent of disintegration and a potential threat to the 'territorial integrity' of such states.

Fourthly, such movements can be associated with the 'classical goal of national self-determination' (Smith 1981:16). It is not now 'national' but 'ethnic' self-determination (Buchheit 1978:228) that is in focus - if there is, indeed, a difference.

Fifthly, such a movement is confined to non-colonial situations (Nanda 1972:321-2). Ethnic secessionism arises within or is aimed at, the territory of an independent state. It is not a term applicable to colonial situations or to internationally-not-accepted annexations (Heraclides 1985:3).

Sixthly, such an ethnic movement is not necessarily directed against another ethnic community but at the state (cf. Esman 1985:439). Its ideology and its goals are aimed at the dismemberment of an already existing state, and only incidentally at any ethnic group dominant in such state. An ethnic nation which is a '...possible self standing ...candidate for nationhood...' (Geertz 1963:111) exists behind the whole enterprise.

Ethnic secessionism is a movement representing the extreme form of modern ethnic nationalism; associated with the sense of ethnic national aspiration, the consciousness of distinct historical origin, a protest of regional ethnic groups against (actual or perceived) discrimination and subordination, and having the supreme goal of national self-determination.

The distinction between 'separatism' and 'secessionism'

Though secession is an old phenomenon (Seton-Watson 1975:1) and experiences of ethnic secessionism are numerous and world-wide, theoretical discussions on the subject have still not settled on the terms which they will employ.

There is a flow of individual case studies and a range of mini-theories on various aspects of ethnic conflict and especially on ethno-regional movements. The majority of scholars associated with studies of ethno-regional movements have tended to employ 'separatism' as a general term. It has been used to denote all types of ethnic homeland movement as well as secessionism, sometimes with the qualifier 'outright' to the latter. Hugh Seton-Watson (1975), W. Morris-Jones (1975), Cynthia L. Enloe (1975), Hugh Tinker (1975), Ruth McVeey (1975), Richard Simon (1975), Joane Nagel (1980), Donald L. Horowitz (1981), Anthony D. Smith (1981), Milton J. Esman (1985), David Brown (1988) are prominent among scholars who prefer 'separatism'.

But as stated by John R. Wood '... political separation and especially separatism are the more vague and encompassing terms covering all instances of political alienation...' (Wood 1981:110). Separatism implies movements of **separateness** within a broader political or social system. Ethnic movements for **autonomy and** self-rule are clear examples of such separatist movements. But for secessionist movements its applicability is confusing. The goal of the secessionists is to sever ties to the existing state system. Thus secessionism is associated with disintegration, while separatist autonomy movements seek the continuation of their association with the total system albeit with regional, political and cultural separateness. This is, as explained by Myron Weiner, 'unity in diversity'; a strategy to achieve national integration in a multiethnic society (Weiner 1965:56). Thus the demand for separatist autonomy is not a vital problem to existing multiethnic societies except where the dominant ethnic groups and their leaders may tend to categorize autonomists as secessionists to justify their denial of the demand for power sharing, denouncing it as a mere prelude to secession.

Peter Lyon, maybe the first to recognize such confusion of meanings, has suggested,

> separatism; meaning a movement seeking to resist further incorporation, subordination within the larger political authority of which it is already a member, and secession, meaning a movement seeking to break away decisively from the existing principal political authority (Lyon 1975:69).

Modern 'ethno-regional movements' (Hechter & Levi 1979:260) are usually distinguished by being associated with one or more of three political goals. First the aim of a homeland movement may be to regain their lost homeland territory which is presently held by another state. As defined by Anthony D. Smith, this is 'irredentism' (Smith 1981:17). Irredentism is associated not only with ethnic nationalism but sometimes with 'official nationalism' (cf. Anderson 1987:80-103) as in the case of the Republic of Ireland's claim for Northern Ireland and Somalia's claims for the North Eastern Frontier District of Kenya and the Ogaden area in Ethiopia. The Kurdish homeland movement in Iraq, Iran and Turkey is a classic example of an ethnic movement which is potent in producing irredentism because of the distribution of its people over several states; Iraq, Turkey, Iran and Syria.

The second type of goal is associated with autonomy or home rule demands. This is 'autonomism' (Smith 1981:17). The goal of these homeland movements is to obtain greater or complete control over their homeland for matters relating to economic, political and cultural affairs, but remaining within the national boundary of the present state. In many cases these movements aim at constitutional reforms and governmental restructuring to establish regional autonomy.

The third type of goal is where ethno-regional movements aim at complete breakaway of their homeland from an existing state to establish a new state. This is secessionism. These groups describe themselves as distinct nations, capable of assuming sovereignty over their homeland. This is not seeking an internal separateness but a complete withdrawal from the state.

Despite the different approach of some scholars like Peter Lyon and John R. Wood, 'separatism' as a concept has been used to cover ethnic movements of all three types. From one point of view, as noted by Donald Horowitz, since the change of political objective by an ethno-regional movement, from autonomism to secessionism and vice versa, remains a possibility (see Horowitz 1981:168-9), such a usage is perhaps justifiable. But it is confusing when one wants to make a distinction between autonomism and secessionism.

For the general purposes of this study, there is a strong case for accepting the distinction between 'autonomism' and 'secessionism', and avoiding using 'separatism' at all. Our study treats 'devolution' as a method of managing ethnic secessionist conflict. In discussing that term the conceptual distinction between irredentism and autonomism is employed but the term separatism is not used.

The confusing and ambiguous nature of the very terms that have been employed in discussions on the subject highlights an existing gap in the field, which is the lack of studies linking 'devolution' and 'secession', considering 'devolution' as a method of secessionist conflict management.

Theoretical discussions of the development of ethnic secessionism

The literature which can be used to understand the development of ethnic secessionism is large and extensive. In the wake of the emergence of varying types of ethno-regional movements in modern states some scholars have made an attempt to categorize the theoretical perspectives which have been employed in the literature on ethno-regional movements (for example see Brown 1988:51-5). Following these discussions we have discerned the following broad perspectives which have been employed in that literature to analyse the root causes of the development of ethno-regional tendencies in modern states.

(a) The first theoretical perspective is found in the studies which have followed some of the basic premises of Marxism or focused on the impact of socio-economic and power disparities as a key to understanding the root causes of ethnic nationalism. Michael Hechter's 'internal colonialism' (1975), Tom Nairn's 'uneven development theory' (1977) and Anthony Mughan's 'regional relative deprivation' (1979) are among the significant examples of this theoretical perspective.

(b) Secondly, there is a theoretical perspective which identifies ethnic groups by reference to their culture and history in a particular homeland territory, and considers elite interests and conflicts for political and economic power as the basic foundations for the emergence of ethno-regional movements in these ethnic groups. The writings of Ernest Gellner (1964 & 1973) and Anthony D. Smith (1979,1981 & 1982) are associated with this broad theoretical perspective.

(c) A third group of studies have followed the basic perceptions of the theory of 'plural society' presented by J. S. Furnival (1948) and later modified by Leo Kuper and M. G. Smith (1969). David R. Smock and Audrey C. Smock (1975), Crawford Young (1976) and David Brown (1988) can be recognized as prominent examples. These scholars have maintained the argument that ethnically plural societies in Asia and Africa are inherently fragile as their post-independence mono-ethnic state machines are no longer capable of uniting culturally discrete groups in the society.

(d) Fourthly, there is the theoretical perspective of scholars known as the 'New Ethnicists' (Birch 1978:331), who '...drew attention to the strength and endurance of ethnic and cultural loyalties' (Birch 1978:331) in analysing the background factors which paved the way for the emergence of ethnic nationalism. Walker Connor, Cynthia Enloe, Daniel Moynihan, Nathan Glazer, Wendell Bell, Anthony C. Birch, Robert Melson and Howard Wolpe are among the scholars who have contributed to the development of the 'New Ethnicist' school.

(e) Lastly, there is a school of thought which, instead of seeking one explanation, lists all possible conducive circumstances and preconditions in understanding the development of ethnic nationalism. This line of analysis can be found in the writings of Arline McCord & William McCord (1977), Raymond L. Hall (1977) and John R. Wood (1981).

The following is a brief survey of the theoretical discussions which have been identified as examples of our categorization.

Marxism and the theories of power disparities

Original Marxist theory provides little help in understanding the development of ethnic secessionism. Except for its consideration of anti-colonial type nationalism, original Marxist theory has paid little attention to ethnically-inspired nationalist movements which are basically cultural. This is mainly due to its predominant assumptions about class interests and the form of economic organization as determining factors of social, economic and political change (Davis 1978:3). Marxist writers as a tradition in both West and East have treated nationalism of any sort as an outcome of class conflict because of their strict adherence to the distinction made by Lenin between '...the nationalism of an oppressor nation and that of an oppressed one' (Richmond 1987:8). For Marxist writers in the former Soviet Union 'national' or 'ethnic' identities are spontaneous developments in human history but 'nationalism' is not. It is a doctrine generated by the dominant class in the nationalist movement, which decides its direction. Thus it is only evident in class-based societies and is an obstacle to social progress. Accordingly they paid much attention to examining the social, economic and power disparities associated with mass mobilization into a particular national movement, and to probing the class basis of the nationalist leadership (for example see Rudenco et al. 1975). This approach has also appeared in the writings of Soviet social scientists who have examined the ethnic phenomenon from the anthropological point of view in recent years. They have devised two related but distinct categories of the evolution of ethnic consciousness; 'the socio-economic and the specifically ethnic' (Bromley & Kozlov 1989:433), and argue that 'under socialism interethnic integration increases as the result of strengthening economic and cultural bonds and the lack of national and class antagonisms' (Bromely & Kozlov 1989:435).

In the 1970s some scholars have tried to use some of the original Marxist arguments to analyse the emergence of ethno-regional movements in the West. Michael Hechter's 'internal colonialism' is the most significant example of recent theories of ethnic conflict derived from Marxist thought. Extending the original arguments presented by Lenin and Gramsci (Hechter 1975:8-9), he suggests the 'core-periphery' relationship of cultural groups in nation states as a paramount influence in shaping ethnic conflict. This is a new application to internal situations of the classical model of colonial exploitation. Hechter argues that centre-periphery manipulations results in structural convergence, which gives a dominant political position to the core ethnic group and an avenue for material exploitation of peripheral ethnic communities, leading to the creation of relatively advanced and less advanced groups. For Hechter this hierarchical arrangement creates a cultural division of labour: economic exploitation by the core of the periphery promotes reactive group responses which eventually give rise to ethno-regional movements associated with autonomism and secessionism (Hechter 1975:8-11,30,265; Hechter & Levy 1979:261).

Tom Nairn has employed the 'uneven development' thesis to explain the recent wave of ethnic nationalism in the West. He recognizes the uneven expansion of industrialization associated with imperialism as an instrument which has created qualitatively different functions for ethnic groups. This uneven economic growth and social differentiation has been adduced as the main basis of nationalism, and the intelligentsia as its leading spokesmen (Nairn 1977:96-8,101,127-8).

Anthony Mughan has made an attempt to develop a theory of ethnic conflict on the basis of power disparities in modern societies using the 'relative deprivation' hypothesis which was first presented by Ted Gurr in his *Why Men Rebel* (Gurr 1970). The original arguments of relative deprivation describe group violence as a reaction to the discrepancy between people's value expectations and their actual achievements. (Gurr 1970:13,24; Mughan 1979:281). The theory recognizes the diverse patterns of modernization as the basic root of group inequalities which have generated politicized conflicts (Mughan 1979:281-2). Mughan in an extension of the theory to ethnic conflicts, identifies two different kinds of power resources; *de jure* and *de facto*. By *de jure* power resources he means democratic political rights like the right to vote. Education, position and wealth are considered as *de facto* power resources. According to this analysis modernization has created an imbalance in the allocation of these power resources in modern nation states, and the consequent gap has led to ethnic group responses associated with political conflict (Mughan 1979:283-304).

Theories on culture, history and elite interest

Ernest Gellner also recognizes the emergence of a modern intelligentsia as a significant turning point in the development of nationalism and the emergence of ethnic secessionism. According to his presentation, one important difference between modern societies and simple societies is the position achieved by the 'culture' over the 'structure' of the society (the two anthropological distinctions in any society). As Gellner argues it, in the process of industrialization and modernization, 'culture' replaces 'structure', rather than reinforcing it as happens in simple societies. In this new atmosphere the resources of an educational system became an essential requirement in the making of citizens of the society, as well as the precondition of the defence of its economy. Thus language becomes the medium of operation of the educational system, and essential for the organization of government in the new industrial society. The social outcome of this process is the creation of an intelligentsia and an industrial proletariat, the prerequisites of an effective national movement (Gellner 1964:149-62).

However, in a society comprising a multiplicity of languages and a certain diffusion of power between the centre and a multiplicity of local semi-autonomous authorities, only one language, probably the language of the old heartland, could become the medium of education and of the organization of government. The creation of such a privileged language generates frustration among the regional intelligentsia who possess different languages and cultures. Apart from the fact that the nation represented by this language is not their own, it requires them to change not only their language but also their cultural traits, which is the most intractable part of the process. Sometimes, entry into the dominant nation (as defined by the language in the cultural sense) becomes almost an impossibility. As industrialization and modernization progresses unevenly in the various parts of the world, the 'uneven diffusion' of modernization and industrialization makes a greater impact upon these intelligentsia (Gellner 1964:162-6). Its uneven wave generates a sharp social stratification which, as Gellner puts it,

> ...unlike the stratification of past societies is (a) unhallowed by custom and which has little to cause it to be accepted as in the nature of things, which (b) is not well protected by various social mechanisms, but on the contrary exists in a situation providing maximum opportunities and incentives for revolution, and which (c) is remediable, and is seen to be remediable by national secession (Gellner 1964:166).

In this way '...nationalism does become a natural phenomenon...'(Gellner 1964:166). The backward regions or populations, led by the intelligentsia, will be influenced to accept secession as the ultimate political goal (Gellner 1964:168-71).

Accepting with slight modifications many of the arguments presented by Gellner on the importance of culture in modern societies and the role played by the intelligentsia, Anthony D. Smith proposes the rise of a scientific and centralized bureaucracy and of a secular intelligentsia on the basis of modern education as the first stage in the development of ethnic nationalism (Smith 1979:28-35). For Smith, educated professionals who have found themselves unable to win a place in the metropolitan culture, especially in the central bureaucracy, are the leading elements in reviving regional ethnic nationalism. Those professionals after failing in their efforts to assimilate tend to turn to their own ethnic culture and history. This is the second stage, according to Smith: the emergence of ethnic nationalism. The outcome of external economic conditions and internal restrictions, as well as the negative policy approaches of governments to ethnic demands, transforms it to its third stage, the politicization of their demands, i.e. autonomism or secessionism (Smith 1979:34-5).

The new ethnicists school

A considerable number of scholars who have examined modern ethnic conflicts assume ethnic characteristics such as race, language, religion and culture to be relatively stable and independently persistent despite changes in economic and political spheres. According to their argument, current ethnic conflicts emerge from this permanently-differentiated social group background (see Heraclides 1985:26-7). These scholars known as 'new ethnicists' (Birch 1978:331) have mainly directed their efforts to the displacing of earlier theories on nation building. The nation building theorists expected that '...modernization in the form of increases in urbanization, industrialization, schooling, communication and transportation facilities etc., would lead to assimilation...' (Connor 1972:322) and so to the completion of nation building. In contrast the new ethnicists found modernization to be a key process in disintegration. For them urbanization, industrialization, schooling, communication, all accelerate ethnic segregation and lead to conflict (Connor 1972:322).

According to the 'new ethnicists' the modernization process removes the social isolation of regional ethnic groups and increases the cultural self-awareness of minorities, by highlighting factors distinguishing their own members from other groups within the larger political society. Walker Connor, one prominent scholar in the 'new ethnicists' school, commented upon the impact of modernization:

> In yet another way, modernization and more effective communications have acted as catalysts for ethnonationally inspired demands. As formal education and globe-girdling communications have spread, the likelihood of people becoming cognizant of historic and contemporary self-determination movements has also spread (Connor 1977:29).

The 'plural society' theorists

The theory of plural society, first introduced by J. S. Furnival and later modified by M. G. Smith and Leo Kuper, presents a social and political framework with which to understand the inevitability of deep ethnic cleavages in multiethnic societies. Plural society has been defined as a (political) society which contains deeply divided, separate cultural communities whose mutual contacts are limited only to economic activities. The other main characteristics of this ideal type of plural society are a cultural division of labour and the absence of common will to a political unity. In the absence of 'common social will' it is the force of the state which binds society together (Furnival 1948:304-12; Smith 1969:33,35-6; Leo Kuper 1969:7,10-16).

Thus the political super-structure in a multiethnic society is an inherent outcome of its pluralistic infrastructure. And its main characteristics, the dominance of the one cultural section in socio-economic and political affairs, and the absence of 'common social will', ensure ethnic resentments in these societies.

Scholars who used the basic propositions of the theory of plural society to examine the politics of cultural pluralism in Asian and African new states (like David R. Smock, Audrey C. Smock, Crawford Young) cited political factors such as the centralization of state power, monoethnic domination in politics and government, the central state's penetration into ethnic homelands and so on, as among the causes for current ethnic resentment in these new states, and also to explain the development of ethno-regional movements.

Discussing the politics of cultural pluralism in two new states (Ghana and Lebanon) David and Audrey Smock (1975) have cited modernization coupled with limited industrialization as a process which 'pierces the shell' of communal separateness in traditional societies and '...sets the stage for communal competition by endowing societies with new opportunities and resources.' (Smock & Smock 1975:4). But they have directed much attention to ascribing the politicization of ethnic conflicts in plural societies to political reasons. The distribution of economic and political positions after independence, the attempts made by governments to establish effective control over their territory, and the increasing centralization of political power are pin-pointed as political causes fostering communal conflicts. On centralization of political power they noted,

> ...the centralization of political power has so advanced, that the citizen feels almost naked before the anonymous and distant government and craves some form of identity in which to clothe himself to impart meaning to his existence (Smock & Smock 1975:5).

David Brown has drawn on a theoretical perspective using a state dominated by one ethnic group in the society (as the key to ethnic secessionist conflict) to describe the development pattern of ethnic secessionism in three South-east Asian states: Burma, Thailand and the Philippines. For Brown the ethnic character of the state (that is, essentially a mono-ethnic domination) ensured state penetration of peripheral areas, with disruptive effects on communal authority structures:

...such disruption of communal authority structures precipitated the de-stabilization of the communities and thus promoted both crises of communal instability and identity at the mass level and a crisis of legitimacy at the elite level (Brown 1988:54).

Then the elite groups in these peripheral communities would try to resolve the crisis by generating ethno-nationalist movements and mobilizing confrontation against the state. This provided a new basis for ethnic unity and identity, legitimating the rise of secessionism (Brown 1988:54-5).

Studies which stress the complexity of conditions

Raymond L. Hall in his *Ethnic Autonomy* (Hall 1979) presents various microvariables to analyse the root causes of ethno-regional tendencies in modern states. He introduces culture, economy, ethnicity, geography, history, patterns of domination and religion as micro variables to explain group differences which provide the basic foundation for the development of ethno-regional movements (Hall 1979:xxv-xxx).

Arline and William McCord (McCord & McCord 1979) examine both subjective and objective variables which can be used to understand the emergence of ethno-regional movements. History and assumptions on future achievements are subjective variables and differential access to power, language, religion, economic divisions, culture and geography are objective variables. Their assertion is that autonomist and secessionist movements would seem to emerge when one or a combination of the above variables characterize a particular situation (McCord & McCord 1979:426-36).

Presenting a systematic programme to search for a theory of secession, John R. Wood discusses the political, geographical, economic, social and psychological preconditions which may precipitate the rise of secessionism in modern states. His programme of analysis includes not only the preconditions of secession but also some considerations on the response of central government and the resolution of secessionist crises by armed conflicts. Amongst the preconditions of secession he discusses the psychological conditions such as ethnic nationalism, xenophobia, and territorial imperatives (Wood 1981:120).

The foregoing theoretical survey leads to at least one general conclusion; there is no one general theory on the development of ethnic nationalism in modern states. Instead we have different theoretical perceptions, often overlapping with each other, but covering a wide range of background factors. Thus they highlight the argument presented by our last theoretical perspective; that the root causes of ethnic nationalism cannot be explained by a mono-causal theory: many different preconditions and conducive circumstances may result in the emergence of secessionist tendencies.

The impact of ethnic secessionism

The emergence of ethnic secessionism has had an enormous impact on the modern state. Its very legitimacy in governing its territory and society, and in representing a national personality on the international stage, has been challenged. Its conceptual foundation, the idea of the 'nation-state', is impugned, creating even greater challenge to the present inter-state system, most of whose legal principles are based on the very same conception. Ethnic secessionism has entered practical politics, de-stabilising both domestic and international politics; arousing animosities between different ethnic groups in the internal society on the one hand, and providing a source of conflict for inter-state rivalries on the other. In the next two sub-sections we will investigate these practical and conceptual implications of ethnic secessionism in more detail.

Practical implications

Ethnic secessionism is frequently seen as an imminent danger to an existing state which happens to have different ethnic groups in its society, some of them with claims to their own ethnic homelands within its territory. In this regard its practical implications are varied and complex. For analytical convenience we will divide our discussion on practical implications into two parts; the internal and external dimensions.

The internal dimension

Ethnic secessionism in its maximal objective is directed at the state, though indirectly challenging the dominant ethnic group's tight grip on political and economic power, together with its cultural dominance in the state. The supreme objective of ethnic secessionism, the establishment of a new state, injures the territory of the existing state. The territorial claim for an ethnic homeland incites the members of that ethnic community to withdraw their allegiance from the state, with disastrous effect upon the 'social will' which according to the theory of plural society is an essential condition for the functioning of a state. The presence of a secessionist conflict, in any multiethnic society, implies that the 'social will' of one ethnic group is drifting towards an imagined nation-hood. This reflects the very features of social plurality but in this regard secessionism is the force which unveils the inherent fragility of the plural state. The state comes to be considered as alien rule or as an illegitimate political domination, which needs to be removed by a national liberation struggle.

As noted by Clifford Geertz

...economic or class or intellectual disaffection threatens revolution but disaffection based on race, language or culture, threatens partition, irredentism or merger, redrawing of the very limits of the state, new definition of its domain (Geertz 1963:111).

Revolution and the introduction of a new state are the two highest modes of political change. Each has its own parameters of time and scale for its successes. Political revolution uproots the existing social economic and political order and changes the social basis of the dominant interests in the state. But it is not necessarily a challenge to the territorial integrity and legitimacy of the state as such. In contrast ethnic secessionism in seeking the division or breakup of the state, challenges both.

This doesn't mean that ethnic secessionism is always entirely distinct from revolution, or not at all associated in practice with revolutionary activity. There may be ethnic secessionist movements, like the Tigray People's Liberation Front (TPLF) in Ethiopia, which aim at both revolution and state formation (see Africa Confidential, 15 December 1989:5). Ethnic minorities are quite frequently associated with class divisions or the division of labour (cf. Enloe 1973:28-9) in society; in which case ethnic movements may join ethnic attachments with class sentiments to achieve their objectives. In this regard the practical implications of secessionism are far reaching and somewhat difficult to cope with.

Ethnic identities, such as language, race, region, culture and religion (the 'primordial attachments' of the people in Clifford Geertz's terms, see Geertz 1963:110, 112-14) are also capable of crossing social class boundaries to unify ethnic communities as *de facto* nations. In this regard ethnic secessionism in its aspirations to new nation-statehood, seems to be the revival of that 19th century nationalism which gave birth to so many of the existing 'nation states'. Today it is not the 'multiethnic empires' of the Russian or Ottoman emperors but the succeeding 'multiethnic nation states' which are required to cope with this phenomenon. Ethnic secessionism has raised the same old banners that were used by the 19th century nationalisms. It is an historical irony for the present nations that they should have to fight against their own slogans: 'nations' rights to self-determination', 'popular sovereignty', 'national liberation' and so on - in the new era of ethnic nationalism. The practical implications of this deep rooted development cannot all be predicted at the moment but one cannot easily be ruled out: that is, the disintegration of the existing intrastate and inter-state systems.

For a successful secession, according to Zalmay Khalilzad, at least one of the following conditions would have to appear: either (a) a total breakdown of the centre accompanied by substantial nationalistic and anti-centre activities in the minority areas; or (b) a commitment by a superior external power on behalf of the ethnic 'separatist' groups without countervailing response on the part of other major powers in support of the centre (Khalilzad 1983:63).

To achieve these preconditions secessionist movements may be tempted to use all-out' methods in their attempt to disrupt central control. When violence becomes the principal medium of a secessionist campaign, a gradual breakdown of social life is inevitable.

Compared with other ethnic movements, secessionism seems to swing more easily from agitational politics to armed violence once the ethnic group is sufficiently aggrieved by persistent discrimination and by the hostile activities of the centre. Any confrontation with an armed movement within its internal boundaries is a heavy burden for the state, a costly exercise which consumes much-needed human and material resources. A determined secessionist campaign may lead to a lengthy social and political crisis at all levels of society. Militarization of political and social life may become unavoidable. As a result government will become ever more authoritarian and repressive. And the secessionist movements may *intend* just that.

Further secessionist violence and counter operations by the central forces may develop into an unqualified war situation in which centre-periphery relations are impaired beyond recognition. Under the existing political conditions in the modern state, as John R. Wood puts it, direct armed confrontation in a set-piece battle between centre and secessionist forces is unlikely; '...guerrilla warfare is more common' (Wood 1981:130). These guerrilla operations and countervailing actions by secessionists and central forces may then beget atrocities such as genocide and lead to severe refugee problems. These are only some of the practical effects of a secessionist campaign on the internal society.

The external dimension

Up until the present decade, it could be said with confidence that the post-1945 system of international relations was basically a 'conservative order' (Heraclides 1990:351) unfavourable to unilateral secession. In any conflict with ethnic secessionism the interstate network would be found cautiously behind the centralized national state (Heraclides 1985:v).

The United Nations' negative approach to 'unilateral secession' was well established and well documented (see Nanda 1972; Buchheit 1978). As Van den Berghe puts it:

> the UN is, first and foremost an organization of states, not of nations, and since most states are, in fact, threatened by the claims of nations, it is little wonder that the UN is pro-state and anti-nation (as quoted in Ryan 1990:26).

Commenting on this particular issue, U Thant, former Secretary General of the organization, once stated that the United Nations '...has never accepted and does not accept and I don't believe it will ever accept the principle of secession of a part of its member state' (as quoted in Nanda 1972:327). The very recent cataclysms in the Balkans and in the territory of the former Soviet Union have perhaps belied U

Thant's belief - but even now, the reluctance of the international community to move to recognition of secessionist communities except under strong political pressure shows the strength of the legal principle. It can certainly be argued that international customary law is still interested more in preserving the territorial integrity of states than in recognising their break-up. The prevailing international legal framework centres on the principle of 'national sovereignty'; and existing principles of 'national self-determination', 'territorial integrity', and 'non-interference' are all protective of present states (cf. Heraclides 1985:v). The principle of 'national self-determination' was developed to deal with liberation struggles in colonial situations (see Nixon 1972:492-7; Nanda 1972:321-8; Bhalla 1991:91-2). Perhaps the complete collapse of federal systems in Eastern Europe has created a new type of situation in which 'self-determination' has to be redefined; but apart from the protection of minority rights, there are as yet no internationally-accepted principles of new state formation which could be used to justify ethnic secessionism. As Lee C. Buchheit noted in his monograph *Secession, Legitimacy of Self-determination*, '...at the present time there is neither an international consensus regarding the status of secession within this doctrine (of national self-determination) nor... is there an accepted teaching regarding the nature of a legitimate secessionist movement' (Buchheit 1978:216).

Normatively, then, as against a secessionist group, the 'nation state' appears '...as Goliath possessing all the advantages in this conflict...' (Wood 1981:125). In addition to its centralized and technocratized internal state apparatus the modern state has the advantage over an ethnic secession movement on the external front: its actions against rebellious secessionists are justified in international law, and it can use its diplomatic channels to muster support from other states while still characterizing such actions as an internal matter. This does not, however, mean that the secessionist group is helpless in international politics (as distinct from law). In a world where vested social interests, ideological differences, and economic competition have generated inter-state rivalry in plenty, it has usually not been difficult for a secessionist movement to find external supporters.

The norms of international customary law are themselves fragile in a clash between great powers. External intervention in secessionist conflicts, in spite of these norms, is far from unknown. Heraclides counted 73 external state involvements in seven secessionist conflicts between 1960 and 1970 (Heraclides 1985:608). An external dimension is inherent in ethnic secessionist conflict in any state, large or small, in any part of the world. Secessionism, as stated clearly by R. W. Sterling, '...straddles the boundary between domestic and international politics (and seeks) to introduce a new actor into the international system. The system itself will undergo greater or lesser change as a consequence of the new member's presence' (Sterling 1979:413). This will usually ensure the emergence of a committed external supporter of the secessionist cause even though the international legal and normative framework discourages such moves.

Cross-boundary ethnic links, refugee problems in neighbouring countries and care for minority rights have been cited as among the more tenable reasons for external interference (see Suhrke & Noble 1977:06-16), and as pointed out by Astri Suhrke and Leela Garner Noble, '...if genocide seems a possibility there are additional moral and legal pressures for outside parties to intervene' (Suhrke 1977:6). Such interferences are inevitable in current international politics and are often associated with the political, economic and strategic interests of relatively big states. Great powers, or particularly at the regional level, a Big Neighbour, can be named as possible interveners.

Experience of post-World War II ethnic secessionist conflicts suggests that the power politics of the Great Powers (and at the regional level, the Big Neighbours) play a dominant role in determining the level and extent of such interferences. If a Great Power or a Big Neighbour decides to intervene, then international principles such as 'non-interference', 'territorial integrity' and 'national sovereignty' will turn out to have little practical validity.

In the period of the 'Cold War', the great powers which dominated most inter-state relations closely followed the patterns of internal conflict in other states, as an inseparable aspect of their global strategies. They had a particular interest in maintaining the existing balance of power in international politics - unless, of course, they could shift it to their own advantage. Any internal conflict capable of becoming an international conflict would be used by these states to increase their realm of influence. As noted by C. R. Mitchell

...external involvement does, then, tend to become an inevitable process, with external parties intervening pre-emptively for fear that rivals will themselves be involved and thus secure an increasing measure of influence in the domestic affairs of another state (Mitchell 1970:172).

In this context ethnic secessionist conflicts present a '...standing temptation' (Mitchell 1970:173) for those external parties to design their strategies and intervene. The external structure of ethnic secessionism may also entail an 'invitational' rather than an 'interventional' process. In their confrontation with each other both centre and secessionists may need outside support to gain a complete victory. Maybe the initial steps will be taken by the secessionists, whose main objective is to counterbalance the advantageous position held by the centre, which can exploit the existing international resources of an already established state. In addition to the centre-biased international legal system, the central regime possesses well established diplomatic, economic and military resources to meet any domestic conflict. Therefore the secessionists may devise an organized campaign to internationalize their grievances, to win the sympathy of world opinion, to counteract the external strength of the state. Appeals may be made inviting intervention by international bodies, great powers and neighbouring countries.

Sometimes these steps may be accompanied by desperate attempts by the secessionists to provoke outside attention, such as terrorist acts, or charges of genocide (Suhrke & Noble 1977:6).

The ethnic kin of the secessionist community, living in various countries, and especially those living in neighbouring countries, may act as the spokesmen, pressure agents and financial supporters of the secessionists, and play a substantial role in the process of internationalization of secessionist conflict. These manoeuvrings on the part of secessionists may provoke the centre to follow suit. If secessionists have found external patrons rather than merely ethnic kin groups the centre may intensify its diplomatic drive, and if the conflict is violent, make efforts to attract special economic and military aid for speedy counter operations. In the process, the centre itself contributes its share towards internationalizing the conflict. Such appeals made by both parties can eventually become an open invitation to a sequence of third party interferences; every external state assistance secured may arouse the attention of other states who may then take measures to protect their interests. Third party intervention in internal conflicts is a well documented aspect of international relations.

In an early essay on the subject, George Modelski noted that '...every internal war is a contest between the incumbents and the insurgents. But every internal war too has a third party, also disposing of internal and external structures' (Modelski 1964:19). These third parties which have intervened on behalf of insurgents '...encourage their struggle and provide moral support as well as economic and military aid, thereby isolating and demoralizing the centre' (Modelski 1964:19). Thus the international system functions as an accelerator '...by strengthening the hands of the insurgents' (Modelski 1964:31).

Most of these external 'political entrepreneurs' (Suhrke & Noble 1977:13) are not interested in secessionist victories, but just want to exploit them to achieve their own strategic, economic and political ends. When the vital interests of great powers are at stake, their involvement in domestic conflicts is inevitable. But in most of these cases their interest may be limited only to minimizing their strategic burdens. A committed involvement in secessionist conflicts may not appear unless the envisioned secession would guarantee them some deep strategic and political gain. Such involvement may prolong the conflict. Whenever external involvements appear on the domestic scene, especially on the side of the secessionists, the centre is faced with a crisis: it has a real threat of partition or secession to deal with, and is caught in diplomatic collision with the external supporters of the secessionist group at international forums. The resolution or management of secessionist conflict then becomes a complex task; it is no more an internal matter, but an inter-state conflict which may have to be settled through international negotiations. Sometimes at this stage both the secessionists and the centre will lose their gains, and their direction, to these different external bed-fellows. If the internal conflict has been used by great powers in this way, there is a strong possibility of the conflict becoming a stage for a competition among themselves, which cannot be resolved unless the great powers decide to change the venue.

Third party involvement in secessionist conflicts is likely to occur to this extent more especially in small states, and not in relatively big states. Where the affected state is a big one, however, the secret involvement of enemy or ill-disposed states is even more likely, providing economic and/or military support for secessionists to sustain clandestine activities against the state.

The external structure of a secessionist conflict may thus bring to the central state both an unwelcome inter-state conflict and prolonged domestic instability. The central state weakened by such a situation then faces a real legitimacy crisis. Now its internal legitimacy (that is, the right of the government or regime to rule the secessionist region, Herz 1978:318) and its external legitimacy (that is, the right of the state to keep it as a constituent part of the 'nation state', Herz 1978:318) are both being contested, not only on the domestic level but also at the international level.

Conceptual implications

When discussing the world-wide impact of all forms of ethnic nationalism, Anthony D. Smith commented,

> Clearly the very term 'nation-state' is a misnomer. Ethnic pluralism rather than ethnic homogeneity appears still to be the norm, despite the acceptance of the principle of self-determination (Smith 1981:10).

Most of the conceptual implications of ethnic secessionism rotate around this misnomer; the 'nation-state'. As has been already illustrated, not only the conceptual basis of the 'nation-state', such as the ideas of 'nation' and 'national self-determination', but also its legitimacy and even the envisaged process of 'nation-building', are contested by this phenomenon.

Despite definitional disagreements at the academic level, 'nation' has been considered as synonymous with 'state' by the present international system in which the existing 'nation-states' function as constituent partners. Accordingly all political societies prefer to be known as 'nations'. In this sense every state has its own 'nationality' for its citizens. This official version which is the conceptual basis of today's 'nation-state' or, if we put it more accurately, the 'state-nation' (term borrowed from Smith 1971:189), dominates the current international legal and normative framework.

As assigned by the charter of the 'United Nations', the central task of the international community is to maintain a conflict-free environment for inter-state relations (Buchheit 1978:226-7). In this regard international law has given central place to the protection of the territorial integrity of the 'nation-state'. Therefore any attempt towards the forcible dismantling of one of these 'nation-states' is unacceptable to the existing international and regional inter-governmental organizations. States are bound to honour the 'territorial integrity' and the attempts at 'nation-building' of other states. This legal and official version further legitimizes the existence of 'nation-states' within the international order.

Most of the conceptual directions in conventional academic discussion on nationalism, national integration, and even today's ethnic nationalism, have been dominated by this official version of 'nation'. Many existing concepts such as 'national integration', 'nation-building', 'assimilation' also have this conceptual bias. Commenting on these issues, Walker Connor asked

> Where today is the study of nationalism ? In this Alice-in-Wonderland world in which nation usually means state, in which nation-state usually means multinational states, in which nationalism usually means loyalty to the state, in which ethnicity, primordialism, pluralism, tribalism, regionalism, communalism usually means loyalty to the nation. ...Indeed careless vocabulary has even proclaimed a realistic assessment of the magnitude of nationalism's revolutionary potentiality (Connor 1978:396).

Even the term 'ethnic' has not escaped; for some social scientists it implies ethnic groups as sub-national groups within the larger political society (Connor 1978:386), or if they possess protected autonomous status, then as 'imperfect nations' (Krejci & Velimsky 1981:34-5) in the political society which allows the central state and the dominant ethnic groups to own 'nation'.

Most of the present nation-states were inherited or emerged from a dynastic state, or by territorial break-up of an empire, or decolonization. In this process the majority of these states absorbed less self-conscious peripheral or minority ethnic groups into their territories. The oldest 'nation-states' such as Spain, Britain and France, which inherited their 'national societies' through the assimilation policies followed by their historical dynastic states (Krejci & Velimsky 1981:23) have been cited as an example of nation-building through assimilation (Deutsch 1963:8). Most of the conceptual terms in the scholarly discussions on national integration have been influenced by this political process. Karl Deutsch asked, '...How long might it take for tribes or ethnic groups in a developing country to pass through such sequence of stages?' (Deutsch 1963:23).

With these conceptual approaches the phenomenon of ethnic secessionism presents a potential confusion. Most of the present 'nation-states' belong to the politically and economically dominant ethnic groups in their respective societies. Thus 'nation' as defined by A. K. Francis '...has to be reserved for the dominant ethnic group...' (Krejci & Velimsky 1981:34) in the state, and its hegemony in economic, political and cultural affairs is imposed on other ethnic groups. Terms like 'assimilation', 'accommodation' and 'nation-building' then become the conceptual instruments of the dominant ethnic group in its efforts to absorb or dominate other ethnic groups in the society.

If any of these minority or peripheral ethnic groups makes an attempt to emancipate itself from this political trap, it is characterized as 'nation-destroying' (Connor 1972:336); a process contrary to 'nation-building'. As Krejci and Velimsky put it '...there is, however, no logical reason why the situation could not be seen the other way round; absorption of the minorities as nation-destroying and their emancipation as nation-building' (Krejci & Velimsky:1981:23). The political message is unequivocal; to avoid secession the modern state should find a viable political and economic environment for peripheral ethnic groups to maintain and deepen their national identities, in order to continue their partnership in the political society.

Our special area of interest in the present study lies in 'devolution of government', a political device practised in many places to grant regional autonomy to peripheral ethnic groups (see below sub-section, devolution and ethnic autonomy), which has received wide acceptance in political and academic approaches towards this important phenomenon (for example Buchheit 1978:214-15; Heraclides 1985:v; Rothchild 1970:615-16; Olorunsola & Rothchild 1983:234,240-1; Horowitz 1985:Ch.15), as a way of managing secessionist and ethno-regional conflicts, short of secession.

Devolution of government

'Devolution' has been commonly treated as the political form of decentralization, a term embodying the simple idea '...away from the centre' (MacMahon 1969:15). However, this common meaning has been presented in various guises in the literature (for example Smith 1967:1; 1985:12-17; Maddick 1963:23; Bogdanor 1979:3; Rondinelli & Cheema 1983:22-3; Rondinelli 1984:138; Cloets 1988:17, Rondinelli et al. 1989:74-5). It is difficult to blend together all those definitions to afford a general meaning for the concept of 'devolution'; but for the purpose of our study we make an attempt.

On the basis of a close examination of many scholarly treatises on the subject, we shall define *devolution* as a political and organizational strategy by which a central government within a unitary system, or within states or regions of a federal system, establishes new units of government with defined boundaries at the regional or provincial level or strengthens the powers and functions of already existing regional governments (MacMahon 1969:19-20; Sherwood 1969:68; Smith 1967:1; 1985:11-17; Rondinelli & Cheema 1983:22-3, Rondinelli 1984:138).

These regional governments have legally-conferred legislative and executive powers in designated fields of policy and administration, so that they may function within these fields as autonomous regional units of governance outside the formal command structure of the central authority. In devolution the centre relinquishes its formal authority over these powers and functions, which have been accredited to the regional governments, and keeps little control or no direct control (Rondinelli 1984:138).

As noted by Yoram Dinstein '...regional autonomy denotes self-government... established in a delineated portion of the territory of a state and relates to all the inhabitants within the area' (Dinstein 1981:291-2). According to Louis B. Sohn, within the regional autonomy framework the concept of self-government implies that for important political or economic reasons a particular area will remain within the territorial jurisdiction of another political entity but will possess political freedom to regulate certain of its own affairs without any interference by that entity except in the case of powers which are in the common interest of both entities (Sohn 1981:5).

In the real world territorial autonomy has never been complete (Smith 1985:9). But in the theory, regional autonomy is certainly incomplete without powers for regional governments to raise their own revenues. Thus assignment of a substantial amount of power for the regions to raise their own finance is central to the regional autonomy arrangement. Sometimes regional autonomy entails powers to maintain law and order in the regions. Where this is so, the regional institutions can enjoy a significant amount of influence over local citizens.

Such regional governments are designed to be perceived by local citizens as managing their local and communal affairs (Rondinelli 1984:138). The important point in this connection is the representative nature of the local government. Territorial autonomy is imperfect, until the process has incorporated provisions to elect the regional leadership. If the purpose of devolution is autonomy for regional communities, regional representativeness is intrinsic and inseparable. Hence devolution can be considered as a step towards further democratization (Leemans 1970:17-19).

Devolution can be instituted either by legislation or by the constitution. Arthur MacMahon provides two individual terms to identify the legal status of devolution; 'Statutory Devolution' and 'Constitutional Devolution' (MacMahon 1969:20):

> constitutional devolution covers federalism in its many applications. It describes a situation in which power is divided between central government and territorially defined constitutional units of self-government under an agreement (the constitution) which cannot be altered by the ordinary law making procedure (MacMahon 1969:20).

Brian C. Smith in his *Decentralization, the territorial dimension of the state* also discussed the comparative characteristics of federal and unitary systems, and observed '...it is possible for a unitary state to devolve substantial powers to provincial governments, so that a quasi-federal arrangement exists' (Smith 1985:14).

This enables us to extend our definition of devolution, treating the formation of a federal system, on the initiative of a central government which is already functioning within an unitary system of government, as the highest form of devolution. We shall call this *devolutionary federalism*, a term borrowed from Benyamin Neuberger (Neuberger 1979:176); here the initiative and the decision of central government in establishing new regional governments covering the whole of its territory by devolving its existing powers, are crucial for the formation of federalism. For example, unlike the early federal systems of the United States and Switzerland, most of the post World-War-II federal systems (e.g. India and Nigeria) were, as noted by John P. Mackintosh in the case of the Nigerian federal system '...created by the subdivision of a country which had in theory been ruled as a single unit... rather than the coming together of separate states to create a federated state' (Mackintosh 1962:223).

With that understanding of the meaning of 'devolution', in the next section we will examine different empirical experiences of devolution of government around the world, with reference to devolutionary arrangements which provide ethnic autonomy to regional ethnic groups.

Devolution and ethnic autonomy

'Devolution' is in fact the most frequently found strategy for the granting of ethnic autonomy; that is self-government or self-rule by an ethnic group within the broader political union of the state. Arranging an independent governmental framework within which dissatisfied ethnic groups may manage their own affairs has long been considered the simplest technique for reducing ethnic disaffections.

Danial J. Elazar has categorized some 18 federal systems, and another 18 as states which have introduced federal-like arrangements to accommodate social diversity in their territories (Elazar 1979-a:19-23), along with more than 90 different examples of autonomy involving 52 states (Elazar 1979-b:215). Not all those autonomy practices are examples of ethnic autonomy; but many of these can be found in a wide spectrum of governmental restructuring arrangements and also in diverse socio-political backgrounds.

Devolution practices are familiar in the Asian and African continents where state formation usually took place within ethnic enclaves created by the arbitrary boundary making of colonialism. Among them India and Nigeria provide clear examples of 'devolutionary federalism' established at independence, directing their future 'state-nation' formation by granting autonomy to regional ethnic groups.

The Indian federal system illustrates how devolution in a multiethnic context is a continuing process. In India carving out new states and strengthening the powers of existing states has been taking place continuously since the original establishment of devolutionary federalism in the 1950s. The creation of the states of Andhra Pradesh (1953), of Haryana (1966), of Nagaland (1963), of Mizoram (1988), the Sikh majority state of Punjab (1966), the hill council of Gorkha land (1988), and the granting of more constitutional powers to the state of Madras (1963), exemplify this evolving process of devolution. These changes, which we shall review in a little more detail below, were made by the central government in response to the communal, autonomist and secessionist impulses that broke out in those parts of India (see Eradman 1979:398,401-2; Horowitz 1985:613-14).

Such a development did not take place in the Nigerian setting because of the disruption of democratic politics by frequent military interventions. The bloody secessionist conflict in Biafra in 1967 was incubated in this political background. However, military take-overs did not eliminate the federalism from Nigerian politics. After their crushing victory over the secessionist Biafra region, the military rulers of Nigeria made an attempt to reduce ethnic tensions by redrawing the territorial divisions of the country. In 1967 the three existing federal regions were divided into twelve states and another seven were created in 1976. The Nigerian example shows how a central government may use devolution as a political instrument to weaken the political strength of ethno-regionalism (Horowitz 1985:604-13), and hence strengthen the long-term viability of the overall state.

In post-war Eastern Europe, three socialist systems viz. the Soviet Union, Yugoslavia and Czechoslovakia (where according to Marxist premises, working class rather than nation should become the driving force of social progress), used ethnic differences extensively in the design of the governmental structure. In the framework of the Soviet system, for example, there were four types of ethnic autonomy arrangement one within another; viz., Federal Republics, Autonomous Republics, Autonomous Regions and National Districts (Farberov 1975:177). In these states devolutionary federalism continued as the formal framework of the governmental system, but modified by a 'unitary party' (Gitelman 1979:159) which maintained a rigid internal hierarchical organization to bind central and regional units of government. Thus the apparent devolution has been characterized as a step towards mere '...administrative convenience and psychological rewards to different ethnic groups' (Gitelman 1979:169). However, since the collapse of Soviet communism, the ethnic basis of the 'devolutionary federalism' in these territories is providing the structure for the political struggle now taking place for new state formation, as well as attempts at the management of secessionist tendencies.

In Western Europe Italy, Spain and Belgium provide further experiences of varieties of devolution. The government of Italy dealt with the South Tyrol (which had been caught up in a diplomatic row with Austria) by devolving powers to the province within the framework of its unitary constitution (Esterbauer 1979 147-50; Schrear 1981:58-63). Post-Franco Spain is an illustration of a common dilemma: in order to reduce tensions in one region, autonomy has to be offered to others where there is little or no ethnic tension. In the attempt to resolve ethnic tensions in Catalonia and the Basque country the constitution inaugurated in 1978 offered regional autonomy to all Spanish provinces; subsequently 17 autonomous provinces have been instituted with executive and legislative powers (Donaghy & Newton 1987:117).

Belgium provides a striking example of an attempt at devolutionary federalism in the western world. After prolonged ethnic tensions and political conflict between Dutch speaking Flemings and French speaking Walloons, political leaders made a grand settlement (the Egmont Pact of 1977) and proposed a system of devolutionary federalism. Under this agreement (which completed its final phase of devolving governmental power in August 1989, see *The Times* 21 July 1989) two linguistic regions with regional legislatures and executive authorities were provided, with powers on matters of education, culture, social welfare and local planning. Brussels is kept as a separate region, where the central government functions as representative organ for all communities (Kane 1980:140-1).

These experiences (and many more which could be adduced) suggest that devolution stands as a policy strategy in which central regimes may try to find a political framework to accommodate peripheral or minority ethnic groups. But they also point to the fact that devolution is not just an organizational strategy but a political process. Once utilized in a multiethnic polity it continues to be an option in the political system.

The political effects of devolution can be looked at from different angles. In the political context of multiethnic states it provides self-rule or self-government for the constituent ethnic groups in the society. Although these self-governing entities have no international personality (Hannum & Lillich 1981:250), unless otherwise granted by the devolutionary law, they certainly possess internal legal personality, and are able to act as independent entities within the boundary of the state.

In this regard devolution provides autonomous status for an ethnic group in its collective efforts to safeguard ethnic interests and identity, strengthening its national character. This creates a political equilibrium of compromise between the ethnic group and the central state, which should reduce tensions and conflicts in centre-periphery or majority-minority relations, by providing a clear-cut institutional framework.

From another perspective, devolution is a formula for both central regime and secessionist movements to make a political compromise, reducing the intensity of the secessionist conflict and redirecting the ethno-centric interests of their communities into mainstream politics.

In the next section we examine this aspect with some notable examples where devolution has been implemented by the central regime either by its own initiative or in agreement with secessionist leaders.

Devolution of government and the management of ethnic secessionism

Faced with an ethnic secessionist movement, a central government has two basic options: (a) repression and assimilation or (b) conflict management of a political kind (cf. Wood 1981:125-26).

Outlawing of secessionist campaigns and military suppression have been cited as assimilative measures. But these measures alone cannot serve the purpose and are unable to deal with the real causes of secessionism. 'When misapplied these policies have counterproductive effects' (Wood 1981:126).

As a political expression of an ethnoregional movement, to a certain extent ethnic secessionism represents '...an unreal conflict' (cf. Elliot 1971:8). The real conflict lies in the social, economic, political and psychological environment of secessionism. To deal with these real causes of secessionism, governments need to make '...attempts to rebuild 'nation' or state in fuller recognition of existing plural divisions' (Wood 1981:126). This needs initiatives to compromise with the ethnic movement or to find a negotiated settlement. In other words it needs conflict management initiatives. As defined by Stephen P. Cohen and Harriet C. Arnone,

> ...conflict management initiatives are attempts to contain conflict, to avert major breakouts, to bring about cease-fires in already violent confrontations, to negotiate political settlements, to lower the level of mutual blaming and recrimination (Cohen & Arnone 1988:177).

In this connection 'devolution' becomes one of these possible initiatives for a central government facing a deeply rooted ethnic secessionist conflict. This has been proved by the experience of many ethnic secessionist conflicts.

Devolutionary practices in the management of ethnic secessionism

Once again we shall begin with the Indian multiethnic state which has provided varying types of experience in the management of ethnic secessionist conflicts since its independence. Our first case is the Tamil secessionist agitation which originated in the southern state of Madras in the 1950s and 1960s. When the agitation turned into violent mass protests, the Indian central government promptly banned the secessionist campaign, but at the same time introduced a constitutional amendment to devolve more powers to the state. However, the Indo-China border war of 1962, reduced the political intensity of the secessionist campaign. In this atmosphere the central government's devolution initiative enabled it to contain the secessionist campaign led by the Dravida Munnetra Kazhagam (DMK) movement, which had suspended their campaign in face of the external threat posed by the border war with China. Their subsequent election victory in the state of Madras in 1967 allowed them to use the newly granted autonomy powers to implement most of their nationalistic objectives within the framework of Indian federalism. The state of Madras was renamed Tamil Nadu. In this way the central government of India was able to accommodate the DMK movement which had once been considered as a highly competent ethno-nationalist movement, able '...to use an international crisis to take Madras out of the Union' (Erdman 1979:402).

The Naga and Mizo secessionist struggles in India which erupted in insurrections in the 1950s and 1960s provide somewhat different stories. When these movements turned into insurrections, the central government deployed its military forces and employed more repressive measures to quell the rebel campaign. Since the early stage of their campaign in the 1950s, the central government had refused to grant even union territory status to the Naga community. But the military assault on the Naga movement went beyond its expected political limits, damaging the image of central government and promoting more Naga resistance. These developments made the later negotiations more difficult (see Maxwell 1980:11-13). When central government established the state of Nagaland in 1963 with the participation of a breakaway section of the Naga movement, the main underground secessionist movement, 'the Naga Federal Government', refused to accept the new state and continued their campaign. The central government made another attempt to find a negotiated settlement in 1964 with the 'Federal Nagas' but failed; largely due to the intransigence of the secessionists (Maxwell 1980:13-18). However in the long run, together with the new autonomy and special development initiatives, the central government's persistent military campaigns against intransigent secessionists succeeded in weakening the social base of the secessionist movement, which later transformed into a tiny guerrilla group. As one analyst commented '...for its part the Indian policy of granting a measure of local autonomy to the Nagas within the framework of the Indian union was a classic case of stealing the other fellow's thunder' (Buchheit 1978:198).

When the Mizos launched their militant secessionist campaign in 1966, the centre also replied by military repression. But those attempts served only to harden Mizo resistance. Five years later, after those futile military operations, the central government granted 'union territory status' for the Mizo homeland (Maxwell 1973:19). But the settlement was inadequate and too late. It took nearly two decades finally to settle the Mizo secessionist conflict in Mizoram in 1986 with an agreement signed by the central government and the Mizo National Front (MNF). This agreement established the new state of Mizoram and the MNF entered into the mainstream of Indian politics (see *India Today* 15 July 1988). The formation of Darjleen Gorkha Hill Council within the state of West Bengal was another successful devolutionary exercise by the Indian central government in recent years to contain a protracted secessionist conflict (see *India Today* 15 August 1988, 15 November 1988).

The current secessionist conflict in the Indian state of Punjab shows that the creation of the present Sikh majority state in 1966 has only given them a more advantageous position from which to organize their secessionist campaign. In the early 1980s militant Sikh secessionist movements launched a violent campaign, demanding a Sikh separate state (Khalistan). In 1985 the central government signed an agreement with a moderate Sikh leadership to settle the conflict through more autonomy concessions (Shackle 1986:15), but Sikh extremism and religious animosities which had been aroused by pre-accord military operations not only disrupted the settlement but also outweighed the strength of the moderate Sikh leadership, creating a vacuum in the consensus politics. Today the Sikh campaign for an independent state has created a situation of near-anarchy in the state of Punjab.

The creation of Bangladesh which (until the recent unilateral secessions in Slovenia and Croatia) is the solitary example of successful unilateral secession since the second world war, was the outcome of the undiluted assimilative approach followed by a central regime in Pakistan. Until the last phase of their struggle, the Awami League's agitation was explicitly directed at autonomy not secession (see Rahman 1975:43-5). But the centre preferred assimilative policies and made attempts to suppress the movement. In the final phase of the conflict, the central regime's reluctance to grant autonomy to the regionally elected Awami party leadership and the subsequent military campaign against the Awami movement transformed the East Bengali autonomist struggle into a secessionist struggle (Rahman 1975:45) which finally realized its goal with the military intervention by India, the Big Neighbour. This will be one of our main case studies in succeeding chapters.

In South-east Asia, the southern Philippines island of Mindanao illustrates another attempt at devolution with mixed results. In 1976 after a prolonged Christian-Muslim conflict and continuous military manoeuvres against the secessionist movement, the then government of Ferdinand Marcos first offered regional autonomy to the thirteen provinces of Mindanao and nearby islands, as a part of an agreement reached between the government and the Moro National Liberation Front (MNLF), under pressure from the Organization of Islamic Conference (OIC) in Tripoli, Libya (Bacho 1987:155). But due to disagreements at the initial stages of implementation, the proposed autonomy settlement was rejected by the MNLF. Their definition of proposed autonomy for a Moro homeland with its own flag, official seal, military, and judicial system was unacceptable to the central government. Further they demanded that special status for the MNLF in the regional government. Another controversial aspect was the government's insistence on holding a referendum to approve the regional autonomy package. Despite the MNLF's intransigence, the central government held its planned referendum which gave an opportunity to the Christian majority to reject the MNLF demands (Bacho 1987:155-6).

On the one hand, this exercise is witness to the central government's reluctance or inability to settle the minority conflict by ignoring the wishes of the majority community; and on the other hand, to the intransigent and extremist approach shown by the secessionists. However the central government's initiatives in honouring its promises in the Tripoli agreement satisfied the OIC and other external parties. As a result, in subsequent years MNLF's external support gradually declined. Further the autonomy issue stirred disputes within the MNLF ranks. In these circumstances the Philippine government enjoyed a peaceful period for more than a decade (Bacho 1987:155-8). Since 1983 MNLF has again launched its political activities, forcing the new Philippine government of Corazon Aquino to enter several rounds of talks with the MNLF. In November 1989, the Aquino government unilaterally held a referendum on the autonomy issue, and received substantial support from some of the Muslim majority provinces in its efforts to establish an autonomous region, called 'Autonomous Region of Muslim Mindanao' (see *Far Eastern Economic Review* 23 and 30 November 1989; 7 December 1989; 6 September 1990).

The regional autonomy granted to Southern Sudan in 1972 stands as an example of democratic devolution established by a military regime. Under the devolutionary package implemented in 1973, the secessionist Southern Sudan received the status of 'self-government' with an elected legislative assembly and a regional executive authority. Further, Southern Sudan was granted powers to keep its own official language and an agreed proportion of posts in the central civil service and military (Shaked 1981:154-8). This devolution settlement brought to an end the prolonged civil war which had disrupted the life of Southern Sudan for more than a decade, and lasted until 1983 when the central regime unilaterally annulled it, attempting a further territorial division of Southern Sudan (Horowitz 1985:615-16) which paved the way for the civil war now being fought.

In the Sudanese setting it is the Muslim majority which has been opposing autonomy for the Christian south, and by their pressure caused the cancellation of the settlement. The present civil war is being fought by the Southerners to regain their lost ethnic autonomy, not secession (see Novicki 1989:44). A political settlement was agreed in 1989 with the Sudanese People's Liberation Army (SPLA), but reluctance to ratify it led to a military coup in August 1989. This, however, has not ended the conflict. The central regime's reluctance to oppose the northern Muslims' demand for the imposition of Islamic (*Sharia*) law over the southern Christians is one of the main obstacles to a settlement (see *The Independent* 9 December 1989).

In Spain even after the introduction of regional autonomy in 1978 the main Basque militant movement ETA still continues its guerrilla campaign for an independent Basque state. The Basque nationalists urged their people to boycott the Basque referendum which was held in 1979 to approve the proposed regional autonomy (Donaghy & Newton 1987:100).

These experiences indicate that the acceptance and implementation of devolution in a secessionist situation is often something of a tricky task for the conflicting parties. Sometimes it is the central government which refuses devolution. As Milton J. Esman puts it '...autonomy is a painful strategy choice for central elites' (Esman 1977:382). Autonomy concessions to one set of secessionists have demonstration effects on other ethnic groups, providing a strong precedent to bolster their campaign for further autonomy or to strengthen their claim to territorial rights. Sometimes a major problem emerges when the secessionist group is not concentrated in one principal region, but dispersed and distributed throughout the state; or else the principal region which the secessionists claim as an ethnic homeland is itself a multiethnic entity. But the denial of territorial right may transform an autonomist movement into a secessionist movement. In this regard the continuing refusal of autonomy to East Pakistan by the military regime in Pakistan, and the East Bengali movement's transition from autonomism to secessionism, provides a clear example.

Majority communities, too, sometimes have deep-felt opposition to devolution for minorities (as in the cases of Sudan and Philippines), and may have their ethnic claims to the territory inhabited by the secessionist community, deriving from their historical memory or from their vested interest in the resources there (like the oil in Biafra or copper in Katanga). If the majority-minority conflict and the mutual mistrust of ethnic groups are highly visible in the background of the secessionist conflict, devolution of power to the region will become a particularly controversial issue in national politics. Sometimes the protests of majority groups may turn to violence, contributing further to the formation of a negative approach towards devolution by the majority-supported central regime.

Even more significant is the attitude of secessionists towards devolution. They may have their own reasons to refuse devolution, as in the cases of MNLF in the Philippines or Sikhs in Punjab or ETA in Spain. Usually, a secessionist movement which has got used to violence is reluctant to accept any but very substantial political concessions. A devolutionary settlement may be damned as a 'sell-out'. After losing the lives of many of their cadres, it may be difficult for secessionist leaders to make an instant return to peace time politics. If they have adequate external support they might prefer to exacerbate the situation and create a point of no return, hoping to achieve international sympathy for the plight of their community.

Certainly, the prevalence of a negative approach by so many conflicting parties may strengthen the pessimism apparent in some academic quarters (see Lijphart 1990:497-9, Nordlinger 1972:31-3) regarding the effectiveness of devolution of government as a method of managing ethno-regional conflict in multiethnic societies. However, given its success in the management of violent secessionist conflicts in some parts of the world (such as Tamil Nadu, Naga land, Mizo land, Gorkha land in India, Southern Sudan between 1972 and 1983, and Mindanao in the Philippines from 1972 to 1988), such pessimism is perhaps misplaced and is not predominant in conflict management theory.

Neither 'secession' nor 'repression', the extreme solutions envisaged by the adversaries in the secessionist situation, is always possible. There are certain external and internal conditions which prevent the achievement of either objective unilaterally. Successful unilateral secessions like Bangladesh in the 1970s, or Slovenia and Croatia in the 1990s, on the one hand, and complete military victories by the central regimes such as in Katanga and Biafra, on the other, occurred under very special circumstances, and required much human suffering to overcome these external and internal constraints. Unilateral secessions are the exceptions not the rule. Ethnic secessionism is still unacceptable to the international community. Samuel P. Huntington's statement still has currency in the present international environment:

> The twentieth century bias against political divorce, that is secession, is just about as strong as the nineteenth-century bias against marital divorce. Where secession is possible, contemporary statesmen might do well to view it with great tolerance (Huntington 1972).

The most common outcome of secessionist conflict is unnecessary loss of human lives, and the complete disruption of social, economic, political and human progress of the society. Devolution of government as a compromise can reduce the violent intensity of the secessionist situation, and create an institutional framework for further reduction of violence and a gradual movement towards fresh 'nation-building'.

It is this belief that shapes our present task which is to determine the conditions under which devolution of government may become the preferred settlement to ethnic secessionist conflict in a modern state. Then, we may hope, it will be the task of the central regime and secessionist leadership in an affected state, the leaders of other states and the international community to establish the necessary political and economic environment for the installation of such a devolutionary settlement in the interest of national reconciliation.

Next we will survey existing theoretical perspectives on devolution as a method of ethnic conflict management, before setting out our formal research problem.

Theoretical perspectives on devolution as a method of ethnic conflict management

We have already referred to some of the academic discussions of devolution as an option in multiethnic societies in finding a compromise settlement to ethnoregional conflicts. Many of these discussions are no more than passing references in studies serving other objectives in the ethnic conflict literature (for example Buchheit 1978; Heraclides 1985). Some of them, however (Rothchild & Olorunsola 1983; Horowitz 1985), have examined the achievements of devolutionary devices in multiethnic societies and conditions conducive to their implementation. For example, Donald S. Rothchild and Victor A. Olorunsola offer devolution as a means to achieve strategic objectives, such as the isolation of conflicting ethnic groups into their own territory, and power sharing in the larger society (Rothchild & Olorunsola 1983 234,240-1). Introducing federalism, devolution, territorial and electoral innovations as 'structural techniques' to reduce ethnic conflicts, Donald L. Horowitz explains their weaknesses and benefits, and the conditions of their implementation (Horowitz 1985:Ch.15). But even these studies do not provide a comprehensive theoretical perspective on devolution as a method of ethnic conflict management.

More promising as a theoretical perspective on devolution as a method of ethnic conflict management are theoretical discussions related to the broad category of 'consociational' political practices, recognized mainly in the politics of ethnically plural modern states.

The pattern of consociational politics was first recognized by David E. Apter in the 1960s (Lijphart 1969:211). In his *The Political Kingdom in Uganda, A Study in Bureaucratic Nationalism* (1961), Apter cited the contemporary Nigerian 'devolutionary federalism' as an example of the consociational pattern. For Apter the consociational model

> ...is essentially a system of compromise and accommodation. Its outstanding characteristic is that it places a high value on compromise among groups which may demonstrate a wide range of ideas and ambitions. (A)t the minimum level a loose alliance stressing common ideological, political and economic benefits is sought (and) at the maximum, (the) federal principle is adopted to achieve greater organization and consensus (Apter 1961:24).

Later consociational political practices have been more clearly recognized and subjected to diverse theoretical treatments, one of which is, in Hans Daalder's words 'the incipient school of consociational analysis' (Lijphart 1977-b:ix).

Among this school it is Arend Lijphart who has successfully popularized a theoretical perspective on 'power sharing' in the management of ethnic conflict in multiethnic societies (McRae 1990:93-6, Lijphart 1990:508). His theory, popularly known as the 'consociational democracy model' was originally intended to disprove a basic perception in the theory of plural society, namely, '...that democracy is not a viable form of government in deeply divided societies' (Lijphart 1977-a:113).

In the consociational model he introduces a system of democracy which could be implemented as a system of conflict resolution in deeply divided multiethnic societies. It is a grand political design for power sharing by the different cultural groups and their leaders through agreement and compromise. After a detailed examination of consociational political practices in some European countries, especially in the Netherlands, Belgium, Switzerland and Austria, and also in non European countries such as Lebanon and Cyprus, he isolated four main characteristics of the consociational democracy model:

(1) Government by grand coalition
(2) The mutual veto or concurrent majority rule
(3) Proportionality as the principal standard of political representation, civil service appointments and allocation of public funds.
(4) A high degree of autonomy for each segment to run its own internal affairs (Lijphart 1977-b:25).

According to Lijphart, the questions of secession and of partition do not arise if the system can successfully maintain a consociational pattern of democracy (Lijphart 1977-a:118). He sees it as the one solution for the '... political problems of a plural society under all circumstances' (Lijphart 1977-b:44-5). In a more recent study he has characterized this model as 'the power sharing approach' in the management of ethnic conflict in multiethnic societies, and extended it to cover regional autonomy and federal arrangements in different parts of the world where the power sharing method has been used (Lijphart 1990:494-7).

In the consociational model an important place is given to the autonomy principle. 'A high degree of autonomy for each segment to run its own internal affairs' is an essential element of consociational democracy. He characterizes segmental autonomy as '... a generalization of the federal idea' (Lijphart 1977-b:43), by which minority groups receive, in Lijphart's words, '...their own governmental and administrative units...' as well as non-territorial autonomy in communal functions (Lijphart 1977-b:51). Then federalism is considered as a special form of segmental autonomy in relation to its most important feature; the granting of autonomy to constituent partners of the state, and the over-representation of smaller subdivisions in the federal chamber (Lijphart 1977-b:42; also see Lijphart 1979:499-515).

This allows us to place 'devolution' in the broad theoretical perspective of the 'power sharing approach' or 'consociational democracy' as a method of managing secession conflict. Many later scholarly discussions provide relevant arguments (for example Daalder 1974; Boynton & Kwon 1978; McRae 1979), but we do not intend to present all of these discussions here.

However, we must pay special attention to some who doubt the effectiveness of devolution of government as a method of conflict management in multiethnic societies. One such is Eric A. Nordlinger's theory on conflict management in divided societies (Nordlinger 1972).

Like Lijphart, rejecting majoritarian democracy as suitable for the regulation of ethnic conflicts in deeply divided societies, Nordlinger features 'open regimes' (Nordlinger 1972:1). Generalizing from successful conflict regulation, he lists practices some of which are similar to the main characteristics of the consociational model, viz. a stable governing coalition, the principle of proportionality, mutual veto, depoliticization, compromises on the issues which divide the conflict groups, granting of concessions by the stronger to the weaker group (Nordlinger 1972:21-9).

He treats federalism and autonomy as outcomes resulting from one or other of these six conflict regulating practices (Nordlinger 1972:31-3). According to Nordlinger, federalism, by providing a greater measure of political security to territorially based social groups, affords a suitable atmosphere for conflict regulation. But he is doubtful about its potency as a direct conflict regulation practice. According to Nordlinger the granting of territorial autonomy may not resolve conflicts; instead it may simply generate more demands for autonomy. The refusal of these demands by the central governments or dominant groups may then lead to secession and civil war (Nordlinger 1972:31-3).

Milton J. Esman (1973) made an attempt to extend Nordlinger's analysis into a broader range of experience by classifying regime objectives and the corresponding methods of communal conflict management available in plural societies. Introducing four classes of regime objectives viz, institutional assimilation, induced assimilation, syncretic integration and balanced pluralism (Esman 1973:56-60), he treats 'territorial' and 'legal-cultural' autonomy as two among four methods of conflict management which have been employed by regimes practising 'balanced pluralism' (Esman 1973:60-2). According to Esman regimes practising 'balanced pluralism' accept pluralism as legitimate and permit ethnic groups to organize and promote their cultural as well as political interests, and then deal with the inevitable competition and conflict within institutionalized political bargaining processes (Esman 1973:60).

Esman sees territorial and cultural autonomy as effective in providing broader powers to ethno-regional segments, enabling them to manage regional resources and facilities such as civil service posts, and educational and economic opportunities; also to give the language and religion of the ethno-regional groups equal status with the national language or religion (Esman 1973:63-4). In respect of Nordlinger's pessimistic approach towards territorial and non-territorial autonomy, he accepts its inherent problems in the allocation of opportunities, resources, representation at the centre, domination of one unit over the other territorial segments, and the dangers of secessionism and civil war.

But he disassociates himself from Nordlinger's explicit exclusion of autonomy, considering it as a feasible method of communal conflict management. He cites examples of successful resolution of ethnic conflicts through autonomy, and suggests it can be effective if its implementation is guaranteed by certain conditions:

> ...while territorial autonomy cannot guarantee successful communal conflict management, it is a feasible option in many situations. The research problem is to clarify the conditions under which federal arrangements are most likely to facilitate conflict regulation and the most appropriate federal practices for each set of conditions (Esman 1973:65).

This authoritative statement provides clear guidance for our own central research problem, and brings an end to this discussion. We clarify our main research problem thus: to clarify the conditions under which devolution of government may be implemented as a negotiated settlement to secessionist conflicts in modern states.

In the foregoing discussion of the literature on ethnic secessionism and devolution of government we have noted many relevant theories and identified several secessionist situations where devolution of government has been considered as a feasible option. But in the secession literature we have not come across any comprehensive and full-length study which examines conditions of implementing devolution of government as a method of managing ethnic secessionist conflict. Although we have placed devolution practices within the broad theoretical perspective of consociational politics, that theory itself does not cover specifically the ethnic secessionist conflict situation. In such a situation claims for an exclusive ethnic homeland are basic and thus central to any negotiated settlement. Without settling this important issue the parties cannot move on to the possibilities of power sharing. This study, as noted at the very beginning of this chapter, is intended to extend the existing understanding of devolution, especially as a method of managing secessionist conflict. But as our discussion has shown, secessionist conflicts have an external as well as an internal dimension. As will be explained below, the study focuses on the external conditions of successful devolution as much as on the internal, and on one condition in particular: the existence of a Big Neighbour.

The research problem

Within the broad aim of extending understanding of the applicability and effectiveness of devolution of government as a method of managing ethnic secessionist conflict, the research problem of the present study is to clarify the conditions under which devolution of government may be implemented as a negotiated solution to ethnic secessionist conflict in modern states. We have, that is, to identify contingencies for the reception of devolution as a compromise settlement, and those which will inhibit such reception, in secessionist situations.

The existing literatures on ethnic secessionism and on devolution are both quite extensive, but a study linking them is still, to the writer's knowledge, awaited. Devolution, as a device of territorial distribution of power, and its alternative modes of decentralization, are well studied in that literature; and devolution can offer both ethnic autonomy and exclusive ethno-regional rights to secessionist communities. But it falls short of the sought-for 'freedom' or complete self-rule for the more extreme secessionists; while being a painful choice, and even an unacceptable option, for central regimes and ethnic majorities simply because it affords special homeland rights to the minority and damages unity. In this situation both parties might think that '... it is worth spilling blood to achieve their objectives' (Birch 1978:340). Military repression (on the part of central regimes), discrimination and intolerance (on the part of majority communities), and intransigence (on the part of secessionists), are likely reactions in many secessionist situations. These unfavourable responses may have deep-rooted social, economic, political and psychological aspects, which are well covered in the ethnic secession literature.

Those reactions, it would seem, are what is to be normally expected. For devolution to succeed as a compromise proposal, therefore, a special concatenation of circumstances must obtain. To elicit these is our research problem.

In an earlier part of the chapter we distinguished between internal and external aspects of a secessionist situation - those endogenous to the nation-state concerned, and those exogenous to it, arising from the country's position in the world of nation-states. Secessionist groups, for example, may have external supporters; central regimes may be influenced by foreign policy or security considerations in their attitude towards the claims of a secessionist community. When external supporters appear on the scene both secessionist and centre may well react as to a challenge, by intensifying their military campaign, rejecting political solutions. If they do not, but rather begin to withdraw from violent action and to negotiate constitutional and administrative accommodations, it must be because of certain very strong exogenous factors operating in that direction. Again, identifying these factors is our research problem.

Working hypotheses

The literature provides several hypotheses for testing against the several secessionist situations we will investigate. For example, we should expect the reception of devolution as a solution to ethnic conflict to be facilitated by such internal conditions as;

(1) a substantial breakdown of central control over the secessionist region accompanied by strong and complete popular nationalism among the secessionist community (cf. Zalmay Khalilzad's two conditions of successful secession, Khalilzad 1983:63);

(2) a relative decline in the capabilities of the antagonists, accompanied by a long period of warfare that brings home its destructive impact (Horowitz 1985:623);

(3) the emergence of an auspicious conjunction such as the inauguration of a new constitution, a change of government, or the revolutionary replacement of the central regime (Horowitz 1985:623).

Among other major working hypotheses derived from our own studies are that, in accounting for a secessionist situation (whether one of violent or of peaceful reactions),

(4) the external dimension of the secession conflict management is of more significance than the internal dimension. The 'external dimension' includes international pressure and launching of conflict management initiatives by Inter-Governmental Organizations (IGOs) or other third parties engendered by, principally,

(a) the affected state's or the secessionist region's location in a highly sensitive geostrategic spot; or

(b) the high dependence of the affected country on the international economic and political system;

But in this external dimension of secession conflict management there is one very influential condition which we have identified:

(5) the existence of a (relatively) Big Neighbour.

By Big Neighbour we mean not necessarily a great power or regionally-dominant power but a neighbouring state which is relatively larger (by any meaningful measure) and which has the capability to intervene in the affairs of the secession-affected country (hereafter the affected-state) by economic, political, or military means.

To bring the scope of our own inquiry within reasonable compass, therefore, we have selected as the central focus for research the role of the Big Neighbour, or 'the Big Neighbour syndrome' in a secessionist situation, with particular reference to the conditions under which devolution of government becomes the preferred solution.

We have discussed already in this chapter, although briefly, the circumstances in which such international normative principles as 'non-interference', 'territorial integrity' and 'national sovereignty' may have little practical validity if a Big Neighbour decides that its interests are affected by an internal struggle beyond one of its frontiers. In the literature on the external dimension of secessionist conflicts there is, indeed, discussion of the role of 'third parties' but no specific analysis of the role of the Big Neighbour. So we shall have to construct our own analytical model.

From the literature and from observation we postulate an elaboration of our working hypothesis as follows;

(6) To the extent that a Big Neighbour shares (or has legitimate interests to do so)

(a) common strategic resources,

(b) a common security zone,

(c) a common territorial boundary,
    and, above all,

(d) ethnic ties with some part of the affected country,

its involvement in the internal conflict of the latter is virtually unavoidable. The first three we shall refer to as components of the 'strategic' dimension, and the fourth the 'ethnic' dimension, of the Big Neighbour's national interests.

A brief discussion of each of these components follows.

Common strategic resources: strategically important facilities such as harbours, air fields, military installations, communication networks, oil refuelling and storage facilities etc., situated within the boundary of the affected state, that might be effectively employed against the national security interests of the Big Neighbour. Against this background a secessionist conflict which could well attract external interests endangers the national security of the Big Neighbour and increases its potential involvement.

Common security zone: this refers to the proximity of the affected state within the Big Neighbour's regional defence sphere thus providing a legitimate reason for the Big Neighbour to be interested in any military activity there.

Common territorial boundary: if the Big Neighbour is contiguous to the secessionist region or any other part of the affected state by land or narrow sea it will become almost inevitably involved in the secessionist conflict for various reasons, e.g. refugee influx, border trespasses by secessionists, terrorist activities in the bordering areas.

Ethnic ties: this refers to the presence both in the Big Neighbour and in the affected state of sizeable groups of people who recognize themselves as 'ethnic kin' or from common ethnic stock. There are four possible significant relationships: the 'ethnic kin' group can be (1) a minority in the affected state but a majority in Big Neighbour; (2) a minority in Big Neighbour but a majority in the affected state; (3) a majority in both; or (4) a minority in both, but of a size to be influential in changing policy directions inside Big Neighbour. In any case, the Big Neighbour can hardly avoid involvement in a secessionist conflict in the affected state.

The other element in the analysis concerns the preference for a 'devolution of government' settlement to the secessionist conflict, rather than any others, given the Big Neighbour's involvement as in (6). Here we hypothesize as follows;

(7)   A Big Neighbour will be disposed towards a devolutionist solution if

   (a)   absorption of the entire affected state or its secessionist region into its own political or territorial union ('annexation') is not a feasible or desirable step on economic or any other grounds; and/or

   (b)   the success of the secessionists in achieving independence by whatever means ('secession'), would be unwelcome; and/or

   (c)   the success of the central regime in the affected state in imposing by oppressive means centralized and uniform rule over the ethnic kin group (without providing a proper institutional framework to safeguard their legitimate rights) ('repression') would be equally unwelcome.

A brief discussion of each of these situations follows.

Annexation: forced absorption of the affected state or a part of it would sometimes deal with the defence and common security problems of the Big Neighbour, but at the expense of taking the affected state's ethnic problem into its own fold. More harmfully, it would mean the creation of occupied territory which can provide a political base for protracted resistance in future, as well as international condemnation. Even with the total support of the secessionist community, support from the international community is not necessarily forthcoming. Thus annexation is not often a desirable option for the Big Neighbour.

Secession: the dismemberment of the affected state by a successful secession means the creation of an additional state on the Big Neighbour's borders. This may have repercussions in disruption of trading links, especially if one strong economy is replaced by two weaker ones: but more significantly, it may be seen as the establishment of two unfriendly states instead of one - hostile to each other as well as to the Big Neighbour, and providing a safe haven to other secessionists in its own territory.

Repression: 'standing idly by' while the central regime in the affected state carried out successful military and other repression would not only expose Big Neighbour to enormous political pressure exerted by its own ethnic kin or refugee groups but also to the appearance of weakness internationally. The 'conflict situation' might be ameliorated, at least for a time, but continued repression being necessary to maintain the 'peace' would extend Big Neighbour's discomfort - quite apart from liberal or humanitarian reactions.

The rejection of any of these options 'annexation', 'secession' and 'repression' by the policy makers of the Big Neighbour might predispose them towards a devolutionary solution to the ethnic secessionist conflict in the affected state. If all are rejected the devolutionary solution is practically the only policy option open to Big Neighbour's policy makers.

Finally, assuming now a commitment to a devolutionary solution rather than an alternative (including the *status quo*), in applying the analytical model to the Sri Lanka and other similar situations around the globe, we discern a number of alternative modes of action for the Big Neighbour pursuing its preferred policy option, viz;

(8) The Big Neighbour may play
    R1   the 'pressure' role;
    R2   the 'big stick' role;
    R3   the 'interventionist' role; or
    R4   the 'invitational' role.

Once again, a brief discussion of each follows.

The pressure role: The Big Neighbour may use many methods short of direct military intervention to exert pressure on each of the parties in the affected state, including offering its good offices to mediate a settlement. Diplomatic, economic, financial, and religious resources may be employed (even in the most extreme situations the use of the 'secessionists' as a proxy military force), to make clear to the central regime what they stand to lose by not ending the conflict; or conversely, what they might gain by doing so. The very ties that bind Big Neighbour to an ethnic kin group can be used to threaten withdrawal of support if goals are not changed, or increased practical subvention if they are.

The big stick role: Even if the Big Neighbour's commitment to a devolution solution effectively rules out its support for either annexation or secession, the perception of this by either of the parties in conflict in the affected state is not necessarily a confident one. It would not be beyond Big Neighbour's diplomacy to put about the possibility of either of these alternatives if the conflict continued; diplomacy could be 'stepped up' by demonstrative armed services 'manoeuvres' on the borders or even in the affected state's airspace, and the like ('gunboat diplomacy'). For the central regime and the majority community the Big Neighbour may well be seen as chronically expansionist; for the secessionists, annexation might be seen as likely to end in client status and not 'freedom' at all. They might thus be persuaded to change their goal from secession to autonomy, while the majority change theirs from suppression to separation - both goals then being realizable through devolution.

The interventionist role: This implies military invasion against international law, in support of the insurgent group, but it could be presented as limited in character, as a 'fire-fighting operation' undertaken to 'prevent further bloodshed' or the like. It would effectively, however, be aimed at establishing a cease-fire and perhaps a 'green line', running along the territorial boundary claimed by the secessionists, thus creating a *de facto* temporary 'autonomy' or 'secession' policed by Big Neighbour. Such a situation is intended to engender both a physical setting and a psychological climate for bringing the two parties together for talks about devolution, as a price for Big Neighbour's withdrawal.

The invitational role: Finally, Big Neighbour may actually be invited into the affected state, in a 'peace-keeping' or 'matchmaker' capacity, by the central regime in that state. That body, seeing no prospect of speedy repression of the secessionists, and willing to move towards a negotiated settlement, may prefer the presence of Big Neighbour's troops or police by invitation to their presence by invasion; and may be able to offer quiet frontiers (plus any other sweeteners currently available) in return for Big Neighbour's weight in persuading the secessionists to accept autonomy rather than partition and sovereignty.

These roles are not always wholly distinct in practice, and the Big Neighbour may move in time from one to another as circumstances change. Ideally (i.e. in ideal-type terms) these moves appear in a cycle as depicted in the diagram 1.1 (see below).

The cycle of Big Neighbour roles

Let us examine the logic of movement by Big Neighbour from one of these roles to another. In a secessionist situation where the involvement and the commitment to devolution by a Big Neighbour are very strong, there seems a strong case for saying that its first choice will be the 'pressure role' (R1). This is the most internationally acceptable and legal method of interference in internal conflicts; and involves least departure from normal relationships between states. If, however, the 'pressure role' proves unsuccessful and the prolongation of the secessionist strife is seen as intolerable, the Big Neighbour may well shift from the 'pressure role' to the 'big stick' role (R2). This can be an almost imperceptible escalation, but at some stage it may trigger international disapproval, especially if it is associated with varying types of military manoeuverings. This is as far as Big Neighbour may go without actually crossing borders.

If wielding the 'big stick' does not succeed in persuading the combatants to a devolutionary settlement Big Neighbour, at this juncture, has two optional roles.

(a) Where the unyielding stance is maintained by the central regime its option is direct intervention on behalf of the secessionist group (interventionist role R3), i.e.

aiming at the creation of a forced cease-fire, or a *de facto* secession or partition. If this is done, it needs to be done in great strength and quickly for it is unacceptable in international law.

(b) Where the intransigence is that of the secessionists, and the central regime is amenable to the suggestion, the option is the 'invitational role' (R4), sending military forces in a peace keeping or policing role into the affected state. The problem then becomes one of ending the role: once invited in, yet still meeting with intransigence, Big Neighbour may have to begin again exerting pressure and waving the 'big stick', in the attempt to achieve the devolution settlement.

The diagram 1.1 sets out the shifting phases of these Big Neighbour roles. But we can intuit some basic conditions for preferring one to another, given a commitment on the part of Big Neighbour to a devolution solution to the conflict.

There are four 'actors' whose views and reactions have to be taken into account by Big Neighbour's policy makers; the international community, the 'ethnic kin' secessionist community, the central regime in the affected state, and Big Neighbour's own 'ethnic kin' group or other secession-inclined minority communities (if any). Outright annexation as a policy would not only go against Big Neighbour's commitment to a devolutionary solution, it would also in all likelihood arouse opprobrium from all four of these actors; the international community because of the breach of international law, the secessionist community because it does not give them independence, the central regime because they lose territory and possibly their existence, and Big Neighbour's own 'ethnic kin' group or other secessionist-inclined minorities because there is no future in it for them. So, in its turn, since it implies annexation as a possibility, the 'big stick' role is a very risky one, depending for its effectiveness on the perception of threat by two of these actors (the secessionist community and the central regime in the affected state), while the other two actors (the international community and Big Neighbour's own minorities) perceive so little threat to their own interests, that they are able to be acquiescent.

The 'interventionist' role is also a risky one, almost certain to create great differences of opinion within the international community because of the possibility of the *de facto* partition situation which may be created by the Big Neighbour's intervention. But it will probably get the support of Big Neighbour's own 'ethnic kin' group and secession-inclined minorities, since they will see it as an encouragement to secession in general - a perception which, given that Big Neighbour is committed *against* secession and in favour of a devolutionist solution, produces a risk of later disillusion and internal conflict. The support of the secessionists in the affected state is essential for success, and likely to be forthcoming. The central regime will of course oppose, at least for public consumption.

The 'pressure' role is less risky because it does not hang on misperceptions on the part of the actors of Big Neighbour's true intentions. The international community takes such pressures in its stride, and would certainly support that alternative to a breach of international law. Though the secessionist community may feel betrayed when pressure is exerted on themselves, since goal-changing is specially difficult for them, it is at least a clear *realpolitik* situation and they are able to calculate where their best interests lie. The central regime should feel no threat to its existence, and their position is really little different in this regard than in many others - governments are always having to balance costs and benefits in this way. The overt commitment on Big Neighbour's part to devolutionary solutions rather than partition or secessionist independence may, however, antagonize its own secessionist-inclined minorities.

An 'invitational' role is still a risky one, but likely to achieve the approbation of the international community (depending on the legality of the regime in the affected state and the Big Neighbour's true commitment to the political resolution of the conflict) as well as of the central regime whose initiative it is. The 'ethnic kin' secessionist community is, however, likely to feel betrayed and ill-dealt-with, since Big Neighbour's police or troops are likely to be deployed against them; and Big Neighbour's own 'ethnic kin' and secessionist-inclined minorities will be more alienated from their own central regime than before.

We can hypothesize as follows. Given involvement, and given a commitment to a devolutionary settlement to the conflict in the affected state:

(9)   The role adopted by Big Neighbour will be chosen according to its policy makers' perceptions of their relative strength and weakness vis-a-vis each of the four actors

A1   the international community;

A2   the 'ethnic kin' secessionist community:

A3   the central regime in the affected state; and

A4   Big Neighbour's own ethnic group or other secession-inclined minority communities in the specific situation at a particular time.

The 'cycle' hypothesis can be stated as follows:

(10) Big Neighbour will first adopt a 'pressure role' (R1), and if that does not lead to devolution will shift to a 'big stick role' (R2). If that does not lead to devolution it will then choose the 'interventionist role' (R3) or the 'invitational role' (R4) according to whether the central regime or the secessionist community are most intransigently against a devolution settlement. Neither role will lead directly to devolution, but either can be the base for further pressure towards mediation or threats of stronger action still. The 'interventionist role' may, however, end up with a *de facto* secession or *de lege* partition.

The analytic model of the role of Big Neighbour thus predicts as follows; the intensity of Big Neighbour's involvement in a secessionist conflict will increase the more of the four predisposing conditions listed in hypothesis 6 are present; its preference for a devolutionist solution will be the stronger the more of the three predisposing conditions in hypothesis 7 are present; and it will choose a role from among those listed in hypothesis 8 according to its current perceptions of the effects upon the balance of power between itself and the four 'actors' described in the hypothesis 9, or enter into the cycle of roles as depicted in the figure 1 (hypothesis 10).

Scope and methodology

The main empirical situation to which the model will be applied is the prevalent ethnic secessionist and devolution conflict in Sri Lanka, together with the role played by India as its Big Neighbour. India dominates Sri Lanka's immediate geostrategic environment, as well as having an intimate interest in the Sinhala/Tamil conflict in Sri Lanka because of its own sizeable Tamil minority, which forms a majority in the state which most nearly adjoins Sri Lanka, Tamil Nadu.

But other Big Neighbour situations can be found around the globe, and if the model has any validity it should serve to illuminate at least some of these situations also. For the purpose of the study we have identified the following Big Neighbour secessionist situations' (Big Neighbour in capitals), viz.

1. INDIA-Pakistan (East Pakistan)
2. TURKEY-Cyprus (Northern Cyprus)
3. AUSTRALIA-Papua New Guinea (Bougainville Island)

as comparable situations to the India-Sri Lanka one. In addition, we shall take note of the roles played by Syria between 1976 and 1982 and in 1989-91 in the ethnic conflict in Lebanon as a comparable example for the 'invitational role' played by some of our selected case study Big Neighbours, and in general to test other internal conditions postulated in the previous sub-section. The limited use of the Syria-Lebanon situation will be further explained at the appropriate place.

The methodology to be employed is a simple historical and comparative one, using (in the case of Sri Lanka) a combination of primary and secondary material. For the other cases secondary material only will be used in the main. Statistical data will be given where available in order to illustrate points being made, but there will be no attempt at statistical analysis as such.

The organization of the book

The book consists of seven chapters including the present one. The second chapter discusses the roots of Big Neighbour involvement in a secessionist conflict situation. It examines the circumstantial factors which may provoke the Big Neighbour's involvement in the secessionist conflict situation, using the four selected Big Neighbour secessionist situations, viz, India-East Pakistan, Turkey-Cyprus, Australia-Papua New Guinea and India-Sri Lanka.

The third, fourth and fifth are the most analytical of the chapters and address directly the hypotheses presented in the analytical model. In Chapter 3, using our

FIGURE 1 THE CYCLE OF BIG NEIGHBOUR ROLES

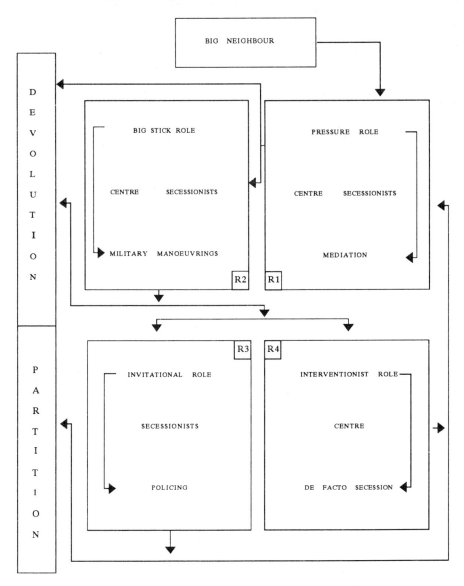

four case study secessionist situations, we investigate the options available to the Big Neighbour as alternatives to 'devolution of government'.

In Chapter 4 we enter the most crucial area of the study, the investigation of the four Big Neighbour roles in a secessionist situation and the implication of such Big Neighbour roles in the reception of devolution of government by the conflicting parties. Using our case studies of the roles played by five Big Neighbour states from different continents here, we will examine the impact of 'the Big Neighbour syndrome', paying due attention to the reaction of other actors, and assess the contribution made by the Big Neighbour's involvement in the successful management of the secessionist conflict in the territory of its small neighbour.

In Chapter 5 we take the other internal conditions and external factors as hypothesized in the analytical model to analyse the implication of their presence in the conflict situation, with particular attention to the role played by the Big Neighbour.

The concluding chapter will integrate the major findings in the study, and examine their relationship with the theoretical model in order to appraise the model's validity in practical politics. Areas of possible further research will also be identified.

2 The Roots of Big Neighbour Involvement

Introduction

The subject matter of this chapter is an analysis of the conditions under which Big Neighbour will be drawn into a secession situation, examining the circumstantial factors which provoked Big Neighbour involvement in the secession conflicts in (East) Pakistan, Cyprus, Papua New Guinea and Sri Lanka. Our hypothesis is that a Big Neighbour will be involved in the secession conflict in the affected state to the extent that it shares a common boundary, a common security zone, and common strategic resources (the 'strategic dimension'), and/or has common ethnic ties with some parts of the affected state (the 'ethnic dimension'). We shall show that in this regard the strategic dimension is of considerably more importance than the ethnic one.

India-Pakistan (East Bengal) situation

As the solitary example of successful unilateral secession until 1991, the East Pakistan (hereafter East Bengal) secession provided us with the most effective Big Neighbour intervention in a secession situation on behalf of the secessionists. Perhaps because it was successful in achieving most of the immediate objectives perceived by the Indian policy makers and, above all, the central goal of the self-determination of the East Bengal people, it has produced a flood of literature of theoretical and empirical importance (e.g. Morris-Jones 1972; Iqbal 1972; Ayoob and Subramanyam 1972; Nanda 1972; Wilcox 1973; Choudhury 1974; Jackson 1975). Much of this literature discusses the Indian involvement in the East Bengal secession conflict as an outcome of the events which followed the tragic incidents of March 1971. The brutal military attack launched against the civilian population by the Pakistan army in this period, the massive influx of refugees which placed a huge human and economic burden on India, and the immobility shown by the international community in preventing further deterioration of the situation, have been considered the major milestones on the way to intervention by India.

The mass exodus of Bengali refugees into Indian territory, as the then Indian Prime Minister saw it, transformed '...an internal problem of Pakistan into an internal problem of India' (Jackson 1975:47). The refugee problem, in her eyes 'a demographic aggression' (Marwah 1979:560), created a powerful argument for Indian intervention. For us it provides a clear case of the influence of 'the refugee problem' in the involvement of Big Neighbour states.

According to impartial accounts at the beginning of December 1971, India received more than 10 million refugees from East Pakistan in the mass exodus of the preceding six months. This raised the estimated total number of refugees in the world from 17.6 million in 1970 to 27.6 million in 1971. Therefore it created a situation where a single country had to bear the burden of more than one third of the refugees in the whole world, mainly due to its neighbour's ethnic conflict (International Commission of Jurists, hereafter ICJ 1972:58).

There was a huge economic cost. India spent well over 500 million dollars for the welfare of these refugees, while the World Bank estimated 700 million dollars for keeping them for a further three months period (ICJ 1972:59). Since international assistance covered just a half of this amount, with no assurance of maintaining even this level of aid continuously, Iawia had to face a huge uninvited economic burden due to this refugee influx.

Even the International Commission of Jurists which recognized the Indian action as a gross violation of international law, was unable to find '...a historical precedent or juridical definition applicable to this situation' (ICJ 1972:58):

> It was not an armed attack in the sense of the Charter, nor even a provocation on the part of Pakistan, nor a blockade - although it gravely threatened India's economy. It must be recognized that India's vital economic interests were at stake and that the only possible solution to the problem was to be found in the creation of political conditions which would make it possible to repatriate the refugees. The United Nations, as we have seen, was doing nothing to bring about those conditions, and it is hard to see how they would have been achieved without the liberation of Bangladesh (ICJ 1972:58).

It was against this background that the Indian intervention in the East Pakistan conflict took place, apparently aimed at the removal of the human and economic burden created by the growing refugee problem.

However, there was a humanitarian dimension too. Though the Indian authorities never argued their mission in East Pakistan as an humanitarian intervention (ICJ 1972:62), by intervening India immensely benefited from the global reaction to the situation there, which was one of growing world anger against the military regime in Pakistan. Their illiberal decision to repress the democratically-elected East Pakistani leadership of the Awami League, and the atrocities committed by the Pakistan army against the civilian population, drew world sympathy for the plight of the Bengali people. The publicity given by the world press and in international forums to human suffering in East Pakistan created an international atmosphere favourable to Indian intervention (about the media coverage of the conflict, see Nanda 1972:322-3, fn.4-7).

Even G. W. Choudhury (a member of the Pakistan cabinet of 1971), while claiming a grand design of the Indian leaders to dismantle Pakistan as their national enemy (Choudhury 1974:ix), argued that,

> The Pakistan Army's brutal actions, which began on the midnight of March 25, 1971, can never be condoned or justified in any way. The army's murderous campaign in which many thousands of innocent people including women, the old and sick and even children were brutally murdered while millions fled from their homes (Choudhury 1974:181).

It was just as the revelations of these atrocities came to the knowledge of world opinion that India launched its rapid large-scale military attack and defeated the Pakistan army. There is no doubt that the world sympathy drawn by the plight of the Bengali people overshadowed the illegality of the Indian action which amounted to the violation of the sovereignty of Pakistan (ICJ, 1972:53-7). The United Nations failed to find a consensus among the member states to deplore it. Pakistan's powerful friends in international politics, especially the United States and China, hesitated to make a counter intervention on behalf of the unpopular military regime (see Iqbal 1972:25-7; Choudhury 1974:193-6).

However, such an analysis of the Indian intervention in East Bengal is incomplete without also considering the ethnic ties between East Bengal (Pakistan) and West Bengal (India), and the security or strategic issues that were perceived by Indian policy makers as arising from further escalation of the conflict in East Bengal.

The common ethnic ties of the East and West Bengali people were frequently used by Indian commentators to justify the Indian involvement in East Bengal. Their central argument was that India had an unavoidable obligation to help its ethnic-kin in East Bengal in their hour of greatest need (see Sharma 1978:55). For example one Indian writer, demanding military intervention by the Indian central government, noted in 1971,

> The embattled people of Bengal Desh are not a distant and unfamiliar race; they speak our language, sing our songs and read our literature. Indeed many millions of Indians have relatives and dear friends across the border (Guha 1971:984).

But the ethnic-kin dimension of Indian intervention cannot be fully explained in this simplistic way. The main reasons for the intercession derived from the dualistic nature of East Bengali nationalism.

The national identity of the majority of the East Bengali people, as it has existed in the South Asian sub-continent since 1947, comes from two different roots. One is their religious affiliation; the Islamic identity. The other is their linguistic and cultural identity; the Bengali identity (Jackson 1975:146). By religion the East Bengali people distinguish themselves from the Hindu majority in India and especially from their fellow Bengalis in the Indian state of West Bengal. But by their linguistic and cultural identity they become a part of the same ethno-linguistic community that exists in West Bengal (for a comprehensive examination of East Bengal identity, see Ghazi 1972).

In 1947 the people of East Bengal became the single largest ethno-regional group in undivided India to join the Muslim League in realization of their vision of a 'religion-based-state', Muslim Pakistan, on the basis of the famous 'two-nation theory' ('...that the Hindus and Muslims of undivided India were two different nations' Rajan 1972:191). At that time the East Bengali community gave pre-eminence to their 'Muslimness', as against 'Indianness', (Qureshi 1973:570) as a way of rejecting the Hindu dominance that existed in undivided Bengal in British India (Qureshi 1973:559).

However this Muslim identity and their hatred of Hindu domination did not ensure them regional autonomy in a confederated state of Pakistan, as expected gw their political leaders at the time of partition (see Jackson 1975:11-12,fn.4). Instead Muslim Pakistan became a typical multiethnic 'state-nation', which gave political and economic dominance to one ethnic group over others. Political and economic discrimination and cultural neglect became the lot of culturally and linguistically discrete regional groups excluded from sharing political and economic power. Of these aggrieved ethno-regional groups in Pakistan the East Bengalis became the most disturbed community. (We do not enter into a detailed examination of the socio-economic and political factors which led to the alienation of East Bengalis as it is a well documented aspect of the conflict; for example, see Owen 1972; Rahman 1975; Choudhury 1974.) Against this background the Muslim Bengalis soon came to realize the importance of their linguistic and cultural identity. The Bengali language and culture became the salient elements of Bengali nationalism, providing an identification for East Bengalis distinguishing them from their countrymen in West Pakistan, a distinction further enhanced by their geographical separateness. As noted by Abidullah Ghazi, in their geographical, linguistic and cultural separateness '...the two parts of Pakistan differed with each other in almost every aspect of their life except their religion' (Ghazi 1972:147).

It was, in fact, the wish of the leaders of the Muslim League to make Urdu the sole official language of Pakistan which provoked open resistance by the people of East Bengal in the early 1950s (Jackson 1975:17), marking the first stage of a developing Bengali ethnic nationalism (Urdu, as spoken in West Pakistan, has links with Persian and Arabic: the Bengali language, like Hindi, is Sanskrit based). In the face of this linguistic and cultural subordination, all the East Bengalis' social and economic grievances against West Pakistan provided further stimulus for the rise of Bengali nationalism. As linguistic and cultural identity came into prominence, the East Bengalis were pushed into side-lining their Muslim identity. This was first symbolized by the decision of the main political organization of East Bengal, the *Awami Muslim League*, to drop the word 'Muslim' from its name as earnest of its secular orientation (Rahman 1975:39).

In this way the East Bengalis, a community which once raised the banner of Muslimness (Qureshi 1972:370) against the idea of secular India (as visualized by the Congress leaders in undivided India) describing it as a continuation of Hindu domination in disguise, returned to the concept of 'ethno-linguistic nationality', now the foundation of the political structure of the Indian federation.

It was against this background that common ethnic ties turned into a vehicle of Indian involvement in the East Bengal secession conflict. Political co-operation was already developing among Bengali politicians in the two states. It was known that the Indian state of West Bengal had provided sanctuary to East Bengali leaders since the 1950s (Jackson 1975:17; Rahman 1975:39). This was strengthened by the movement of refugees towards Indian territory, and the seeking by the secessionist leaders of military intervention from the Indian side in late 1971. When the conflict in East Pakistan transmuted into open civil war, a strong political agitation emerged from the Indian side of Bengal, asking for direct intervention by the Indian central government (see Guha 1971:984).

While the humanitarian and refugee dimensions, along with common ethnic ties between the secessionist Bengalis and the Bengali people in India, facilitated a political environment favourable to Indian intervention, certain security and strategic issues emerged as possible eventualities of the conflict, to give the policy makers in Indian central government serious thought.

In the early stages of the conflict in East Pakistan the official Indian strategy was to get the United Nations into the conflict situation as an intermediary, and to influence world public opinion about the plight of the East Bengali people, in order to pressurize the central regime in Pakistan to find a political settlement to the conflict (Jackson 1975:60). It is widely accepted by many analysts that India did not foresee any kind of military intervention in East Bengal at this stage (see Kumar 1975:489-498). But the brutal military suppression that took place in East Pakistan marked the point of no return for the Bengali community, and provided the opportunity to India to take the side of the secessionist Bengali people against its hostile enemy in the sub-continent. At this point, Indian intervention became necessary for two short term strategic reasons.

The common ethnic ties on both sides of Bengal themselves provided a security threat, to the Indian mind in Delhi. From the point of view of India, any prolongation of the conflict, with a huge and increasing presence of Bengali refugees in Indian territory, created the possible emergence of an all-Bengali nationalism, a security threat for the Indian federation (Wilcox 1973:34), especially on India's Eastern frontier, which had already become a breeding ground for several secessionist groups (see Dommen 1967). In addition to this threat of all-Bengali nationalism there was another possibility, of the transformation of the secessionist Bengali organization into a Communist guerrilla movement, vulnerable to Chinese involvement as already manifested by the Naxelite movement in West Bengal (Guha 1971:984). The guerrilla movement in East Pakistan was carrying out a successful resistance without the physical presence of pro-Indian Awami League leaders, and in the later stages, the leadership of the liberation movement suffered a rift between its moderate and its leftist and radical elements (Jackson 1975:77-8). For Indian policy makers, delay in direct intervention would risk filling the vacuum with these unacceptable options.

On the other hand, at this later stage they found that United Nations involvement had become a shield for the Pakistani rulers' prolongation of the conflict. As pointed out by Robert Jackson, a decision by the Indian central government to abandon further involvement, allowing a UN-sponsored settlement between India and Pakistan, was seen by the Indian side not as a resolution of the East Bengal conflict but a further escalation of it with '...many more years of continuing savage repression' (Jackson 1975:68). Such an eventuality would damage the image of the central government and add another headache in its troubled frontier state of West Bengal (Jackson 1975:68). Therefore Indian intervention can be seen as an effort by the Indian policy makers to keep control of the events unfolding at its most sensitive frontier. Indian anxiety was clearly expressed by Mrs Indira Gandhi in the following words,

> I do not think any people or any government could have shown greater restraint than we have in the face of such tremendous provocation and threat to our safety and to our stability. ...With all our restraint we are not getting any nearer to a solution. On the contrary, the military confrontation, as the other confrontations which I mentioned, political, economic, social, administrative, are steady getting worse. People have asked me how long can India manage? Actually that date has long since passed. I feel I am sitting on the top of a volcano and honestly do not know when it is going to erupt (as quoted in Kumar 1975:496).

Quite apart from that, by a successful intervention India might be able to change the regional balance in the sub-continent. From the point of view of Indian policy makers the dismemberment of Pakistan would remove the greatest obstacle in the sub-continent to India's long-held ambition of playing a greater role in the region and the world. In the short run the birth of the new Bangladesh would disconnect the most prosperous and populous part of Pakistan, reducing the size of its heartland to a territory that is less than one-tenth of that of India, and occasioning great military loss to Pakistan. As Wayne Wilcox puts it:

> The well-equipped Pakistani army of about 350,000 men was supported by a society of over 120 million and Pakistan's foreign exchange earnings were large. Without East Pakistan, the country would shrink to about 55 million, a little less than half of its foreign exchange earnings would be lost, and it could not afford to maintain such a large military establishment. It was a golden opportunity for India to eliminate the Pakistani threat (Wilcox 1973:35).

As the conflict in East Bengal transmuted into an all out civil war, with the large majority of the East Bengalis wanting to make it the point of no return in their conflict with West Pakistan, S. Subramanyam, a prominent Indian strategist, commented,

> What India must realize is the fact that the break up of Pakistan is in our interest and we have an opportunity the like of which will never come again (as quoted in Iqbal 1972:22).

Here, then we see in place the refugee, humanitarian, ethnic-ties, and short- and long-term strategic conditions for the involvement of the Indian Big Neighbour in the secessionist conflict in East Bengal.

Turkey-Cyprus Situation

The Turkish involvement in the ethnic conflict between the Greek Cypriot and Turkish Cypriot communities in Cyprus stemmed directly from on the one hand the ethnic affinity of the Turkish Cypriot minority with the majority Turks in mainland Turkey, and on the other the security and strategic interests of the Republic of Turkey affected by it. In the Turkey-Cyprus situation, these two roots of Big Neighbour involvement are closely interconnected.

The conflict in Cyprus, as noted by Mehmet Ali Birand '...is the by-product of a struggle which Turkey and Greece have been carrying on for years in order to increase or secure their respective influence in the (Eastern Mediterranean) region' (Birand 1988:173). Official Turkish involvement in the Cyprus conflict first started in 1952 when the government of Greece unsuccessfully tried to raise the issue of the self-determination of the Cyprus people at the United Nations' General Assembly (see Souter 1984:658-61). The real intention of the Greek government was perhaps to provide an opportunity for the majority Greek Cypriots in the island of Cyprus to realize their long held political ideal of *Enosis* (union with Greece) through their right to self-determination. Thus Greek interest in the island derived from the main currents of Hellenic nationalism prevailing in the region. First there was the 'Great Idea' held by ethnic Greeks in mainland Greece and in Asia Minor including the islands like Crete and Cyprus, which aspired to establish organic links and political unity within a larger Greek State. Second was the 'Enosis' ideal held by Greek Cypriots since the 19th century, expressing their nationalist vision of joining with the Greek motherland (Markides 1977:10-11, see for a brief analysis of this Kitromildes 1990).

As Greek irredentist nationalism made its claim for Cyprus, concurrently with 'Enosis' in Cyprus, the policy makers of the Republic of Turkey found both unacceptable, as either would endanger Turkey's strategic and security interests in the region. Having concluded a bitter war with Greece some twenty two years before, and concluded a treaty demarcating the maritime boundary, they rejected any annexation of Cyprus by Greece, bringing the frontier with Greece to an island that lies just forty miles away from its southern coast.

As a Turkish spokesman commented,

> In view of its geographical location so close to the Turkish mainland, Cyprus is politically and militarily of vital importance to Turkey as its occupation by a foreign hostile power may endanger Turkish security. A take-over of Cyprus by Greece would moreover disrupt the delicate geopolitical balance established between Turkey and Greece after the First World War with the Treaty of Lausanne in 1924 (Idiz 1975:7).

Until this time, Turkish nationalism had refrained from making official claims to territories inhabited by ethnic Turks or formerly belonging to the Ottoman empire. To quote one such official statement,

> Although our nationalism loves all Turks ...with a deep feeling of brotherhood, and although it desires with all its soul their wholesome development, yet it recognizes that its political activity must end at the borders of the Turkish Republic (Tachau 1959:265).

However, in the case of the strategically important island of Cyprus, awaiting its decolonization and inhabited by a large population of ethnic Turks, this had become too expensive a principle to be maintained. There was a violent nationalist protest in the Turkish capital, demanding that the government of Turkey launch an active policy towards Cyprus (Tachau 1959:269-70,271). At this stage, Turkey for the first time involved itself in Cyprus affairs by making known its disapproval of the Greek demand, resisting Greek irredentism by diplomatic means (Tachau 1959:269).

The anxiety shown by the Turkish minority in the island towards 'Enosis' provided a pan-Turkish background for Turkish involvement. Turkish Cypriots who had enjoyed a privileged position in colonial society under Britain found that in addition to becoming a permanent minority in the future Cyprus society, they were in effect going to be colonized by Greece. They saw 'Enosis' as a threat to their survival and joined with the Turkish mainland against the 'annexation' and 'Enosis' aims perceived by Greece and Greek Cypriots respectively.

It was understandable for them to seek assistance from the Turkish government, as an ethnic community which shared religious, cultural and linguistic unity with Turks on the mainland, who identify Turkish Cypriots as *Soydas* - Kin or brothers (Ryan 1984:167). As Sunni Muslims by religion, they shared the same Islamic values practised in Turkey. They spoke the same Turkish language - even according to Nancy Crawshaw, 'a purer form of Turkish than that spoken on the mainland' (Crawshaw 1978:21). They were descendants of immigrants who came to the island from Anatolia during the period 1570-1825 when the island was a possession of the Ottoman empire (Ryan 1984:168).

Moreover, in association with this ethnic affinity, Turkey made a claim for the island of Cyprus as the heir-apparent to the former territories held by the Ottoman empire. According to their version the island was handed over to the British imperial government in 1878 in virtue of their promise to protect Turkey from the Russian threat. Their argument was that Cyprus had belonged to the Turkish empire for nearly 300 years and had never belonged to Greece: '...if there should be a change in the status of Cyprus its should be returned to Turkey since it was the natural extension of the Anatolian peninsula and a former Ottoman possession' (Ryan 1984:161). In strengthening their irredentist claim for Cyprus, the Turkish commentators had further arguments. To quote one such statement:

> Turks were in the majority a century ago, when the island was leased to Britain by the Ottoman Empire at the end of a disastrous war with Tsarist Russia in 1878. Their number decreased due to heavy emigration to the Turkish mainland for various reasons (Idiz 1975:7).

The Turkish involvement in Cyprus had another dimension, related to the historical hostility that had prevailed between Turkey and Greece for supremacy in the Eastern Mediterranean. Both countries engaged in persistent armed conflict and finally a bitter war in the 1920s. This created deeply rooted anti-Greek feeling among the Turkish people as an integral aspect of Turkish nationalism or 'Turkism'. As described by Frank Tachau,

> Indeed the birth of the present day Turkish Republic was attended by a long and vicious war between Turks and Greeks. The resultant hostility was so bitter that an exchange of populations on an unprecedentedly large scale was thought necessary to prevent further bloodshed. ...The average Turk, in conformity with his habit of classifying nations as either friends of Turkey or

enemies of Turkey, continues to think of the Greeks as national enemies (Tachau 1959:263-4).

Since the outlook of the ordinary people was associated with a hostile attitude towards Greeks, the plight of their ethnic kin in Cyprus and the Greeks' claim for the island easily became national issues in Turkish politics (Ryan 1984:162). Against this background, policy makers in Turkey were compelled to take the necessary steps to prevent Greece getting control of the strategic island of Cyprus, which could '...command the routes of access to the ports of Southern Turkey, which are the only ones that have remained relatively free of foreign domination...' (Tachau 1959:263) in the recent past.

Having entered the Cyprus conflict in this way and through successful diplomatic manoeuvrings, Turkey achieved a permanent role in the affairs of Cyprus, before and after independence in 1960. Until 1974 it played a key role as the guarantor power as well as the main backer of the Turkish Cypriots in achieving what they called the 'partnership Republic' of 1960 (Ertekun 1990:47), putting pressure on the Greek side to maintain the 'status-quo' situation created by that constitution. However, the situation in Cyprus deteriorated into persistent inter-ethnic conflict after 1963, as will be discussed in the next chapter, influencing Turkish policy makers to become involved more closely in Cyprus affairs, playing different roles as the concerned Big Neighbour of Cyprus.

The Turkish military intervention in Cyprus in 1974 destroyed the uneasy political equilibrium that had existed since independence in the island. It paved the way for the *de facto* secession of Northern Cyprus, creating a 'green line' between two warring factions in the Cyprus conflict. Turkey decided on this intervention despite the advice given by the United Kingdom, one of the guarantor powers of the Cyprus constitution, and by the United States, its major ally in the NATO block. As argued by the Turkish side, their action was necessitated by the change in the political situation in Cyprus following the military coup of 1974 by officers of the Greek Cypriot National Guard against President Makarios.

As there were reasons to suspect an involvement by the Greek military regime in the Cyprus coup and since the new leader of Cyprus, Nikos Sampson, was known to the Turkish community as a 'Turk Killer' (Denktash 1982:65) as well as being the extremist leader of the 'Enosis' movement, Turkey declared that the situation in Cyprus had become a risk to its national interest and a threat to the very existence of its ethnic kin in the island. Thus, intervention in the end was the Turkish response to a political situation which raised the spectre of 'Enosis', which would threaten the security of the Turkish Cypriots and the security of Turkey (Ryan 1984:211).

Australia-Papua New Guinea (Bourgainville) Situation

The present and any future involvement by Australia in Papua New Guinea's (hereafter PNG) secession conflict in Bougainville Island (or North Solomons Province) are largely determined by Australia's regional strategic interests and the common security interests that are shared with its former colonial possession, an archipelago lying about 100 to 160 kilometres north of Australia's northern shore.

There are no common ethnic ties between the peoples of Australia and PNG or its secessionist region, Bougainville Island. Ethnically the majority of the people in PNG belong to the broad Melanesian stock which is common to many of the mini-states in the South Pacific. But the people of Bougainville Island claim a distinct territorial, historical and ethnic identity from the mainland Papua New Guineans. Bougainville is culturally and geographically a part of the Solomon Islands chain though politically it belongs to Papua New Guinea. Bougainvilleans are conscious of their historical, cultural and geographical identity, and even their colour is distinct from mainland Papua New Guineans. Leo Hannett (one of the leading spokesman of the Bougainville secession movement in the 1970s) explains:

> The Bougainvilleans are a culturally, ethnically, historically and geographically distinct group from the rest of Papua New Guineans... We are generally jet black people, having common ancestry with more people down Western Solomons rather than with any group in Papua New Guinea...We have always had a common history of ourselves as distinct from Papua New Guineans (quoted in Griffin 1990:4).

However, PNG has something in common with Australia as it uses English as the principal language of instruction in the school system (Baldwin 1978:15). Since English speakers are considered one of the three largest linguistic groups in PNG (Baldwin 1978:18), this cannot be considered just a colonial legacy.

On the other hand, to a certain extent, the patron/client-like relationship which has been continuously maintained by the two countries since PNG independence has created a psychological attachment in the Australian mind - an obligation to protect the territorial integrity and the economic well being of PNG. At the 10th anniversary of PNG independence, the then Minister of Foreign Affairs Bill Hayden admitted,

> ...Australia and PNG are for better or for worse permanently thrown together. The importance of the relationship between us will always be given the highest priority. Geography and history make it inevitable that our concerns must overlap and, in different ways, be shared. We should use this anniversary of independence as a measure of the progress we have achieved together and the challenges that lie ahead (Hayden 1985:813).

As reflected in such expressions both countries since PNG independence have committed themselves to maintain a close relationship, giving Australia a key role in assisting and advising in PNG's economic and defence matters. In 1977 the then Australian Prime Minister Malcolm Fraser and Prime Minister Michael Somare of PNG jointly set out their commitment towards the security of PNG by declaring,

> ...that it was their governments' intention to consult, at the request of either (on) matters affecting their common security interests and about other aspects of their defence relationship (as quoted in Babbage 1987:87).

Since its independence in late 1975, PNG (which was kept as an integral part of Australia's economic, monetary and defence system until the last moment of its independence) has received large sums in economic aid from the Australian government in continuation of its colonial obligations, to help the new state develop self-reliance in defence and economic management. For the last 15 years successive Australian governments have honoured the pledge given at its independence.

The main Australian aid goes to PNG as a direct annual grant to its annual budget. In the late 1970s Australia provided 40 to 45 percent of PNG's budgetary resources (annually US$200 million) and 45 to 50 percent of its foreign exchange requirements (Baldwin 1987:6). At that time, according to a World Bank Study Report, this grant amounting to '...nearly US$ 80 per capita, giving Papua New Guinea one of the largest per capita aid figures of any country in the world...' (Baldwin 1987:6), was considered as the lifeline of PNG's political and economic structure (Baldwin 1987:6). This high dependency on Australian aid has now become a salient element of PNG's economy. For 1989-90 it received US$ 275 million in budgetary aid and US$ 20 million in project aid (Evans 1990:28).

The most important aspect of this Australian assistance is their total commitment to the development of the defence and security capabilities of PNG. This has become an Australian responsibility, according to Ralph Premdas, partly '...because of the suddenness of the Australian decolonization process... (and their neglect in developing) ...the PNG army for an independent existence' (Premdas 1976:269). It is worth noting that even in the 1960s Australians were unable to make up their minds about the future of PNG. Some colonial administrators considered self-government was not within PNG's reach for the next 100 years (Hayden 1985:812-13) while some envisaged incorporating it as the seventh state of the Australian Federation (Baldwin 1978:21). On the other hand, since Australia had turned over its former defence structure in PNG to the new state thereby compelling PNG to maintain it to Australian standards, they had an obligation to help the new state (Premdas 1976:269).

In its first year of independence, PNG received nearly half of its defence budget from the Australian government (Premdas 1976:269) following an assurance that they would continue their training programmes for the PNG Defence Force

(PNGDF). As a part of this programme a total of 2500 personnel have trained in Australia since independence. Further they sent military advisers, engineers, technicians and even pilots to assist PNGDF. There were some 750 Australian personnel in PNG at independence for this purpose, and in the 1990s this has been reduced to 80 Australian personnel (Bullock 1991:3). These defence obligations reached their 15th year in 1990, and under Australia's Defence Co-operation Programme - DCP - ('the general objective of which is to promote Australia's security interests in South-east Asia and South Pacific, and to facilitate co-operative defence activities with countries in those regions', see Baldwin 1991:1), the Australian government provided US$ 41 million to PNG, a US$14 million increase from the previous year (Evans 1990:29).

Since 1987, accepting the necessity of formalization of their decade-old close relationship, both countries have established a permanent Ministerial Forum to conduct their bilateral relationship, including activities in economic, development and defence co-operation. Further to that both governments have entered a mutual agreement on defence by the Joint Declaration of Principles (JDP) issued in 1987. Under the terms of JDP both governments are now bound to

> ...consult, at the request of either, about matters affecting their common security interests, in the event of external armed attack threatening the national sovereignty of either country (in order to decide) what measures should be taken, jointly or separately, in relation to that attack (as quoted in MacQueen 1989:539).

In this continuation of Australian assistance to PNG's economic management and development, and above all in establishing such a close relationship of mutual defence, both countries have common political and strategic interests as close neighbours belonging to the same geographic region.

The Australian policy makers have strong reasons to consider the location of their small neighbour as an integral aspect of their defence structure. As the only South Pacific country which shares a common territorial border with Indonesia, and in effect becoming the central divide between the South Pacific and South East Asia, PNG would provide enormous strategic advantage to a hostile power, should any such power occupy PNG, as noted by an Australian analyst:

> (It) would not only increase the potential threat in the Taurus Strait and Gulf of Carpentaria regions but also generate an axis of threat down the east coast of Queensland and, in a broader sense, to adjacent countries in the South-West Pacific. The occupation of PNG by such a power would also deny Australia access to potentially important air and naval facilities to our north and hence restrict Australia's strategic reach in some areas of the Central-Western Pacific (Babbage 1987:88).

Further, given such objectives as '...fostering a strategic outlook among the Pacific island countries which accords with Australia's; (and) encouraging (those) small island countries to look to Australia for guidance on defence and security issues...' (Hegarty 1988:311), which have become the present strategic objectives of the overall Australian security perspective in the South Pacific, a country like PNG which lies well within strategic reach cannot escape from Australian defence calculations. Thus, as far as the political elite in PNG is willing to continue it, Australia has to maintain its existing guiding role in PNG's economic management and defence build-up.

On the other hand, the political leadership of PNG has its own reasons to continue defence ties with Australia, because of its common border with Indonesia's troubled Irian Jaya province (formerly West Papua) and the security issues emerging from that due to the secessionist activities of the *Organisai Papua Merdeka* (OPM) or Free Papua Movement which has been receiving some support from Melanesian brothers in PNG (May 1986:148,155; Bullock 1991:9). This 750 kilometre-long border which lies along terrain difficult for the PNG security forces to patrol, has long been considered a potential source of trouble in inflaming a conflict with Indonesia. Interestingly, this threat perception is not a post-independence phenomenon but a colonial inheritance. It was the Australians who first understood the security threat to the Australian national interest arising from this troubled area and developed a border defence system, spending more than US$ 40 million (Verrier 1986:31). As such Australia has an obligation to support PNG's defence planners in facing their powerful South East Asian neighbour.

Further, the historical impression of an expansionist neighbour, given by the Indonesian administrators to the countries in the region by their irredentist campaign against the Malaysian Federation in the 1960s (see Keesing's 1963:19262-3 & 19746-7), the incorporation of Irian Jaya after the end of Dutch colonial rule (Premdas 1986:241,242), and the forcible annexation of East Timor (see Crouch 1986), has also greatly influenced the people and the political leaders in PNG to give serious attention to the OPM related issues in Irian Jaya (see Seth 1985:115; Crouch 1986:172-3; Premdas 1976:272-3). Most Papua New Guineans consider Indonesia's border violations in pursuit of OPM dissidents from Irian Jaya province, and accusation over the OPM activities in PNG territory, as premeditated attempts by Indonesians to provoke an encounter with them. This line of thinking has given Indonesia the colour of an imperialist power waiting to intervene in the affairs of PNG (Crouch 1986:167). When Indonesia annexed East Timor in 1975 most Papua New Guineans saw their country as the next territorial target of Indonesia (Mackie 1986:81-3). For this they had some grounds. For example, Jose Ramos-Horta one of the founders of the Fertiline resistance movement against Indonesian Occupation in East Timor, alleged,

Papua New Guinea is the next objective of Indonesia's expansion after its virtual take-over of East Timor. Fertiline troops in Timor have captured documents which prove Indonesia (is) behind the Bougainville secessionist movement and other civil unrest in Papua New Guinea (as quoted in Lawless 1976:965).

These thoughts about Indonesian expansionism, and a possible threat arising from that country against PNG, are not limited to PNG itself. A considerable number of Australian strategic thinkers are willing to share these assumptions. Many of them consider Indonesia not only an external threat to PNG but also to Australia itself. Though they do not perceive any external power with the capacity to launch a major attack against Australia, for them Indonesia appears to be the only regional power capable of making strategic gains against Australia (see Seth 1985:115-16). This was, as noted by Nancy Viviani perhaps '...because of Indonesia's capability to disturb or enhance the regional balance of power, because Indonesia can facilitate or check Australian entree to regional forums and because of great power interests in Indonesia' (Viviani 1976:201). Above all, most Australian foreign policy administrators believe that they will eventually have to meet Indonesia in a regional conflict, due to the special attachment as well as common strategic interests embodied in the PNG-Australia framework. While discussing the possible conflict between Indonesia and PNG, an Australian foreign policy administrator once explained this quite clearly,

Where certain Indonesian development priorities have seemed to destabilize relations with neighbouring PNG, and the area adjacent to Australia's border, or transgressed basic human rights, this concern is shared by the Australian government. The situation is made more complex by the depth of feeling in Australia for the course of PNG independence. Any possible threat to the internal interests and national security of PNG, which this year celebrates its 10th anniversary of independence, will be viewed with grave concern (Holloway 1985:513-14).

Against this background, then, the more than 15 years old secessionist conflict in Bougainville Island,[1] which has transmuted into a civil war in the 1990s, is not just an internal problem for PNG. A request from PNG for assistance in its efforts to put down such an anti-state movement could not be ignored by the Australian

---

1. Bougainville declared secession first in September 1974 less than three weeks before PNG obtained its independence. The conflict was resolved (temporarily) by the PNG leaders by establishing a devolved governmental structure at independence (Premdas 1977-a:65) but most of the hot issues of the conflict remained unanswered, creating further resentment among the island population.

policy makers. Australia is not in a position to become a bystander. It cannot maintain neutrality without facing the danger of losing its strategic alliance with the PNG leadership. As early as 1978, T. B. Millar while discussing the security problems in the South Pacific region identified this more precisely:

> If either of these movements (the secessionist movements in Papua and Bougainville) succeeded, we would be involved at least in terms of providing logistical support for ground forces. It is not inconceivable that if Australia refused to provide the arms, helicopters etc., that the PNG government considered necessary to enforce its authority, it might turn elsewhere for them (Millar 1978:223, words in brackets added).

Since there is no state with appropriate military or economic potential in the region, except Australia, to provide such assistance, any outward looking approach from the PNG leadership would have to bring extra-regional powers into the South Pacific region.

Further, if PNG disintegrated into a number of mini-states it would create a very difficult situation for the Australians. Their immediate South Asian autocratic neighbour, Indonesia, would be one of the potential contenders for the resources-rich territories of PNG. There are many others - even the Libyans, who happen to be the most recent intruder to raise alarms in Australia (see Pugh 1987:127; MacQueen 1989:537) - waiting for such an occasion to get involved in the affairs of the South Pacific region. In brief this is contrary to Australia's long held strategic objective in the region viz. '... the denial of strategic access [in the region] to hostile or potentially hostile powers' (Hegarty 1988:311). Therefore, as Ross Babbage puts it, '...it is in Australia's interests for PNG to remain united with a strong central government maintaining internal cohesion' (Babbage 1987:88).

Finally, coming to the secession conflict in Bougainville Island itself: there is a unique economic dimension which needs to receive serious attention from the Australian policy makers. In their struggle to establish an independent state in an island of just 3000 square miles, apart from their ethnic and regional differences from mainland Papua New Guinea, the Bougainville secessionists have been largely influenced by the economic potential of their territory. This is mainly related to the success of the Panguna copper mine which started production in 1973 and has now become the fourth largest copper mine in the world with an annual production of 180,000 tons of copper (see *Financial Times* 9 September 1989). According to George B. Baldwin, Bougainville Copper Limited (BCL) received a profit of A$158 million and paid out over A$80 million in cash dividends in its first year of production. The project was established on a paid-in capital of A$134 million with two thirds of the project financed by debt. However, in its second year of production by earning A$181 million before tax the BCL returned to stockholders their total investment plus a return of 16.5 percent (Baldwin 1978:84).

By its copper and gold production the Panguna mine now provides 40 percent of PNG's export earnings and up to 20 percent of government income (Keesing's January 1990:37188).

The conflict between the Bougainville Provincial Assembly and the central government over the allocation of additional funds for regional development, one of the major areas where the Bougainville secessionists have sound arguments against the centre, is also derived from these economic realities of the successful operation of the Panguna mine. For example, in 1976, the Bougainville leaders saw the central government's refusal to allocate an additional US$3.5 million to the Provincial Assembly as unjustified since the central government was extracting more than US$50 million annually from the island as its share of the copper reserves alone (Premdas 1977-a:78).

However, the secession movement in Bougainville cites other important issues related to the Panguna mine. The native Bougainville people have grievances against the environmental damage caused by the production process of the mine, that go back to the colonial time. Another issue was the method of paying compensation to the native people. As Ralph Premdas puts it '...the natives were to be compensated for their land, trees, and buildings, but not for the loss of their subsurface mineral rights contrary to traditional village practice' (Premdas 1977-b:255). Further the natives have grievances over the disproportionate share of the royalty granted to the native people and to the central government. The majority of the work force in the mine are not from Bougainville island. More than 60 percent of them are from the mainland areas of PNG. In addition, there has been a growing migrant population arriving in the island from other parts of PNG to reap the economic benefits brought by the prosperity of the copper mine. To this has been attributed the disruption of the orderly life of the native society. The growing non-Bougainville population and their strength in the work-force of the mine have provided sufficient grounds for the 'jet dark' Bougainvilleans to raise their ethno-nationalist cry against the domination of the mainland Papua New Guineans or 'redskins' as they were nicknamed in Bougainville (for these various issues related to Copper in Bougainville, see Premdas 1977-a:72-3, 1977-b:252-5,260-1; Griffin 1990:8-15; Okole 1990:16-24; Filer 1990:73-85).

Against this background, every time secessionist violence occurred it was the disruption of the working of Panguna copper mine that was the main target of the secessionists. Though the mine has brought economic prosperity to the island, strengthening their argument about the economic viability of Bougainville as an independent state, the secessionists have expressed their readiness to '...pay any price to keep (their) human dignity, even if that meant closing the Bougainville copper mine indefinitely' (Premdas 1977-b:261). The most recent occasion was May 1989. The secessionists attacked the mine and forced it to close indefinitely, registering the beginning of the present secessionist crisis in Bougainville. The mine was continuously closed for the rest of the year, even affecting prices in the World copper market (see *Financial Times* 9 September 1990), and causing BCL to lay off 2000 workers from its total workforce of 2300 in January 1990 (Keesing's 1990:37188).

Because of the dominant position held by the Panguna copper mine in PNG's economy as well in the government revenue, its continued closure has severely affected the PNG economy. In view of this situation in January 1990 the PNG Finance Minister was compelled to announce an emergency adjustment package including a decision to devalue the PNG currency by 10 percent, a freeze on credit from Banks and cuts in government expenditure. Further the PNG government requested US\$ 130,000,000 from the International Monetary Fund and the World Bank (Keesing's 1990:37189).

Since Australia has undertaken the obligation of supporting the PNG's annual budget, such an economic crisis certainly became a burden for the Australian policy makers. In recent years the Australian government has announced its eagerness to relieve itself of this heavy economic burden, while supporting PNG's recent initiatives to explore other avenues to replace Australian budgetary aid (Evans 1986:156). Therefore the conflict in Bougainville island, as a cause of the weakening of PNG's economic viability (Bullock 1991:14), demands the attention of Australian policy makers. In the context of Australian PNG relations they are obliged to assist the PNG government to establish its authority in the island. There is no doubt that such an Australian involvement must take account of the 'Australian mining interests on the island' (Kemelfield 1990:71), especially those of the giant Australian multinational corporation *Conzinc Riotinto of Australia* (CRA), which has held the majority of shares in Bougainville Copper Limited (BCL) and received 36 percent of its earnings since the beginning of the Panguna copper mine (Bullock 1991:13).

The Australian government's decision to increase its defence assistance to PNG for 1990 by US\$ 7.5 million and to supply four helicopters to assist the PNGDF in their operations in Bougainville island (see Evans 1990:28-9), symbolizes those Australian commitments to the territorial integrity and the well being of PNG. At a PNG/Australian joint ministerial forum held in February 1990, the Hawke Government expressing its support to PNG government agreed to fund, train and equip 600 men for the PNGDF to meet the crisis in Bougainville (Bullock 1991:16). As conflict intensified, creating threats for the Australian nationals in the island (one Briton working in Bougainville was killed by the secessionists), the Australian Foreign Affairs Minister Gareth Evans went so far as to say that '...he cannot rule out "a limited" military action against secessionists' in Bougainville' (*The Times* 23 January 1990).

In May 1990, in answering an Opposition question in Parliament regarding his government's position upon PNG's decision to impose economic sanctions on the island of Bougainville in March 1990 (discussed later, see chapter four), the Australian Prime Minister Bob Hawke stated,

We will continue at all times to consult with our friends in PNG to do anything that we properly can within the context of that relationship to which I referred to assist them in trying to bring to a peaceful end a problem which presents for the Government of PNG very significant economic and social problems. ...Whether they make the decision to impose sanctions, that is their decision. They are not a second-class nation. If they make the decision to impose sanctions, that is their decision (*Australian Foreign Affairs Record* 1990,61(5):288).

Here, then, is a situation where the strategic interests of the Big Neighbour, though backed by historical colonialist rather than by ethnic ties, compel a rather reluctant involvement in a secessionist conflict on the side of the central regime, whatever views might be held on the rightness of the secessionist claims.

India-Sri Lanka situation

Indian involvement in the secession conflict in Sri Lanka has to be seen in the context of the close linguistic and cultural connections between the Tamils in the Southern Indian state of Tamil Nadu and those in Sri Lanka.

The Tamil community in Sri Lanka[2] belongs to the same ethnic stock as the Tamils in India. Historically Tamils in both countries maintained close cultural relations, though the Sri Lankan Tamils developed their own social and caste system, and in particular the territorial attachment that enabled them to claim a distinct identity. In the 1950s and 60s the Sri Lanka Tamils closely followed the political campaigns carried out by the Tamils in South India, in their campaign for regional autonomy. The rise of the *Dravida Munnetra Kazhagam* (DMK) movement in India (see below), according to Radhika Coomaraswamy, created a Tamil cultural renaissance in Sri Lanka (Coomaraswamy 1987:74,79).

The Tamils in India, nearly 50 million people, comprise just six percent of the total population of 797 million in the Indian federation (Keesing's 1989:36695,37004). Though they are a small minority in comparison to the large

---

2. The ethnic communities in the Sri Lanka population are (percentage in brackets, source: Department of Census and Statistics 1984:14) Sinhalese (73.9%), Sri Lanka Tamils (12.6%), Sri Lanka Moors (7.1%), Indian Tamils (5.5%), Burghers (0.2%). The Indian Tamils are Tamils of relatively recent Indian origin - dating back to the 19th century arrival of Indian immigrant workers to work in the plantations - as compared with 'Sri Lankan Tamils' who were of a native stock. They are not committed to the secessionist demands raised by the leaders of the Sri Lanka Tamils. In the discussion 'Tamils' or 'Tamil' mean the Sri Lanka Tamils unless otherwise specifically stated.

population of the Indian federation, the Tamils in India enjoy the position of an outright majority in the south Indian state of Tamil Nadu, which in turn is the largest in size amongst the four Southern Indian states populated by people who belong to the Dravidian linguistic family.

This Tamil-majority state commands an influential position in the Indian federation and in recent years became a dominant partner in the making of Indian foreign policy towards Sri Lanka's secessionist conflict. Its political importance derives from many different roots.

First, the Tamils in India receive special attention from the policy makers at the centre as being themselves a potential secessionist community within the Indian federation. This largely derives from their leading political parties' past and present political and ideological leanings towards a greater ethnic and political autonomy, as well as their deep opposition to the majority Hindi domination at the centre. At one time, the leaders of the DMK party, one of the major political parties in Tamil Nadu, functioned as secessionist campaigners in Southern India, associating themselves with a demand for the secession of the four Dravidian states from the Indian federation.

The *Dravida Munnetra Kazhagam* (DMK) party and its offshoot the *All India Anna Dravida Munnetra Kazhagam* (AIADMK) party, the two leading contenders for political power in Tamil Nadu state, still feature the Tamil ethno-nationalist ideology which provoked the Tamil secessionism of the 1950s and 1960s. In the past they explicitly preached against the Hindi majority in Northern India branding it as 'North Indian Imperialism' (Ghai & Sharma 1987:60). The current political objectives of these two parties demand the preservation of a separate Tamil culture and linguistic identity with maximum political autonomy within the Indian Union (see Ghai & Sharma 1987:62,65-7). Thus, by their political allegiance to the cultural and linguistic unity of the Dravidian people coupled with their uncompromising stand against the acceptance of Hindi as the official language of India, these parties still carry the seeds of secession.

The second relevant factor in the political importance of Tamil Nadu in Union affairs is the close political association since the 1970s between the ruling parties at the centre, in particular the Congress(I) party, and the AIADMK and DMK parties in Tamil Nadu. The leadership conflict in the Congress party in 1971, at the time of Mrs Gandhi's take-over of Party hierarchy, created a new alliance between Mrs Gandhi and the DMK against the old guard. Since then DMK, and the AIADMK after it gained power in Tamil Nadu in 1977, have both provided electoral support for the ruling Congress Party in central government, by using their dominant position in Tamil Nadu state (see Ghai & Sharma 1987:65-8). This electoral alliance with the ruling Congress Party at the centre has given Tamil Nadu politicians a strong position in the policy making process of the central government (see Ghosh 1985:9).

When the secessionist conflict in Sri Lanka developed into a civil war in the early

1980s, the ethnic-kin dimension of Sri Lanka's relations with its Big Neighbour began to work. Beginning with the 'ethnic holocaust' of 1983, which took the lives of nearly a thousand ordinary Tamils and made more than 100,000 people refugees in various parts of the country (see Manor 1983:450), the repeated reports of violence against Tamils in Sri Lanka, and the international outcry fostered by the world press and the various non-governmental organizations highlighting the hardships faced by the Tamil community in Sri Lanka, aroused an emotional reaction in Tamil Nadu. Tamil Nadu politicians united to demand active intervention by the Indian government on behalf of the Tamil minority in Sri Lanka.

In 1983 the Chief Minister of Tamil Nadu state government and leader of the ruling AIADMK party, himself led an all party delegation from the state to meet the then Indian Prime Minister Mrs Indira Gandhi, submitting a memorandum which stated,

> The grim and inhuman killings in Sri Lanka cannot be discussed as the internal affairs of the country... We definitely feel that the time has come for the Indian government to intervene effectively, actively and urgently to save the Tamils in Sri Lanka (as quoted in Sivaraja 1987:9-10).

Public sympathy and protests were expressed by demonstrations and meetings in various places in Tamil Nadu state, and the opposition DMK party (in association with other opposition groups to the AIADMK government) went to the extent of demanding '...a Bangladesh-type intervention by India in the Sri Lanka conflict' (Sivaraja 1987:10).

The exodus of more than 100,000 Tamil refugees to Tamil Nadu state (*Tamil Times* 1987,2:17; Sivaraja 1987:20), and the communal attacks directed against Indian nationals and the stateless 'Indian Tamils' in Sri Lanka (see *Lanka Guardian*, 1983,6(7-8):16, Mrs Gandhi's statement to the Lok Sabha on 13 August 1983) - both dimensions being new phenomena in Indo-Sri Lanka relations - added to the growing resentment felt by the people of Tamil Nadu state.

The political imperatives of Tamil nationalism in South India too, had played a role in influencing the centre. As the inheritors of the ethno-nationalist politics inspired by the early Dravidian movement in South India both the AIADMK and the DMK had been using every single issue related to the cultural and linguistic identities of the Tamil community to their political advantage. For them, the plight of their Tamil brethren on the other side of the Pork Strait provided a convenient emotional and nationalistic issue on which to organize a mass campaign in Tamil Nadu state.

The DMK party, the main opposition party to the pro-centre AIADMK government, took a more extreme stance. As noted above, it demanded an Indian military intervention to establish a separate state for the Tamils in Sri Lanka, arguing that without the establishment of *Tamil Eelam*[3] there is no solution to the Tamil problem in Sri Lanka (Sivaraja 1987:11). In its campaign against the violence in Sri Lanka the DMK collected ten million signatures to a memorandum to the UN, asking the government of Sri Lanka to grant rights of self-determination to the Tamils in Sri Lanka (Sivaraja 1987:11). The DMK leadership did not hesitate to criticize the central government's policy on Sri Lanka's ethnic crisis. For example in 1986, addressing a conference held in Madurai in support of the Tamils in Sri Lanka, the DMK leader Karunanidhi '…condemned the government of India for not raising the issue in international forums' (Sivaraja 1987:12).

Against this background, in 1983 the Indian central government were obliged to promise the Tamil Nadu leaders that '…the centre is dealing with the Tamil question in Sri Lanka as a national issue' (Sivaraja 1987:13). In the midst of the ethnic violence in Sri Lanka, the then External Affairs Minister Narasimha Rao went to the Sri Lankan capital on a fact finding mission, while his Prime Minister Mrs Indira Gandhi was telling that '…Sri Lanka could not treat India as just any country' (Rao 1988:420).

In her briefings of the Indian Parliament, Mrs Gandhi presented her involvement in the Sri Lanka conflict in terms of the ethnic connection with the Tamils in Sri Lanka. She commented,

> India stands for the Independence, unity and integrity of Sri Lanka. India does not interfere in the internal affairs of other countries. However because of the historical cultural and such other close ties between the peoples of the two countries, particularly between the Tamil community of Sri Lanka and us, India cannot remain unaffected by such events there (as reported in *Lanka Guardian* 1983,6(7-8):16).

This registered the beginning of the official involvement by the Indian central government in Sri Lanka's secessionist conflict. The government of Sri Lanka accepted the good offices of the Indian government to start negotiations with the Tamil leaders. Mrs Gandhi appointed as her special envoy S. Parthasarathy, who is believed to have been behind the document 'Annexture-C' (Tiruchelvam 1987:18), the draft proposals submitted by the Sri Lanka President to the All Party Conference in 1984 for the establishment of a devolved administration in the Northern and Eastern provinces.

---

3. The desired political goal of the Tamil secessionist movement was to establish an independent state, called Tamil Eelam, in an area which roughly encompasses the present Northern and Eastern Provinces of Sri Lanka. According to K. Sivathambi 'Eelam is the ancient Tamil name for Sri Lanka; what is being demanded is the Tamil portion of Eelam' (Sivathambi 1984:13).

In later years, as the Sri Lanka security forces intensified the military campaign against the secessionists, there were fresh waves of refugees from Sri Lanka. During the period 1983-87, the state government of Tamil Nadu was involved in providing facilities for more than 130,000 Sri Lankan refugees, who became a permanent burden for the entire period (*The Guardian* 28 May 1987). In this context, the Indian government's inability to influence the situation in Sri Lanka caused understandable frustration among the concerned parties in India in the late 1980s.

There were signs of further political alienation in Tamil Nadu state. Some critics blamed the centre for maintaining a 'step-motherly' attitude to the problems of the people of South India. For example Mr A. P. Venkateswaran, a former Foreign Secretary of India (during the time of Mrs Gandhi) said '...the government was not as sensitive to the problems of southern states as to those of the northern heartland. Had any linguistic group of North India been persecuted like the Tamils of Sri Lanka, the centre would have reacted more decisively' (*Frontline*, 2-15 May 1987). There were comparisons between the Bangladesh and Sri Lanka situations:

The people of Tamil Nadu are beginning to feel that Delhi has adopted a double standard. When there was a problem in Northern India, that is in East Bengal, the whole country was mobilised and Bangladesh was liberated. But now, problems in the South have not bothered the people of North India (Patrica 1987:16).

Against this pressure the central government was pushed into playing an active role in Sri Lanka's secession conflict, not only as a mediator but as a protector of the Tamil minority in Sri Lanka; not so much because of the common blood relationship of the Tamils in India and Sri Lanka, but in response to Tamil ethnic nationalism in Tamil Nadu state. Active involvement by the Indian government became a grim necessity, as an Indian commentator puts it, at least to contain the alienation of Tamil Nadu (Patrica 1987:16).

However these emotional attachments were by no means the only, or even the most important, factors in the Indian movement towards involvement in the secession conflict in Sri Lanka. The geo-strategic and security implications were very serious.

Sri Lanka as an island at the tip of India possesses an unique geopolitical position in the South Asian regional waters of the Indian Ocean. It lies just twenty miles away from India, at the oceanic location where the waters of the Bay of Bengal meet the Arabian sea. Its close proximity to the Indian mainland, appearing on the map '...like a pendant dangling from the triangular landmass of India' (Priydarshini 1987:45), is considered by the Indian strategic thinkers as one of the focal points in India's strategic and security planning in the region. This is further enhanced by Sri Lanka's naturally protected harbour at Trincomalee on the east coast, which runs inland some eight miles, and is an ideal naval basin suitable to accommodate '...the full fleet of any of the world's great powers' (Wriggins 1960:375), .

In this context Indian politicians and strategic thinkers have looked on Sri Lanka as an inseparable part of their defence system since independence. The existence on her doorstep of an independent Sri Lanka with strategic naval facilities was considered a defence risk: a potential bridgehead for any outside power hostile to the national interest of India. Ideally, they wanted to see Sri Lanka sharing her strategic facilities with India. For example, as early as 1949, K. M. Pannikkar, the earliest authority on Indian defence strategies, argued that '...Burma and Ceylon (Sri Lanka) must form with India a basic federation for mutual defence whether they will it or not' (as quoted in Kodikara 1982:23).

During the early years of independence, Indian politicians made efforts to establish an Indian doctrine for Sri Lanka. The President of the Indian National Congress in 1949 declared:

> India and Ceylon must have a common strategy and common defence strength and common defence resources. It cannot be that Ceylon is in friendship with a group with which India is not in friendship - not that Ceylon has not right to make its own alignments and declare its own affiliations - but if there are two hostile groups in the world, and Ceylon and India are with one or other of them and not with the same group, it will be a bad day for both (as quoted in Kodikara 1982:23).

As secessionist violence and counter operations by the government security forces intensified in the second half of the 1980s, creating a civil war in the Northern and Eastern parts of Sri Lanka, this bad day finally arrived.

The availability of support from Tamil Nadu state to the Tamil secessionists in Sri Lanka created a two-sided security dilemma for the Indian federation. One direct outcome of that situation was the seeking by the government of Sri Lanka of assistance from extra-regional powers to counterbalance the external support for the secessionists deriving from Indian soil, which raised the spectre of a Sri Lanka transformed into a '...spring-board for a security threat to India' (Jetly 1988:301). The other side of the security dilemma was posed by the possibility of the Tamil secessionists in Sri Lanka themselves becoming a security threat to India, by searching for assistance beyond the borders of the Indian federation.

In reality, India had well understood these possible dangers from the conflict in Sri Lanka at the time of the ethnic holocaust in 1983, when the internationalization of Sri Lanka's secession conflict reached its height. As reported in the Indian media, the government of Sri Lanka, fearing an Indian invasion of Sri Lanka, sought military assistance from the United States, the United Kingdom, the People's Republic of China, Pakistan and Bangladesh, (Baral 1985:63; Rao 1989:89). This action on the part of the Sri Lankan government met with an immediate reaction from the Indian central government. The then Prime Minister of India, Mrs Indira Gandhi, took the opportunity to enunciate an Indian security doctrine for the South Asian region. She declared:

> India will neither intervene in the domestic affairs of any states in the region, unless requested to do so, nor tolerate such intervention by an outside power; if external assistance is needed to meet an internal crisis, states should first look within the region for help (Rao 1989:88).

However, as the conflict in Sri Lanka dragged on with intensified armed hostilities between the secessionists and the government forces, Indian policy makers found that the territory of its southern neighbour was becoming 'open house' for various extra-regional powers whose intentions had always been of grave concern to them. As it became more nervous about Indian involvement in Tamil secessionism (more precisely, about an Indian intervention on behalf of the Tamil secessionists), the government of Sri Lanka found external support from a variety of sources to deal with the Tamil insurgency - supplies of arms, ammunition, helicopter gunships, gun boats, naval equipment, training facilities for its military personnel, expert knowledge of anti-terrorist strategies, intelligence coverage and even mercenaries.

India's rivals in the regional sphere, Pakistan and China, appeared prominently in the list of these external bed-fellows. China became the major arms supplier to the government of Sri Lanka, providing 50 percent of the arms and ammunition used by the Sri Lanka security forces during the 1984-87 period (Manchanda 1986:582). Apart from this the Chinese had a definite policy towards Indian involvement in Sri Lanka's secession conflict. In 1983 welcoming Mr H. W. Jayawardane, brother of the Sri Lankan President as his special envoy, the then Chinese Prime Minister Zhao Ziyang declared:

> nations should not utilize others' ethnic disputes to accomplish their own aims (and) the big should not bully the small (as quoted in Rao 1989:96).

Pakistan was the only South Asian country to respond promptly to Sri Lanka's request for military assistance. According to Indian sources it sent arms in civilian aircraft violating the Geneva convention (Rao 1989:95). In 1984 the Presidents of Pakistan and Sri Lanka visited each other's countries and both visits were followed by fresh loads of arms from Pakistan to Sri Lanka. They included AK-47 and M-16 rifles, ammunition, and four helicopter gunships. After the visit of President Zia-Ul-Haq, according to reports, Sri Lanka received a Pakistan military mission which followed the sending of 230 military personnel by Sri Lanka to receive military training in Pakistan (Rao 1989:95). In 1987 when the Prime Minister of Sri Lanka visited the Pakistan capital, the government of Pakistan avowed its support to Sri Lanka, offering defence equipment worth about $1 million. (*Tamil Times* 1987,6(6):24).

During his visit to Sri Lanka in 1984, Pakistan President Zia-Ul-Haq called upon other friendly states to offer their moral, political and economic support to the government of Sri Lanka to protect its territorial integrity. His message was:

> We can not allow states to be wrecked from within. What is happening to Sri Lanka today can happen to Pakistan tomorrow (as quoted in Rao 1989:95).

Pakistan's stand on Sri Lanka's secession conflict was strategically influential in the conflict between the government of Sri Lanka and the Tamil secessionists. The Muslim solidarity inspired by fundamentalist Pakistan in Sri Lanka was seen by Indian spokesmen as an attempt to weaken the linguistic base of 'Tamil Eelam' by creating a wedge between Tamil speaking Moors and Hindu Tamils in the Eastern province - attested to by the much publicized visit to the Moor-dominated terrorist-stricken Eastern Province by the Pakistan President and several follow-up visits by officials of the Pakistan embassy (Rao 1989:96).

The other aspect of this particular dimension was that it could have roused feelings in the Arab and Islamic world towards the plight of Muslims in Sri Lanka, giving the Sri Lanka government an opportunity to approach those Muslim countries for help. Pakistan also played an important role in keeping the support and goodwill of the Islamic world for Sri Lanka in spite of its dealings with Israel (discussed next) as its third significant external partner. As an Indian commentator puts it,

> Colombo's success in getting the Arab nations and the Islamic world in general to look the other way is as much a gain for Sri Lanka as it is for Pakistan, whose President, General Zia-Ul-Haq acting almost as ambassador of goodwill for Sri Lanka, appears to have convinced most governments in this region that Colombo's dealings with Tel Aviv do not adversely affect Islam's larger purposes and should only be seen in the bilateral India-Sri Lanka context withstanding the India-aided Tamil militants' onslaught against Sri Lankan Muslims and Sinhalese (Khergamvala 1986:9).

Among the external supporters invited by Sri Lanka, Israel was the one most resented by the Indians. Israel had been excluded from Sri Lanka in 1970 by the severance of diplomatic ties in conformity with the consensus reached by the Non-Aligned Movement (NAM) on the Palestine question. But in Sri Lanka's desperate search for military facilities beyond the region, its leaders were ready to accept Israel as a useful partner.

In 1984 Israel established an 'Israel Interest Section' in Colombo, interestingly in space provided in the American embassy to Sri Lanka. Apart from its supplies of arms, ammunition, helicopter gunships and other military equipment, a most important aspect of the Tamil insurgency, Sri Lanka's requirements for expertise on counter insurgency activities, had been met by the Israelis. They provided training for the Sri Lanka security forces in techniques of tackling terrorist activities, police and criminal investigations (Rao 1989:97, also *Tamil Times* 1987,6(9):19). Agents of the Israel intelligence service, Mossad, and the internal security agency, Shin Bet were sent to Sri Lanka. According to reports since 1984 there were 100 such agents in Sri Lanka though the number, according to Sri Lankan authorities, was four to six Israeli experts (*Tamil Times* 1987,6(8):14). They were responsible for the establishment of Sri Lanka's Special Task Force (STF) which later became the country's counter insurgency commando unit.

Indian strategic thinkers found many grounds for suspecting that the Pakistani and Israeli involvements were subsidiary elements of Western strategy in South Asia in general and in particular in Sri Lanka - that these countries had not been playing an entirely voluntary role but were acting as surrogates of the West (Rao 1989:97-8). To give strength to this line of thinking they even speculated about a covert role by the United Kingdom government. They pointed to the involvement of ex-SAS men in Sri Lanka's counter insurgency activities and the availability of British made arms, equipment, aeroplanes and naval gunships in Sri Lanka. The Channel Islands-based security company Keenie Meenie Services (KMS) - which was implicated in the Iran-Contra arms scandal in Washington - was involved in sending these ex-SAS men as mercenaries to Sri Lanka (Rao 1989:93). Along with Israeli agents, KMS gave assistance to the Sri Lanka government to train its STF commandos (Manchanda 1986:580). According to some reports they sometimes manned Sri Lanka's helicopter gunships in the Northern and Eastern Province (see *Tamil Times* 1987,6(5):01,12-13). Though the British government denied any involvement in this affair (Rao 1989:93), it was pointed out that such mobilizations of ex-SAS men would be unlikely to proceed without the approval of Whitehall (see *Tamil Times* 1987,6(5):12-13).

During the period 1983-87 Sri Lanka used British made aeroplanes, Cougar patrol boats, rifles, ammunition and armoured cars in its campaign against the Tamil secessionists. The governments of Sri Lanka and the United Kingdom maintained that these weapons and equipment were commercial purchases of the Sri Lanka government. But there was speculation about possible financial assistance from the British Government for the purchase of this weaponry from British companies. One example used by Indian sources was the credit facilities provided by the British government in 1986 to purchase 10 British naval gunships costing 1.3 million each (see Manchanda 1986:581).

However, in the minds of Indian policy makers the prime mover of this Western strategy was the United States which, according to them, '...was worried about the developments on the island, the Indian intention in particular' (Rao 1989:97). They had much evidence to suspect a covert role by this global super power in Sri Lanka's secession conflict. During the first six months after the ethnic riots of July

1983 and the much publicized request for military assistance by the Sri Lanka government, Sri Lanka played host to several important American dignitaries in its capital. First, the then US defence secretary Casper Weinberger arrived in Colombo in October 1983. Then came the visit of US Ambassador-at-large, the trouble shooter Vernon Walters. After this visit, Chairman of the House Defence Appropriation committee, congressman Joseph Addabo and, a month later, Deputy Assistant Secretary of State Howard B. Shaffer, visited Sri Lanka (see Rao 1989:89).

While these visits were taking place in Colombo, three important decisions taken by the government of Sri Lanka during the 1981-83 period received much publicity in the Indian and Sri Lankan press. First was an arrangement between Sri Lanka and the American broadcasting Agency Voice of America (VOA). By an agreement signed in December 1983 with VOA the government of Sri Lanka (extending the previous agreement signed in 1981) permitted VOA to replace its transmitters with more powerful transmitting equipment. Some interpreted this, an effort to establish the most powerful broadcasting network in the South and South-eastern region, '...as providing facilities to link the United States electronic surveillance system in the Indian ocean with a ground tracking station in Australia' (Fernando 1982:214).

Second was Sri Lanka's decision to rent out the oil storage complex of 99 oil tanks used by British forces during World War II, located in the strategic harbour at Trincomalee, to a Bermuda based oil company, Oreleum. As Oreleum was an associate of the US Coastal Corporation of Texas which undertakes supplies to the US navy (Rao 1989:89), some analysts described it as an important concession to the United States (Fernando 1982:214).

Thirdly, coinciding with this important deal, the Sri Lanka government decided to lift the more-than-ten-years-old ban on foreign military vessels visiting Trincomalee harbour (Phadnis 1986:264).

Though the leaders of the government of Sri Lanka explained these decisions purely in economic terms (Phadnis 1986:264), in its wider strategic calculations the government of India treated all these events as integral parts of an American design in the Indian Ocean area directed at the Indian federation (see Phadnis 1986:260-5; Chadda 1987:24-5).

Adding fuel to such suspicions of the Indian strategists, some sources speculated about a secret deal between Sri Lanka and the United States (Fernando 1982:214; Rao 1989:90), highlighted by a map published by the US Joint Chiefs of Staff in one of their pamphlets which showed Trincomalee as one of the ports available to US Navy personnel for rest-and-recreational facilities (Phadnis 1986:264). As revealed by Indian newspapers, Sri Lankan officials and representatives of two American companies acting on behalf of the Central Intelligence Agency of the American government prepared a draft agreement regarding operational rights in Trincomalee harbour in mid-1986. Under the terms of this agreement '... in exchange for its support for Sri Lankan actions against the Tamil militants and 'checking India...'

the Sri Lanka government would confer exclusive operational rights in Trincomalee harbour, the Oil Tank Farm (excluding one tank for Sri Lankan ships) and a substantial land area in the near vicinity and Sinhalese dominated areas around the harbour (*The Hindu International Edition* 30 January 1988; *Lanka Guardian* 1988,10(19):5-7).

These covert and overt involvements of unfriendly states, especially of extra-regional powers, in Sri Lanka's security build-up against the Tamil secessionists became of grave concern to the Indian policy makers. For the last two decades the policy makers of India, as their security objective toward Sri Lanka, according to Maya Chadda expected '…to keep Sri Lanka genuinely non-aligned and dissuade her from moving closer to states unfriendly to New Delhi' (Chadda 1987:25). For Indian policy makers, the developments in Sri Lanka were leading towards a situation which would thwart India's whole Sri Lanka strategy.

It was against this strategic and security background, then, that Indian policy makers decided to use the ethnic-kin dimension to front an active policy of involvement in Sri Lanka's secession conflict.

Conclusion

We can derive from these empirical observations two sets of principles which receive further treatment in the forthcoming chapters. The first is that, generally, the issues which provoke Big Neighbour involvement can be categorized into two groups:

(a) Issues that have an intrinsic relationship with the national interest of the Big Neighbour, viz. common ethnic ties and the strategic dimension. These make inevitable a linkage between the politics of the Big Neighbour and the secessionist conflict in the 'affected state', as they relate to two basic elements of the physical make-up of the Big Neighbour viz. the ethnic character of its society and the geographic location of its territory.

(b) The second group concerns issues that emerge as a result of the escalation of the conflict, e.g. refugee problems, humanitarian issues, economic costs etc. Usually they afford an immediate background and a pretext for Big Neighbour involvement, as calculated by its policy makers in accordance with its ethnic kin and strategic interests.

The above categorization will be useful in understanding the relative importance of the issues involved in the process of provoking Big Neighbour involvement, which is the central theme of this chapter. In this connection, the prime finding is that one set of issues, namely, the strategic dimension, dominates the decision-making process of the Big Neighbour and swamps all other issues. As seen in the case of the Australia-PNG situation, the strategic dimension can influence the policy makers of the Big Neighbour to take a stand in the secession conflict without the presence of other issues. As has perhaps been illustrated well enough in the foregoing investigation, if the Big Neighbour's vital strategic interests are at stake from the spillover effects of a secessionist conflict, it needs just a pretext to initiate an active involvement in the ethnic conflict of its small neighbour. These strategic interests of Big Neighbour may be evoked in many different ways. For the Big Neighbour perhaps the most sensitive development is the intrusion of unfriendly regional or extra-regional powers into the internal affairs of the affected state. In this regard the central regime and the secessionists could both be playing into the hands of such unfriendly states as was perceived by the Indian policy makers in their consideration of the secessionist conflict in Sri Lanka. Thus, one of the intentions of Big Neighbour involvement is to contain this kind of unacceptable venture by the two adversaries.

Then the common ethnic ties, and other issues like refugee influx and humanitarian issues may become pretexts for the Big Neighbour's pursuit of its strategic objectives. Since an uninvited intervention in the internal conflicts of another state is treated as a violation of international law, and likely to become an issue in international politics, the Big Neighbour needs a more justifiable reason for intervention than its own security. In this regard the plight of their ethnic kin, the refugee problem and humanitarian issues provide strong public grounds of such Big Neighbour involvement.

The Turkey-Cyprus situation provides an example of the continuous use of common ethnic ties by the Big Neighbour in protecting its strategic interests. As the central regime in Cyprus was very closely associated with the territorial ambitions of Turkey's historical enemy, Greece, the Turkish policy makers were compelled to involve themselves persistently in the affairs of Cyprus to protect their national interests. The continuous violence that it claimed took place in the island against its ethnic kin provided the 'legitimate' reason for Turkey to play a role as the guarantor of the rights of the Turkish Cypriots. In the end the leaders on the Turkish mainland preferred the present *de facto* secession situation in Northern Cyprus, as they perceived in it an opportunity to realize their objective, *Taksim*. This is the Turkish word for partition - but really means dividing Cyprus between Turkey and Greece and then annexing Northern Cyprus, the most sensitive part of Cyprus for the security of the Republic of Turkey.

The Indian intervention in East Pakistan provides another example of a Big Neighbour intervention aimed at broad strategic gains. But it was the refugee problem in conjunction with humanitarian issues which provided the immediate background for Indian intervention. The common ethnic tie remained as an additional argument, but it had only theoretical validity. Arguments were raised by Indian spokesmen regarding the common ethnic identity shared by East and West Bengal, but in fact it was a short lived one. After independence the new state of Bangladesh returned to its Muslim identity and distinguished its society from that of Hindu West Bengal, though their leaders declared Bangladesh a secular state. On the other hand, since there was evidence to suggest that in the early stages of the conflict the Indian authorities had encouraged the flow of refugees, to strength their hands if intervention in the conflict became necessary, it can be easily argued that the real motivations of the Indian involvement in East Pakistan lay in the strategic objectives of the Indian policy makers.

As will be illustrated further in the forthcoming discussion, the same argument can be led in the case of the India-Sri Lanka situation. The ethnic dimension of Sri Lanka's internal ethnic conflict had remained inert in Indo-Sri Lanka relations since the independence of Sri Lanka, which as one analyst puts it, were based on a 'friendly spirit of give and take' (Kodikara 1978:61). It did not inspire any Indian involvement until 1983. There had been serious violence against the Tamil minority since the 1950s, the last such occasion being in 1981 (before the ethnic holocaust of 1983). But India repeatedly refrained from involving itself in the ethnic conflict in Sri Lanka and did not evince any concern, even to show sympathy, about the plight of their Tamil ethnic kin in Sri Lanka.

This situation changed dramatically after 1983. India launched its new Sri Lanka policy which amounted to an open intervention, declaring its concern about the development in Sri Lanka and pronouncing that it was not 'just another country'. The significant difference between the pre- and post-1983 period was that after 1983 Sri Lanka was openly entertaining on its soil powers hostile to India and offering them some important strategic concessions which would endanger India's security and regional interests.

Our last suggestion is that the ethnic kin dimension has its own importance in the secessionist conflict of the affected state, though it may play only a supportive role in achieving the strategic objectives of the Big Neighbour. The common ethnic tie prevailing in the two societies can influence the ethnic kin citizens of the Big Neighbour to organize an emotional agitation, asking for active intervention by the Big Neighbour. Their pressure usually cannot be ignored altogether, for a number of reasons. The policy makers' inertia might be seen as weakness; these groups may claim that their own nationalistic aspirations are being neglected; opposition political groups and other nationalist elements in Big Neighbour's own society may try to make political capital out of the situation, by creating ethnic backlash.

The most important contribution of the common ethnic tie issue is its role in providing legitimate grounds for the Big Neighbour to represent the interests of the secessionist community. In this connection Big Neighbour has a special role to play as a protector of the secessionist community. The most likely outcome is to give Big Neighbour a role as a mediator, to guarantee the secessionists a fair deal. Such a role is most welcome by the policy-makers of the Big Neighbour as it provides them with strong grounds for international acceptance of its involvement, thereby influencing others to refrain from intervening in the conflict. If the Big Neighbour successfully accomplishes such a role it is in a strong position in countervailing other external parties and finally, in managing the situation to achieve its preferred policy option.

In the next chapter we shall present more evidence in further elaboration of these conclusions, and analyse the alternative options available to the Big Neighbour in a secessionist situation.

3 Big Neighbour Response in Secessionist Situations

Introduction

As noted in the foregoing empirical survey our four Big Neighbours have chosen from three options in deciding their response to their respective secessionist situations, namely, (a) Secession (India-East Pakistan), (b) Annexation (Turkey-Cyprus), (c) Devolution (Australia-PNG and India-Sri Lanka). There was a fourth theoretical option in our original hypotheses, viz. repression, where the Big Neighbour decides to assist or merely stand idly by in the face of military subjugation of the secessionists by the central regime. Apparently this option was unacceptable to any of our case study Big Neighbours.

The present chapter, using these empirical situations, examines the conditions under which devolution of government rather than secession, annexation or repression becomes the preferred option of the Big Neighbour. To address this issue we shall proceed by an analysis of those alternative options, i.e. repression, secession and annexation, paying special attention to exploring factors which may influence the Big Neighbour to dissociate itself from these alternative options to devolution, or simply, abandon them as unacceptable.

Repression

Repression here means the launching by the central regime in the affected state of coercive measures against the secessionists such as draconian legislation, arbitrary arrests, imprisonment, violence, economic sanctions, fuel embargoes, communications interruption etc., and seeking a military solution to the conflict (cf. Duff 1976:24-5; Stohl & Lopez 1984:7; Lopez 1984:70) is an obvious response of a central regime coping with an ethnic secessionist movement that has produced violent expression of its own. (There are various reasons that can be adduced for the adoption of violence and the abandonment of peaceful methods by the secessionists, and also for the resort by the central regime to repressive methods. But we do not deal with them here as they are outside the scope of the present discussion.)

The employment of repressive methods against a secessionist community is not simply the state using force to claim the rightful allegiance of its members in the political society. They appear as constituents of a regime strategy that uses governmental coercion to eliminate the political dissent (cf. Duff 1976:25) of an aggrieved ethno-regional group in the society, reflecting the central regime's unwillingness to offer power sharing concessions or to use political methods to deal with the ensuing autonomist or secessionist movement. In an atmosphere of majority-minority conflict and of the state becoming an instrument of the dominant ethnic group, such a strategy from the central regime is hardly likely to achieve its objective, or to influence the secessionists to abandon their goal or go to the bargaining table.

As happened in Sri Lanka after 1981 and PNG during the period between September 1989 and March 1990, the most likely outcome indeed is further alienation of the minority and the production of more militant expressions, displacing any moderate tendencies previously prevailing among the secessionist community (in this regard for Sri Lanka, see Leary 1981:25-35, 41-59, and for PNG, Spriggs 1990:26, 30). As noted by K. Sivathambi (assessing the impact of the repressive measures introduced by the Sri Lanka government against the Tamil secessionist) the result would be:

> The militants' movements are proscribed by law and actions taken by the government against them and the activities the militants indulge in, make them necessarily militaristic. Militarism has become the *raison d'etre* of their existence for they are now guerrilla fighters openly fighting against the state. The more militaristic a group is, the more effective they are in terms of defending the people and advancing their cause. Thus a high degree of militarism has been the keynote of the organizational upkeep of the militants (Sivathambi 1984:13).

Further, this will speed up the polarization of the society dividing it into majority-minority armed camps. In this situation where central regime and secessionist group engage in direct confrontation and above all where the state uses force to restore its authority against secessionist violence, the normal social and political life of the society comes to a standstill. As was witnessed in Sri Lanka in 1983, the situation is susceptible to an ethnic backlash against the minority community, and then may give way to a vicious circle of communal violence between the communities. As noted by an analyst:

> An awful existential fact in a society that has become totally polarized is that

its minority of activists, populists and terrorists on both sides hold the entire society as its hostage. And the sad fact is that the main body of the people caught in between ...are inexorably seduced and forced into taking sides as the spilling of blood on both sides heightens the emotions and sentiments cohering around such primordial themes as kinship, people, religion, language and race (Tambiah 1986:120).

Once an entire society is caught up in such an intolerable dynamic, the spillover effects will inevitably cross the territorial borders of a Big Neighbour. In addition to the creation of a refugee influx, as we have seen, these developments may stimulate the sentiments of ethnic kin and of democratic public opinion in Big Neighbour's society, to which policy makers will have to respond.

The most recent example of a Big Neighbour being obliged to respond to its own critical public opinion was the critical stand taken by Australian and international human rights groups, opposition political parties and media regarding the PNG government's military actions during 1989-1990 against the Bougainville secessionists. There were repeated accusations of human rights violations and indiscriminate killings of civilians in Bougainville Island (see *News Week* 17 Dec. 1990; Spriggs 1990; Havini 1990) which the Australian human rights groups demanded the government investigate. For example, a documentary film, *Blood on Bougainville*, produced and broadcast by the *Australian Broadcasting Corporation* (ABC) on 24 June 1991 held the Australian government indirectly responsible for atrocities committed by the PNGDF:

> the evidence of Australian helicopters being used against civilians is overwhelming. ...Bougainvilleans say their island has been raped by our miners, and worse by the Australian-trained army that put down their revolt. And *Four Corners* has clearly established that some of the atrocities committed against people of Bougainville, involved equipment supplied to Port Moresby by Canberra (*Australian Broadcasting Corporation* 1991:1-2).

In this context, the government of Australia was compelled to give an assurance of an investigation into these allegations, and to dissociate itself from the repressive actions taken by the PNG government (*The Australian* 27 June 1991), which included economic sanctions and communication disruption. The opposition political parties in the Australian Parliament characterized these actions as inhibiting efforts to find a negotiated solution to the conflict (see *Australian Foreign Affairs Record* 1990,61(5):287).

This is another important factor which may influence the Big Neighbour to find repressive measures taken by the central regime unwelcome. If the Big Neighbour is already committed to a negotiated settlement, repression which clearly disrupts its 'devolutionary policy' and efforts to find a peaceful settlement is unacceptable.

In the middle of 1987 when the Sri Lanka government decided to launch an all-out military assault against the secessionists, the Indian attitude was very much in line with this argument, as reported by an Indian newspaper:

> India according to Mr Gandhi, was seriously opposed to military operations which endanger civilians. It was serving to intensify the process of alienation and making India's task more difficult in finding a political solution. The pursuit of the military option could not but lead to serious consequences, it was pointed out. India was absolutely clear that there could be no military solution to the ethnic problem (*The Hindu International Edition* 30 May 1987).

The refugee influx into the Big Neighbour's territory and claims of human rights violations, as inevitable outcomes of repressive policies, contribute to the process of the internationalization of the secessionist conflict. Genocide, human rights violations and other atrocities may become regular themes in international forums, with a corresponding impact upon the Big Neighbour's attitude.

Firstly these developments create an uneasy security environment on its door-step. The unstable situation provides immense opportunities for extra-regional powers to become participants in the ongoing conflict, both combatants indiscriminately seeking external supporters. When the central regime resorts to militaristic methods it needs constant resources for its counter insurgency activities. In this situation, as happened in the India-Sri Lanka confrontation, foes can become friends, and pave the way for powers hostile to Big Neighbour's interests to establish their influence in the affected state. Therefore the intensification of repressive measures by the central regime may be seen by the Big Neighbour's policy makers as a security threat to its own territory.

There is another aspect which could complicate security perceptions, arising on the Big Neighbour's own territory. The continuous flow of refugees into the Big Neighbour's territory might bring not only an economic and social burden but also possibly the entire operational command of the secessionist movement, its leaders and activists using the territory of the Big Neighbour as a safe haven, perhaps including military facilities i.e. training camps, communication centres and so on. That situation is quite a familiar one around the world, from Ireland to South America and Indochina, as well as Sri Lanka/Tamil Nadu, giving grounds for the central regime's claims of Big Neighbour's involvement in supporting the secessionists, using this in turn as excuse for seeking external support beyond the region.

The worst scenario of all is when the continuous presence of refugees and the clandestine military activities of exiled secessionists within its territory become an internal security problem for the authorities of the Big Neighbour. Since 1983 India has experienced such a situation due to the activities of Sri Lankan Tamil militants in the state of Tamil Nadu, including violent clashes among rival Sri Lankan secessionist groups themselves, and also between the secessionists and the local community (see *Tamil Times* 1986,6(1):1-3,24). On several occasions the central government had to order the Tamil Nadu government to restrict the movements of the Sri Lankan secessionists and curb their military activities (*Tamil Times* 1986,6(1):3,24). The other side of the same coin appeared during the East Pakistan conflict. As predicted by the policy makers of India, the continuation of repressive actions against the secessionists in the affected state, by increasing the flow of refugees would in effect create a danger of encouraging ethno-regional conflict in Big Neighbour's own territory (discussed in Chapter 2).

Therefore, giving due consideration to the Big Neighbour's obligations to international law, to its ethnic kin groups, to democratic public opinion in its society and, finally, to the security threats emanating from the continuous violence in the affected state, it is a very fraught and risky option for any Big Neighbour to become a mute spectator or supporter of repressive governmental actions in the affected state, aiming at a military solution to the conflict.

Secession

Until Bangladesh achieved its independence in 1971, the success of unilateral secession was treated as an impossibility by the international community. The bloody experiences of the failed secessionist attempts in Katanga (Congo) and Biafra (Nigeria) seem to have influenced the international community to refrain from helping secessionist tendencies in other states. On these two occasions it was the United Nations (UN) which took a clear stand against the forcible dismemberment of existing states through secession. The role of the UN in these conflicts (organizing an international intervention against secessionists in Katanga and ignoring the bloody civil war that had been taking place for more than a year in Biafra) clearly manifested its expectation of total commitment from member states to the territorial integrity of existing states against secession demands (see Nanda 1972:325-8; Nixon 1972:492-6; Islam 1985:217-19).

But the secession of East Bengal, backed by direct military intervention by India, introduced a new element into the prevailing international animus against secession demands. To a certain extent it removed the existing international misgivings about the success of unilateral secession and the role of other states in such conflicts (Islam 1985:211-12). Since then many have argued in favour of altering the principle of self-determination to enable the international community to apply it under special circumstances to non-colonial (secessionist) situations (for example see Nanda 1972:321; Islam 1985:219-20).

Though secession is now on the agenda, it still has special risks for Big Neighbours, whose very size may run them into numerous dangers if they accept secession as an option in conflicts within their regional environment. This is exemplified in the contradictory options preferred by one of our Big Neighbours,

India, in two different situations. India responded differently to the East Bengal conflict in 1971 and Tamil secessionist conflict in Sri Lanka. Though it made a military intervention to help the Bengali secessionists achieve separate statehood, it is clear enough that this is a most delicate option for Indian policy-makers in the Sri Lanka situation. In the latter, India has openly committed itself to a devolution settlement and opposed the dismemberment of Sri Lanka. This needs an explanation.

Our theoretical model implies that any Big Neighbour which has a stake in a secession conflict in its regional environment has to consider, firstly, the strategic implications of the entry of a new state into its regional environment as a result of the forcible break-up of one of its small neighbours. Secondly, it has to take account of the spillover effects of this entire process in its own society, which is (because of its size) in all probability a multiethnic entity, perhaps engulfed in numerous secessionist convulsions, including possibly that of the ethnic kin of the affected state secessionists.

The ethnic kin dimension, though it obviously tempts the Big Neighbour to involve itself in the conflict and represent the interests of the secessionist community, or to make efforts to find an honourable settlement for them, has a very discouraging influence upon the Big Neighbour considering selecting secession as its ultimate option. One should never assume that a Big Neighbour sharing the same ethnic identity with the secessionist community will necessarily help them to achieve separate statehood in its regional environment, especially within the strategic reach of its own territory. It could perhaps become an acceptable option where (as in Turkey-Cyprus) the policy-makers of the Big Neighbour see secession as but a transitional stage to annexation (see next section). But otherwise the establishment of a separate state by an ethnic group sharing an ethnic identity with a part of its own society and within its strategic reach would create a paradoxical situation. Such a state with the same ethnicity in near proximity might become a rival 'homeland' or ethnic representative, disturbing Big Neighbour's national interests in the international scene, especially if the new state should become the surrogate of a hostile extra-regional power. Such a security and political threat cannot be ruled out: the world has witnessed something of the sort in the rivalry until 1970s for the representation of the national interests of the Chinese nation between Nationalist China (Taiwan) and the People's Republic of China, though the situation was not the outcome of a secessionist conflict.

The establishment of a new state for its ethnic kin as a result of a secessionist conflict is even less acceptable to a Big Neighbour where its own ethnic kin group is a sizeable minority in its own territory, capable of having separate statehood of its own. The India-Sri Lanka situation provides an interesting case here. The establishment of an independent Tamil state in Northern and Eastern Sri Lanka would pose a challenge to the Tamils in South India whose state, Tamil Nadu, at present enjoys the status of the motherland of all the Tamils in the world. A new

Tamil state would deprive it of this leading role, as described by Dr Ameer Ali;

> By virtue of historical facts, South India is the custodian of Tamil culture and
> the universal spokesman on Tamil interests. This situation is bound to change
> if an independent Tamil country is going to be established somewhere in the
> world even on a one acre piece of land. This country will be a sovereign
> state, will have a national flag and will have representation in the international
> community of United Nations. Thereafter, for all intents and purpose, that tiny
> country will be the spokesman on Tamil affairs. After all Tamil Nadu is only
> a state in India ...it is very difficult to think that South Indians will easily
> surrender their hegemonic position to a tiny Eelam (Ali 1990:16).

The most obvious way of resolving that paradox would be either annexation of
the new state into the Indian federation (see next section) or the realization by the
Tamil Nadu Tamils of their historical ideal, the establishment of an independent
state for Tamils in South Asia, incorporating the seceding Tamil areas and making
impregnable its leading role as '...the home of Tamil civilization' (Ali 1990:16).
Such a development would of course, destroy the territorial integrity of the Indian
federation. If South India joined the secessionist bandwagon in India as Marshal R.
Singer puts it, '...an independent Tamil Eelam (in Northern and Eastern Sri Lanka)
could easily become a safe sanctuary and staging area for Sikhs, Assamese and other
militant separatist groups in India' (Singer 1986:18). These possibilities are not
mere academic speculations. In 1990 the Indian security services claimed to have
found evidence to connect Sri Lankan Tamil militants in Tamil Nadu with Sikh and
Assamese secessionist movements, and of their providing arms training to some
members of Dravida Kazhagam (*The Hindu International Edition* 26 May 1990, 19
January 1991). Meanwhile some Tamil Nadu politicians openly speculated about
the rise of secessionism in Tamil Nadu, pointing to the close attachment shown by
DMK leaders towards the militants of the Liberation Tigers of the Tamil Eelam
(LTTE) in Sri Lanka (see *Tamil Times* 1990,9(6):16-17), which waged a guerrilla
war against the Indian Peace Keeping Force (IPKF) stationed in Sri Lanka during
the period 1987-1990 (see next chapter).

However, long before these matters came into public knowledge, New Delhi had
decided its final policy objective towards Sri Lanka's secessionist conflict, rejecting
secession in (Northern and Eastern) Sri Lanka:

> The central line of official thinking was that Eelam was against India's national
> interests (for the reflex influence in Tamil Nadu) and that there was need to
> ensure that the 'Tamil Problem' as such be (kept) out of India's national
> boundaries (Joshi 1990:9).

The approach was entirely the reverse in East Bengal. Here, it was not secession but the denial of secession, which was seen as a security threat for the territorial integrity of India. As noted in the previous chapter, since the central regime of the affected state, by its own deeds, had created a point-of-no-return situation, the policy makers of India found that they had to cope for the foreseeable future with an unstable East Bengal that had already led to a continuous flow of refugees, with the secessionists using Indian territory as a sanctuary. Therefore, they had reasonable grounds to believe that the denial by the central Pakistan regime of secession for the East Bengal people would create a long-term risk to the security of Indian territory, especially in the Indian state of West Bengal. During the early days of the conflict, arguing for a direct Indian intervention against the regime in Pakistan, an Indian writer noted,

> Delay on our part will ensure the decimation of the moderate democratic leadership of Bangladesh and the rise of a guerrilla leadership, thoroughly disillusioned by our betrayal of their hopes and looking to China for guidance which it will then only be too happy to offer. Then Bangladesh may become the base for the spread of Chinese-inspired revolutionary secessionist movements in West Bengal and in view of its disillusionment West Bengal will be emotionally just ripe for such movements (Guha 1971:984).

Against this background, and also giving considerations to the strategic gains expected from the break-up of Pakistan (as discussed in the previous chapter), 'secession' appeared to be the most desirable policy option available to the Indian policy makers to stop the spillover of East Bengali ethnic nationalism into West Bengal society.

The acceptance of secession by the Indian policy makers in the East Bengal conflict does not contradict our argument regarding the negative outcomes for the Big Neighbour of a common ethnic identity. The secession of East Bengal is not a true case of a common ethnic affinity between the people of the Big Neighbour (or a group of them) and the secessionist community in the affected state. Although ethnic affinity had been used (among others) as an argument for Indian involvement, India's decision to adopt secession policy was not based on the proposition that they were going to help East Bengalis to create an independent state, while their kin in West Bengal were doomed to live in a federated state of India. It was intended rather to create a political environment in which the East Bengalis would want to distinguish themselves not only from their fellow Muslims in West Pakistan but also from their Hindu ethnic kin in West Bengal. There were deep discussions in New Delhi on the possibility of an independent Bangladesh becoming a step towards the formation of a pan-Bengali state. However the Indian policy-makers decided to look on the opposite side of that argument (see Ayoob & Subramanyam 1972;169), correctly calculating that the religious content of East Bengali nationalism, which had led them to secede from undivided India in 1947, would lead them to become a separate nation on their own. So it has proved. As noted by Saleem M. M. Qureshi:

> After all, Bangladesh now is the next largest Muslim nation to Indonesia and the very fact that it exists as a political entity separate from the culturally similar West Bengal is evidence enough of the survival of one form of Muslim nationalism (Qureshi 1973:570).

Now we move to examine the strategic implications for the Big Neighbour's policy makers of adopting an active secessionist policy towards the conflict in the affected state.

If the success of the secession is the result, the image of Big Neighbour in international and regional politics might well be damaged by its action in participating in the dismemberment of another state. Once associated with such an action amounting to a violation of international law, it can hardly sincerely participate in any similar international action for the preservation of international law. Its mere participation in international and regional organizations could be censured by its opponents. An assessment of the international repercussions of Turkish intervention in the Cyprus conflict in 1974 may provide an illustration of these dimensions. How much its Cyprus intervention cost Turkey in international politics is a matter of debate. But the arguments raised by some speakers in international forums regarding the paradox of Turkish participation sixteen years later in the international action against Iraq's invasion of Kuwait (see *The Guardian* 13 April 1991), and the unyielding stand taken by successive Greek governments in opposition to Turkey's admission to the European Community (see McDonald 1986:185) are important evidence.

It can be argued that the 'erring' Big Neighbour can use its regional strategic position and international alignments to counter these negative responses of the international community, e.g. Turkey's role in NATO. But at the regional level, it is not such an easy task. The image-destroying effects of its involvement in splitting another regional state are likely to be reflected in the foreign policy postures of other regional states for a long time. Other small states in the region whose political co-operation is an essential requirement for the maintenance of the Big Neighbour's regional power status, may understandably, from this one instance paint the Big Neighbour as 'expansionist' or a 'regional bully', and set themselves to find alternative allies to counter the errant Big Neighbour's influence in regional politics. In this context the likely outcomes would be the alienation of the small states from the Big Neighbour's sphere of influence, and perhaps the intrusion of extra-regional powers into regional affairs, creating a permanent security threat in the Big Neighbour's regional environment. Then any internal conflict in any of the other regional states would become a sensitive issue for its national security.

In this connection the reception of India's secessionist policy in the East Bengal conflict is instructive. Even though Bangladeshi independence received international acceptance within a very short period, the Indian role in that historical situation still haunts the minds of foreign policy decision-makers in small states in the South Asian region (see Tiwari 1989:262; Razvi 1989:319). For them, it provided another example of 'Indian expansionism' in South Asia. For example, Sri Lanka's desperate efforts to find external assistance outside the region in its attempts to contain Tamil secessionism in the early 1980s were derived mainly from this psychological mindset, an integral element of Sri Lanka's foreign policy posture in the early years of its independence (see Kodikara 1978:61-2; Wilson 1990:45-6). Although the Indo-Sri Lanka accord of August 1987 (see chapter 4) and the subsequent Indian military assistance against the secessionist guerrillas of the Liberation Tigers of Tamil Eelam (LTTE) have gone far to prove that India's long-term strategy in Sri Lanka's secessionist conflict was the preservation of the territorial integrity of its southern neighbour, a strong section of Sri Lanka's political elite is still unwilling to distinguish India's Sri Lanka policy from its policy in the East Bengal conflict (see Kodikara 1989:716-18).

In the regional environment, the Big Neighbour has two more important factors to take into account before moving to an active secessionist policy. First, it has to calculate the reactions of the central regime of the affected state towards Big Neighbour's role in dismembering its territory. Second, it cannot overlook the emerging new pattern of power relationships in the regional environment as a result of the arrival of a new international actor.

For this we shall first consider the Indian experience in the Bangladesh conflict. It was our argument in the preceding chapter that India's role in the Bangladesh secession was largely influenced by its policy-makers' calculations regarding India's strategic gains in changing the existing power equation between India and Pakistan in the South Asian region. In this situation India did not need very long to consider the reaction of the regime in Pakistan, as the very existence of that country had been considered by Indian strategists as a political threat to the Indian federation (see Rajan 1972:191-2; Subramanyam 1980:297,299). For the Indian strategists, as long as Pakistan could manage to hold its two wings together (despite their geographical separation by more than a thousand miles of Indian territory), the 'two nation theory' (which gave birth to the partition of British India) constituted an ideological threat to the unity of their multiethnic society. The dismemberment of Pakistan gave them an opportunity to '...expose the inherent fallacy of the so-called two nation theory' (Rajan 1972:191). Above all, Pakistan's efforts to sustain an unrealistic military balance vis-a-vis India (Rajan 1972:192) had influenced Indian policy makers to use the golden opportunity of the East Bengal conflict to achieve the maximum strategic gain against Pakistan, by breaking the existing power equation which was a direct result of the involvement of extra-regional powers in Pakistan's military build-up (see Subramanyam 1980:299-300). Indian policy makers rightly saw such an outcome as a major milestone on the way to their strategic ambition - to achieve regional hegemony in South Asia (see Wariavwalla 1974:18). As events witnessed India achieved all of these strategic gains after 1971.

But Big Neighbours cannot find Bangladesh-like situations everywhere. In this connection, what India learnt as the negative aspects of its Bangladesh adventure remain as lessons for similar regional powers around the globe.

Just after the independence of East Bengal India found the Bangladeshis themselves openly questioning India's motivations in assisting their liberation struggle. The presence of the Indian army in Bangladeshi territory after liberation, and their economic dealings with the new government, were subjected to severe criticism from the Bangladesh political elite (see Kodikara 1979:27-9). There were even allegations of carrying off military equipment and armaments acquired from the surrendered Pakistan army (Franda & Rahman 1985:262).

The friendly atmosphere which India and Bangladesh nevertheless maintained in South Asian politics after 1971 ended after the first military coup in Bangladesh. During the subsequent period the country was ruled by military regimes. Some of those military regimes openly associated with India's rivals in international politics. Bangladesh did not after all remain in India's sphere of influence. Today the countries are not enemies, but neither are they on good terms. They have disputes over the sharing of Ganges water, over the maritime belt between India and Bangladesh, and over the sovereignty of Purbash Island in the Bay of Bengal (see Hossain 1981).

What, we may ask, would be the likely scenario after such an Indian intervention to dismember Sri Lanka? By an active secessionist policy India would lose an independent political entity which had been at least a neutral and often friendly state in respect of India's regional interests since the 1940s, a situation altered only in the 1980s when Sri Lanka's dealings with extra-regional powers created anxiety in India (as discussed in the previous chapter). But this in turn was for no other reason than India's own deeds, which had given to its own role in the region the appearance of an expansionist Big Neighbour. Had it not been for the perception of that threat rooted in the Sri Lankan mind, Sri Lanka would perhaps not have misunderstood India's long-term objectives in the conflict with the Tamil secessionists.

For a Big Neighbour which enjoys a dominant position in its regional environment and does not want to see any other regional state or an extra-regional power disrupting it, cannot afford the image of an 'expansionist state' or a 'regional bully', particularly harmful internationally as well as in its relations with the affected state. This was accepted as one of the reasons for Australia's support for the Port Moresby government against the secession in Bougainville. Professor Hedley Bull noted in 1974:

The considerations I have mentioned are enough to show that Australia's interests cannot lie in extending active support to a secessionist movement, and probably require at least passive support of the central government.

Australia's refusal to continue military assistance to Port Moresby in the event of a secession would be tantamount to support for the secessionists. It is particularly difficult to imagine Australian support for Bougainville, which, whether or not it was, would be interpreted by the Third World as a replay of the secession of Katanga from Congo, with Australia playing the role of Belgium and Bougainville Copper Company that of *Union Miniere* (Bull 1974:14).

Above all, the forcible break-up of the affected state is a risky option for a Big Neighbour. If it is not on good terms with the affected state, such action will further strengthen the animosity felt by the people and the leaders in the affected state towards the Big Neighbour. The truncated state may become a national enemy of the Big Neighbour, acting as a keen supporter of Big Neighbour's enemies or anti-state movements in its society. This is what India and Turkey experienced on the international and domestic front from their respective small neighbours. For example, after 1971 Pakistan intensified its arms build-up against India in the region and became an open supporter of India's international rivals. The Indian policy makers had to live with the fear of Pakistan's (in reaction to their East Pakistan adventure) taking her revenge by helping Sikh and Kashmir secessionists in India. A similar fate befell Turkish policy makers after their intervention in Northern Cyprus; Cyprus sought support from the Soviet camp and the Non-Aligned Movement, and allowed separatist movements in mainland Turkey, such as the Armenian Nationalists, to use its territory as a base for organizing their campaign (see Gunter 1985:44-5).

This is also the likely scenario in the India-Sri Lanka situation. If India were indeed to help the Sri Lankan Tamils to achieve separate statehood as 'Tamil Eelam', the truncated Sri Lanka state would inevitably become another Pakistan to India. But its strategic location in an island at the southern tip of India is of far greater significance for Indian security than that of the northern neighbour, Pakistan. While an independent 'Tamil Eelam' as already seen would become a security liability in respect of keeping Tamil Nadu in the Indian federation, the truncated Sri Lanka state would have a free hand in offering its strategic resources to India's enemies in international politics. The ultimate result would be to create two unfriendly mini-states, instead of one state which was not essentially an unfriendly one. As a regional power living with the fear of disintegration of its vast territory from secessionist upheavals, India clearly cannot afford such a situation on its southern flank. Thus for its part in dismembering Sri Lanka it would get no strategic gains, but a long-term security threat, which might well be a step towards the disintegration of India itself.

Apart from this ethnocentric dimension of a likely post-secession situation in Sri Lanka, India would have to consider the security impact of the emergence of two mini-states in its regional waters. The creation of additional mini-states not strong enough to defend themselves from external manipulation is not a sensible option for any regional power. Because of their geographic proximity to the Big Neighbour's territory, those weak mini-states may well attract the interest of extra-regional powers eager to dip their hands in regional politics, and not be strong enough to resist such meddling.

Indian military involvement in the Maldives in November 1988, in assisting the government of Maldives to quell a mercenary attack (incidentally by the members of one of the pro-Indian Tamil secessionist group in Sri Lanka) and a plot against the government of President Abdul Gayoom, provides an illustration of the security burden falling on a Big Neighbour from the existence of weak mini-states within its strategic reach (see Tripathi 1989).

In the PNG situation too, this remains as the probable outcome of the success of unilateral secession. Australian policy makers have long made plain their dislike for the creation of more mini-states in their regional waters. One-time Australian Prime Minister Mr E. G. Whitlam was well known for expressing the Australian perspective on this particular aspect:

> Some observers have noted in the past Mr Whitlam's penchant for suggesting new arrangements for small states - more notably his suggestion that the Solomons and the New Hebrides should combine. It has been claimed that he 'genuinely' had an obsession about the stupidity of creating small nation states (Viviani 1976:203).

To this has been attributed Australia's reluctant acceptance of Indonesia's *de facto* sovereignty over East Timor, though successive Australian governments have declined to condone the way Indonesia achieved it. One might argue that Australia's decision to accept Indonesia's *de facto* sovereignty over East Timor is not compatible with PNG's anxiety over Indonesian expansionism in the region (Viviani 1976:226). But this decision, registering Australia's disapproval of the creation of another mini-state in its regional waters, is quite consistent with its stand against the disintegration of PNG. If Bougainville, an island of just 3000 square miles, were to achieve secession from PNG, not only other islands in PNG but also many small islands belonging to other states around Australia would find it an attractive precedent. Considering the vulnerability of the existing mini-states in the South Pacific region to external involvement (Viviani 1976:203), Australia is unlikely to accept the secession of any of the islands in PNG, which is the nearest country to the Northern shore of Australia.

To sum up, then: the occasions when an active secession policy in respect of an internal ethnic conflict in a neighbouring state will have benefits outweighing its costs to Big Neighbour are probably exceedingly rare.

Annexation

What might be the Big Neighbour's gains and losses from annexing the secessionist region or part of it, or the entire affected state? Is it feasible for such a regional power to do so without the consent of the central regime of the 'affected state'? According to Roger Scruton,

> annexation is primarily a term in international law, denoting the act of a state, whereby territory not previously held under the sovereignty of that state is acquired (Scruton 1982:16).

Under these legal provisions, annexation which has not been consented to by the state that formerly enjoyed sovereignty over the annexed territory is rejected, and considered unlawful in the eyes of international customary law (Scruton 1982:17). In this regard the world community has developed an international 'doctrine of non recognition of territorial changes brought about by force or the threat of force' (Hough 1985:305). Then it becomes an illegal occupation amounting to an international conflict, which requires collective international action against it, taking the form of verbal condemnation, economic sanctions or war. Therefore forceful annexation would become a conflict between the occupying power and the international community of states (Hough 1985:327, 447-65).

It is true that in practical politics the Big Neighbour, like any other regional power, may evade such international actions against it: international law is inherently weak in implementing collective action against big powers. The difference between legal theory and political practice in international relations is not a matter of text book discussions only: the recent history of international politics illustrates it. The reaction of other states towards an incident of violation of international law will be determined by their several vested interests and in accordance with their relations with the states involved in the conflict. As an analyst puts it,

> morality and ethics have no place in politics ...we are against aggression and violations of human rights when our adversaries are guilty ...but then we become lukewarm when these very same acts are committed by friends and allies... (Kourvetaris 1988:192-3).

In the secessionist situations we are considering, the Big Neighbour's relations with the major power-brokers in international politics, and its policy-makers' ability to capitalize their debts or credits amassed in the past, can be considered among the determinants of an intervention policy directed at annexation of the territory of the affected state. This does not mean that the Big Neighbour can always evade condemnation of its action under international law and in international organizations.

It may well have to face international opprobrium, and yet in practice count on being able to continue its illegal occupation just as illegally without facing serious repercussion from the international community.

Our case in point is the current Turkish occupation of Northern Cyprus which according to George K. Kourvetaris, has '...followed four major processes - invasion - partition - colonization - annexation' (Kourvetaris 1988:195). Several post-world war II examples of the annexation of territories by other states, such as the annexation of East Timor/Indonesia, Sikkim and Goa/India, West Bank/Israel, Kuwait/Iraq provide other useful illustrations of such practices. Only in the last case was international action swift and effective (see Greenwood 1991; White & McCoubrey 1991).

However, international vested interests have their own limitations. They are not potent enough to legitimate any action in violation of international law. Many of those annexation situations mentioned above, including the Turkish occupation in Cyprus, tell us that no Big Neighbour can get general international approval for a forcible annexation. This applies even more strongly in a secessionist situation, because of the role of the UN in upholding international principles of the sovereignty of states.

In a secessionist situation Big Neighbours contemplating annexation can never just ignore the interests of the other states. Their inherent external dimension ensures that secessionist situations attract the attention of many different external actors, their degree of involvement determined by their reaction to the emerging new balance of power. Regional rivals or, if the affected state is in a strategically sensitive area, great powers, and the other small states in the region, may have genuine reason to feel and express concern about the incursions of the Big Neighbour: '...every potential whale thinking of swallowing a sprat has to weigh up what it would tell the rest of the world about the nature of the whale' (Alford 1984:367). If these vested interests and perceptions are widespread and powerful enough to isolate the Big Neighbour in international politics, the implementation of international law against its action would receive serious consideration in international forums.

At this point the humanitarian dimensions of the conflict and the reactions towards the Big Neighbour's action of the people in the annexed territory (as distinct from their rulers) would come into play. If the populace of the annexed territory were prepared to welcome the Big Neighbour's intervention, and if also there were claims of human rights violations against the regime in the affected state, these would be strong grounds in justification of the Big Neighbour's action. The way in which Turkey used its influential position in NATO and the willingness of its ethnic kin in Cyprus to co-operate with its strategic interests by ignoring the international condemnation of its occupation of part of Cyprus exemplifies this particular proposition (discussed in the next chapter).

The Indian intervention in East Bengal also has relevance. Indian military intervention in the East Bengal conflict did not turn into a forcible occupation, as was suggested by the regime in Pakistan, because of the prompt reaction from the international community accepting the independence of Bangladesh. If the situation had instead prompted international opposition to the secession demand, the Indian intervention had every possibility of becoming an illegal occupation. Coupled with the physical qualifications of East Bengal for separate statehood, its geographical separation and the size of its population (a majority in united Pakistan), it was the humanitarian dimension which influenced the world community to accept the independence of Bangladesh, saving India from such embarrassment.

Is the prevalent situation in Northern Cyprus a strong enough reason for its Big Neighbour to adopt annexation as an option ?

The Turkish policy of annexation has created an international stalemate, the resolution of which is the responsibility of the international community of states. After seventeen years of its occupation of Northern Cyprus, Turkey has succeeded in persuading the international community to accept neither the legitimacy of its action nor the *de facto* secession of the Turkish Republic of Northern Cyprus (TRNC), which it created in 1983. As some observers argue, although the policy-makers in the Turkish mainland may have expected their prolonged occupation to legalize the partition of Northern Cyprus (Birand 1988:174), it has not influenced the international community of states to change their stand against Turkish occupation in Cyprus. Instead the situation has been subjected to intense diplomatic initiatives under the direction of the UN Secretary General, to find a negotiated settlement between the communities in Cyprus.

However, the Turkish intervention has successfully separated the conflicting parties. The prolonged Turkish occupation of Northern Cyprus has helped the Turkish Cypriot community to strengthen their bargaining position vis-a-vis the Greek Cypriots (see Ryan 1984:196-9). In recent years the leaders of that community have openly expressed their willingness to resolve the conflict on the basis of devolution of government. What Turkey can expect from such an outcome is some strategic concessions but not annexation. Therefore, as will be discussed in the next chapter, Turkey's role in the Cyprus conflict provides empirical evidence in our analysis of the role of the Big Neighbour in the adoption of devolution of government as a solution to the secessionist problem.

For any Big Neighbour, the first lesson of the Turkish action (in pursuing territorial annexation as a way out of the ethnic conflict in Cyprus) is the role of the international community in accepting or rejecting the forcible annexation of the territory of another state. The international community cannot disregard an attack on the territorial integrity of a state whose sovereignty has once been accepted by them. They are bound to safeguard the sovereignty of even the smallest and weakest member of the present international community, at least to the extent of withholding approval of its violent overthrow. Such an attack would create permanent embarrassment for the occupying power, in the end probably forcing it to abandon its grip on the territory and allow the international community to initiate negotiations.

The second important lesson of the Cyprus conflict is the role of the people of the annexed territory. Any Big Neighbour which is interested in annexing territory from a state coping with a secessionist conflict needs at least the consent of the people who reside in that particular territory. Without the support of the people in the area an occupation is a security liability for the occupying power. The support received by Turkey from the Turkish Cypriots for their occupation in Cyprus is not forthcoming in every secessionist conflict. Even there it did not last long, and is not in the same spirit today (see McDonald 1989:47-51). What are the prospects of success of a policy of annexation in our other Big Neighbour situations?

Since Australia is the former metropolitan state of PNG, it is very unlikely that the Australian policy makers would consider such a policy towards a state whose sovereignty it voluntarily relinquished. Forcibly annexing a territory from that country, for no identifiable political advantage, would harm Australia's influence in the South Pacific and would destroy its image as an ex-colonial state. The only conceivable gain that might offset this would be the economic attractiveness of the Panguna mine. Since Australian mining interests in Panguna are already threatened by the conflict, for Australians this is not a strong reason to accept annexation as an option in the Bougainville secessionist conflict.

It is true that in 1971 some sections of the Indian establishment had considered this option in the East Bengal conflict (see Iqbal 1972:29). But for the Indian policy makers it was an unacceptable option mainly because of the religious component of East Bengali nationalism. If it had happened, India would have created the paradox of two states for Bengali people, East and West, within the Indian federation. This would certainly have meant a constitutional crisis as the Indian constitution does not accept religion as a basis for the establishment of states within the federal union. Thus in East Bengal, the Indian policy makers preferred secession rather than annexation. But we have to remember that India accepted this option at the last minute, and after failure to find a negotiated solution to the conflict. In the Sri Lanka case before accepting annexation as its policy option India would have to consider its strategic implications. Like the establishment of an independent Tamil state in Northern and Eastern Sri Lanka, to have the Sri Lankan Tamils joining the Indian federation would be a risky option for India, as it would strengthen the hands of its own secessionist elements in Tamil Nadu state. Thus, it would not resolve the immediate security threat deriving from the secessionist ideal of the Sri Lanka Tamils. However, a careful consideration of the linguistic, cultural and psychological dimensions of Tamil nationalism in Sri Lanka (see Coomaraswamy 1987; Arasaratnam 1964; Kailasapathy 1979) suggests that it is highly unlikely that the Tamil secessionists in Sri Lanka would have agreed to co-operate with India in annexing their territory to the more powerful Indian federation.

At the same time Indian policy makers would have had to consider the implication of such an option in relation to the demographic map of the 'traditional homelands of the Sri Lankan Tamils'. Although the majority of the population in these two provinces are Sri Lanka Tamils, nearly 35 percent of the population belong to the other two ethnic groups viz. the Sri Lanka Moors and the Sinhalese. In annexing the 'traditional homelands of the Sri Lanka Tamils' India would incorporate into her society these two communities, which are quite unwilling to become Indian citizens. Though India has a large Muslim population in its territory, the Sri Lankan Muslims have a history and identity distinct from their fellow Muslims in India. The Sinhalese minority in those regions would become the first such ethnic group in Indian territory. India could not expect any support from these communities, but rather, implacable resistance to its action. Therefore annexation of the secessionist region in Sri Lanka might simply bring the existing ethnic conflict in Sri Lanka into Indian territory (see Nagarajan 1984:352).

Yet another important aspect to be considered by the Indian policy makers is the impact of such an action upon the interests of the 'Indian Tamil community', residing in the central parts of Sri Lanka - encircled by majority Sinhalese areas. These people who have a very recent Indian origin (originally immigrants from India in the 19th century), have been separated from the Sri Lankan Tamils in Northern and Eastern provinces not only by their geographic distance but by their standard of living and most importantly, the conservative Hindu caste system of the Sri Lanka Tamils. While the Sri Lankan Tamils engaged in their demands for a separate state, this community has continuously demonstrated their willingness to co-operate with the Sinhalese political elite and now a majority of them have received Sri Lankan citizenship. Until the 1980s it was not the Sri Lankan Tamils but the Indian Tamils who received close attention from successive Indian governments. If India decided to pursue a policy of annexation in the secessionist areas it would gravely endanger the safety and the interests of the Indian Tamil community in Sri Lanka (see Tambiah 1986:177-81, Vaidik 1986:105-6).

Annexation, therefore, as a policy option of a Big Neighbour in resolution of an ethnic secessionist conflict on its borders, provide just as few examples of successful completion as did repression or secession.

Conclusion

It should be clear by now why 'repression', 'secession' or 'annexation' is unwelcome or unattainable by the Big Neighbour as its final policy objective towards the secessionist conflict in the affected state. The reasons which restrain Big Neighbour from settling firmly on these options, rest on Big Neighbour's own external and internal compulsions, and its policy-makers calculations on the gains and losses pertaining to these alternative options. Thus, they themselves explain why the Big Neighbour must pursue an active policy of containment of the secessionist conflict, urging the conflicting parties to settle the conflict through 'devolution' or some other power sharing arrangement.

As we noticed in the cases of India-Sri Lanka and Australia-PNG, if the Big Neighbour considers the break-up of its small neighbour is a security threat, and therefore, maintaining of the territorial integrity of the affected state is of crucial importance to its own national interest, the Big Neighbour's only option is to influence both contenders to accept devolution of government as a compromise settlement. Even in a secessionist situation where the Big Neighbour prefers 'secession' or 'annexation' as its final objective, as exemplified by the lessons of East Pakistan and Northern Cyprus, its policy-makers must keep the 'devolution' option open because of the indispensability of international acceptance in legitimizing such outcomes.

It appears, therefore, that it is 'devolution of government', which the policy makers of the Big Neighbour will prefer as their policy objective towards the secession conflict, in order to safeguard the national interest of their state. If there is to be any involvement in a secessionist conflict at all by a Big Neighbour, there is also no doubt that it is a Big Neighbour's commitment to this fourth kind of objective, a devolutionary settlement, that would be most welcomed by the international community. The explicit objective of a devolutionary policy is to secure the territorial integrity of the affected state while providing an aggrieved ethnic community with an opportunity to realize their nationalistic aspirations through regional autonomy.

However, the Big Neighbour's own commitment to a devolutionary policy, and the blessings of the international community for such commitment, do not alone guarantee the speedy and painless management of a secessionist conflict. Because of its ethnic and strategic ties to the secessionist situation, there is always the possibility of misinterpreting Big Neighbour's commitment to a devolutionary settlement by both adversaries. Furthermore, the policy makers of the Big Neighbour may have to cope with the intransigence of both adversaries, and above all, their efforts to bring other external actors into the conflict situation, which may severely test Big Neighbour's commitment to conflict management. Thus it has different roles to play in the conflict situation, to overcome such refusals, intransigence and disruptive movements of the conflicting parties and to bring them by political and diplomatic means to the bargaining table and finally the reception of 'devolution of government' as the preferred settlement to the conflict. In the next chapter we will investigate these different roles played by the Big Neighbour in a secessionist conflict.

4 The Role of the Big Neighbour

Introduction

As we hypothesized in our model of conditions in chapter one, the Big Neighbour in its efforts towards the containment of the secession conflict in its small neighbour's territory may play one or more of the following roles at different stages of the conflict:

(a) the 'pressure role',
(b) the 'big stick role',
(c) the 'interventionist role', and
(d) the 'invitational role'.

This chapter, using as empirical material our four Big Neighbour secessionist situations as well as the Syria-Lebanon situation (though they do not all carry the same weight for this particular form of Big Neighbour involvement), will examine these different Big Neighbour roles in relation to the reactions of the other actors in the conflict. The central argument of this analysis is that the Big Neighbour's committed participation in the conflict situation through one or more of these roles is designed to have profound effects upon the conflicting parties, influencing them to go to the negotiation table, and to accept devolution as a compromise settlement to the conflict.

The pressure role

This refers to methods used by the Big Neighbour to exert pressure upon the adversaries in the secession conflict to settle their conflict through a political settlement. They range from political, diplomatic and economic activities to providing covert or overt military assistance to one of the combatants, merely as a method of exerting pressure upon the other party in the secessionist conflict, or upon other possible participants.

Where such external involvement is threatened, the Big Neighbour situations produce different behaviours from the internal parties to the conflict and the Big Neighbour's method of pressure differs accordingly. In this regard we can discern two patterns of Big Neighbour secessionist situations: (a) the situation where the secessionist community and the people of the Big Neighbour have a common ethnic tie i.e. 'the ethnic-tie situation' (b) the situations where the secessionists are not ethnic kin of the Big Neighbour people but the affected state and the Big Neighbour have close relations for mutual defence i.e. 'the strategic-tie situation'. From our Big Neighbour situations, India-Bangladesh, Turkey-Cyprus and India-Sri Lanka illustrate the ethnic-tie situation, the other, Australia-PNG, the strategic-tie situation.

Where it is the secessionists who seem to be the most likely of the internal actors to seek assistance from external parties, and to turn to enemies of the Big Neighbour for it, Big Neighbour has two kinds of options in trying to avert or contain such actions: 'moderate' and 'drastic'. The moderate method is to make its present felt in the conflict as a peace-maker, offering its good offices for mediation; and perhaps go to the extent of providing sanctuary to the secessionists in its territory, as a way of gaining control over the secessionist movement. The drastic option is to provide military and other assistance to the central regime, not to encourage 'repression' but as a method of exerting pressure on the secessionist movement.

The drastic option is an obvious response in the strategic-tie situation where understandably, the Big Neighbour may pronounce its commitment to the territorial integrity of the affected state, and provide military, logistic and economic support to the central regime because of its close relationship with the latter. As we saw in chapter three, in view of the continuous violence in Bougainville Island, the government of Australia stepped up its military and logistic assistance to the PNG government in September 1989, supplying four Iroqois helicopters to the PNGDF and major shipments of small arms and ammunition. The Australian Prime Minister defended the PNG government's decision to impose sanctions on Bougainville Island when opposition politicians raised this as an issue in the Australian Parliament (discussed in chapter 2).

Such an open and outright commitment on the part of the Big Neighbour proved effective in the Australia-PNG situation, by frightening off any outside power, and influencing the secessionists to enter negotiations with the central government. The Australian presence in the conflict as PNG's defence benefactor effectively precluded support from outside powers for the secessionist movement. Many neighbouring states from the South-east Asian and South Pacific regions, including Indonesia and the Solomon Islands (with which the Bougainvilleans connect themselves), came forward to declare their commitment to the territorial integrity of Papua New Guinea (Keesing's 1990:37458). The Solomon Islands' government signed an agreement with PNG to prevent secessionists infiltrating its territory (Keesing's 1990:37882).

There was no shortage of states within the region to offer their good offices for mediation on PNG's request, while the Australian Foreign Minister openly accepted his government's unfitness for the job, saying that it would not be seen as 'neutral', because of Australia's interest in Bougainville (see *The Economist* 17 March 1991). In February 1990 PNG and the secessionist movement signed a cease-fire agreement, widely known as 'the Endearoura Accord', since New Zealand had provided one of its naval ships 'Endearoura' for use as the venue of the talks, and another vessel to transport secessionist leaders from the island (see *New Zealand External Relations Review* 1991,41(2):20; Keesing's 1991:37880).

The second round of peace talks was convened at the Solomons' capital Honiara at the end of 1990, under the aegis of the Solomon Islands' government, the result of which was the second ceasefire agreement, 'the Honiara Declaration' of January 1991. Under the terms of the 'Honiara Declaration' a Multinational Supervisory Team (MST) mainly from the military and police forces of the South Pacific Forum countries (including Australia and Canada) would be deployed in Bougainville, to supervise the implementation of the ceasefire agreement (see *Far Eastern Economic Review* 7 February 1991).

Both sides entered the negotiations realizing the futility of their militaristic approach. However, the lessons learnt by the secessionists appeared much more emphatic than those of the central regime. They emerged as a rebel movement exhausted in resisting the central regime's military and economic onslaught, and with trying to keep the secessionist region under its effective control without any outside support or recognition (Keesing's 1991:37879-80, Spriggs & May 1990:117).

This suggests that without external assistance, in the face of such a strong commitment from the Big Neighbour to the integrity of the affected state, no secessionist group can persist in intransigence towards mediation by the Big Neighbour or any other third party. The Big Neighbour's advantageous position, however, depends upon a known commitment to a political settlement, preferably a devolutionary settlement. Without that, the Big Neighbour's actions in providing increased military assistance to the central regime of the affected state could provoke international condemnation. In so far as the Big Neighbour is openly advocating a devolutionary settlement it can justify its action against a secession movement which is unwilling to give negotiation a chance.

Again, the Big Neighbour's decision to provide additional military assistance to the central regime would not be effective as pressure towards negotiations unless it accepts responsibility for checking the use made of the assistance. There is always a danger of the central regime interpreting Big Neighbour's support as a licence to seek an outright military solution. As noted in the previous chapter, any indulgence in repression would negate the Big Neighbour's commitment to a negotiated solution to the conflict. Therefore this kind of tactic requires constant vigil on the central regime, persuading it to restrict its actions to non-military methods. Such methods as economic sanctions, naval and air blockades so on, or at worst deploying its military forces along the borders of the secessionist area as a deterrent, also carry danger to the climate for negotiations, such as shortages of food and medicines. But Big Neighbour cannot reject all such alternatives to excessive military force in containing an intransigent secessionist group, though they damage its own reputation internationally.

Following this scenario, it was with the tacit approval of the Australian government (see *Australian Foreign Affairs Record*, 1990,61(5):287) that the PNG government in mid-1989 decided to withdraw all its security forces from Bougainville Island and impose a naval and air blockade of the Bougainville secessionists instead (*Far Eastern Economic Review*, 25 October 1990), while building up a strong military force in the nearby Nissan Island (see Keesing's 1990:37880) - a change of policy which occurred after an attempt at military victory over the secessionist movement failed, amidst allegations of human rights violations by Amnesty International amongst others (see Havini 1990:31-2,37; *News Week*, 17 December 1990).

In the ethnic-tie situation, by contrast, it is the central regime of the affected state that is the most likely collaborator with the enemies of the Big Neighbour, especially where its policy makers see their Big Neighbour as irredentist or expansionist. Then an effective pressure tactic is to use the secessionist movement as a proxy military force against the central regime and its external bedfellows, giving it covert military assistance and sanctuary.

The Big Neighbour by such 'cold war methods' (cf. Scott 1964:154-5) can weaken the affected state economically and militarily and thus exert pressure towards a negotiated settlement. This can also be effective against external supporters of the central regime. The Big Neighbour has the political advantage over them, in so far as it is committed to a negotiated solution vis-a-vis the central regime's inclination to a military solution. It only needs the situation to provide some incidents of human rights violations by the security forces of the affected state for Big Neighbour to create an international uproar in sympathy with the plight of the secessionist community. External powers are then in an invidious position in opposing the Big Neighbour's involvement in assisting the secessionist movement, for they cannot reasonably support a central regime which has become 'notorious' for its ill-treatment of its minority community, or come to the assistance of such a regime in its efforts to suppress an aggrieved 'liberation struggle', even if it is common knowledge that the rebel forces are playing a proxy role for the Big Neighbour's strategic interests.

The policy makers of the Big Neighbour in using such cold war tactics are at the same time strengthening their influence over the secessionist movement. By providing military and economic assistance in its struggle, the Big Neighbour wins the confidence of the secessionist community, while developing a closer understanding of their leadership and the different factions in the movement. It is an advantage that the secessionist movement become dependent on Big Neighbour's assistance, providing strong leverage to the policy makers to discourage the secessionists from any attempt to find alternative support beyond the borders of Big Neighbour's territory and in particular, from its enemies in international politics. The more the secessionists come to rely on Big Neighbour, the more it enhances the Big Neighbour's position in pressurising the affected state central regime to accept its mediation.

Among our case studies, India's involvement in providing military assistance to the Tamil secessionists in Sri Lanka can be cited as an example of this process. During the period 1983-1987 while still offering its good offices and mediation to find a negotiated solution to the conflict, India provided financial and military assistance (sometimes through the Tamil Nadu authorities) to the Tamil secessionists who enjoyed sanctuary in the Indian state of Tamil Nadu during this time. India allowed the Sri Lankan Tamil secessionists to use Indian soil for military training, sometimes with the help of retired Indian military personnel (see *India Today* 31 March 1984, 31 May 1992; *New York Times* 29 April 1984). Up until 1987 there were 36 military training camps in the Indian state of Tamil Nadu with the knowledge of the Indian authorities, according to a statement made by the leader of the DMK party Mr M. Karunanidhi, who was the Chief Minister of the Tamil Nadu state government at the time of this statement (*The Hindu International Edition* 19 January 1991).

Similar involvements by Big Neighbours could be found in the Turkey-Cyprus and India-East Pakistan situations. The military assistance provided by the Indian government to the *Mukti Bahini* guerrillas in East Bengal in 1971, during the early stages of their secession conflict (when India was openly calling for a political settlement to the conflict), and Turkey's involvement in promoting extremist elements among the Turkish Cypriot community such as the *Turk Mukavemet Teskilati* (TMT) or 'Turkish Defence Organization', which envisaged partition of Cyprus as against the 'Enosis' ideal envisaged by the Greek Cypriots, are now well documented in the literature (in this regard for East Pakistan, see Ayoob & Subramanyam 1972:156-7; Choudhury 1974:99, and for Cyprus, see Black 1977:58; Souter 1984:663).

Beyond our selected Big Neighbour situations, China in the 1950s provided military assistance to the Kachin secessionist movement in Burma (now Myanmar) and used its connections with this particular secessionist movement as leverage in pressurising the Burmese government to make territorial concessions on the disputed Sino-Burmese frontier (see Keesing's 1957:86-92). Another instance was the military assistance received by the Kurdish rebellion movement in Iraq in the 1970s from the then Iranian ruler Mohammad Reza Shah Pahlavi. The Shah's main intention was to use the Kurdish movement in Northern Iraq as an instrument of pressure on the Ba'athist regime in Iraq in the settlement of many outstanding issues confronting the two countries, the central issue being the territorial dispute widely known as the *Shatt al-Arab* dispute (Saikal 1980:170). He achieved this objective by bringing Iraq to the negotiation table in 1975, using his involvement in Kurdish rebellion as the central bargaining chip. In return the Shah promised not only to terminate his assistance to the Kurdish movement in Iraq but also to check their activities on Iranian soil (Harris 1977:73-9; Saikal 1980:169-70). This same method was used by the Shah's successors, the Islamic regime which came into power after the Islamic revolution in 1979, during the time of the Iran-Iraq war in the 1980s. On this occasion Iran not only supplied military equipment to the Kurdish rebels but, going well beyond 'cold war' tactics, also sent the Iranian Revolutionary Guards to join them in their attack on oil installations in the Iraq city of Kirkuk (Aguado 1990:160). This time it was publicly acknowledged by the Iranian authorities that '...the Kurds have become one of the most important instruments of pressure on Iraq' (Aguado 1990:160).

However, there were significant differences between these Chinese and Iranian involvements and our selected Big Neighbour situations. The Chinese and Iranian authorities' dealings with the secessionists in their respective secessionist situations were not directly associated with any devolutionary policy; they used the secessionists as proxies to put pressure on the central regimes for the settlement of wider issues. By contrast, the immediate intention of Indian assistance to the secessionist movements in East Pakistan and Sri Lanka, and also Turkey's assistance to the Turkish Cypriots (though they also had wider strategic interests), was to protect the minority community from the repressive policies carried out by the central regime or from the periodic violence organized by extremists of the majority ethnic group.

It is true that both India in East Pakistan and Turkey in Cyprus went on to military intervention in these secession conflicts. But the policy-makers of India and Turkey were until the last moment expecting to use the secessionist resistance as an instrument of pressure against the central regimes, aiming at power sharing concessions to the minority community. Unlike these two Big Neighbour situations, the Indian action in assisting the Tamil secessionists in Sri Lanka occurred at a time when India was providing its good offices for mediation with the approval of the central regime in Sri Lanka. This Indian involvement in 'cold war' tactics was at its height during the period 1983-1985 when Sri Lanka was desperately seeking direct military assistance from extra-regional powers like the United States and the United Kingdom, and receiving such assistance from Israel, South Africa, China, Pakistan and the Channel Island-based private security firm, Keenie Meenie Service (discussed in chapter 2).

The realities of the Indo-Sri Lanka tangle were that secession and annexation were both unacceptable options for the Indian policy-makers (discussed in chapter three). The best option for the Indian central government was, therefore, finding the road to a devolutionary settlement to end the conflict. Neither the central regime's militaristic policies, nor their embracing of external powers hostile to India, were on that road, hence the use of the secessionists as an instrument of pressure upon the government of Sri Lanka.

The covert involvement allowed the Indian authorities to establish direct and regular contacts with the various Tamil secessionist groups, which were broadly divided on ideological lines.[1] As was revealed by the Tamil leaders themselves, the close relations maintained with the Indian authorities induced the Tamil activists to believe that India would make a direct military intervention against the Sri Lanka government if it failed to contain the militaristic policies of the central regime in Sri Lanka (*The New York Times* 8 July 1985). According to both Indian and Tamil commentators, India at one time mapped out such a military intervention with the knowledge of the secessionists (see Sawhny 1987:135; Vaidik 1986:95; Ram 1989:88-9). In reality India had two purposes in providing sanctuary coupled with military and financial assistance to the Tamil secessionists.

First, it wanted to keep the Tamil groups within its sphere of influence. Professor A. Jeyaratnam Wilson, who was once involved in mediations between Tamil United Liberation Front (TULF) and the Sri Lanka government because of his close relationship with the Tamil political leadership (see Wilson 1982), later disclosed,

> At various times, to my knowledge, Indian policy-makers had contemplated intervention and plans had been drawn up to that end. This had given hope to the TULF and the leaders of the Tamil militant groups. Whether this was done deliberately in order to mislead the Tamil leaders can only be conjectured, but the result of such aid being offered was that the Tamil leaders placed all their eggs in one basket - the Indian one. Had India not been so forthcoming, the Tamil resistance would have become internationalized and other resistance organizations and anti-western states would have offered support to the Tamil movement. But by offering hopes of India's possible military involvement the Indian government contained the Tamil movement within the frontiers of India, and pre-empted its becoming involved in other international terrorist organizations (Wilson 1988:203-4).

---

1. Five main militant groups maintained contacts with the Indian and Tamil Nadu authorities, namely the Liberation Tigers of Tamil Eelam (LTTE), the People's Liberation Organization of Tamil Eelam (PLOTE), the Tamil Eelam Liberation Organization (TELO), the Eelam Revolutionary Organization of Students (EROS) and the Eelam People's Revolutionary Liberation Front (EPRLF), apart from the moderate Tamil political party the Tamil United Liberation Front (TULF) whose leaders (of whom many were members of the Sri Lanka Parliament unseated in 1983 by a constitutional amendment) resided in India as the guests of the Tamil Nadu state government until 1987 (see for more details Oberst 1988:190-195).

Second, aid to the secessionist militants was a form of warning to the central regime in Sri Lanka. It is worth noting at this point that both Mrs Indira Gandhi and her son Rajiv Gandhi, the successive Prime Ministers who led the Indian administration during this stormy period of Indo-Sri Lanka relations, openly declared their commitment to the territorial integrity of Sri Lanka. Prime Minister Rajiv Gandhi once went so far as to advise the Tamil leaders not to '...expect a separate state or federal state but something similar to what India has' (Wilson 1988:183).

So through its support of the armed struggle of the Tamil movement 'short of secession', Indian policy-makers sent two warning messages to the Sri Lankan regime. One was that Sri Lanka couldn't achieve a military solution to the conflict by suppressing the Tamil uprising. The other was that Sri Lanka should look to India, not to any other party, in finding a settlement to the conflict, because only India as the main benefactor of the secessionists could bring the Tamils to the negotiating table.

This two-pronged Indian strategy of exerting pressure upon both side of the conflict had some success. The Tamil secessionists did on many occasions respond positively to the Indian request to give mediation a chance. However, there were occasions when the Indian authorities had to face intransigence from some sections of the secessionist movement. On these occasions the Indian strategy was to exploit differences among the militant groups.

It has been revealed that the Indian Intelligence Agency, the Research and Analytic Wing (RAW) deliberately provoked disputes between hostile Tamil secessionist groups in order to 'divide and rule' among them (see Wilson 1988:204). For example, India sent the TULF leaders to the Sri Lanka capital for direct negotiations with the Sri Lanka government at a time when more militant secessionist groups were demonstrating intransigence to Indian-sponsored mediation (see for more detaails *New York Times* 3 August 1986; *The Hindu International Edition* 4 October 1986).

So far in this section, we have discussed the Big Neighbour's options in pressurizing the main actors to the conflict, supposing one of them to be working against the wishes of the Big Neighbour while the other maintains close relationship with its policy-makers. However, supplying assistance to one of the main actors against the other is undoubtedly a risky tactic. It must create suspicion and anger in the minds of the very party which has to be cajoled into negotiations; and there is always the risk of that internal actor launching counter measures that will directly injure the Big Neighbour's economic and political stability. Thus sometimes the Big Neighbour will prefer to use less risky and less controversial methods; political, diplomatic and economic means of pressure less likely to endanger its wider interests in the conflict and in regional politics.

Among such less risky means, the policy-makers of the Big Neighbour may use public platforms, within its national boundary or on the international stage, to bring 'verbal' pressure on the rivals in the secession conflict. Such platforms would include meetings of the national legislature, international and regional forums, regular press briefings, specially organized press conferences, and public assemblies of one kind and another. Expressing their views and policies on the secessionist conflict in such ways can hardly be found unacceptable by the international community. Yet political rhetoric of this kind can certainly play a 'pressure role' during attempts at Big Neighbour mediation. These occasions can be used to disclose the issues confronted by the Big Neighbour's official mediators and the negative approaches of the central regime and/or the secessionists towards them, alerting public opinion both in the society of the affected state and internationally.

The aim is not so much to send messages to the fortresses of the conflicting parties as to isolate a recalcitrant party in international and regional forums. Once the Big Neighbour is involved in the conflict, the greater the support for its stance it can derive from international public opinion, the greater are the opportunities it has in the containment of the internal actors in the conflict. In gaining more formal international support, the most effective mechanism available to the Big Neighbour is on the diplomatic front. It is natural for any Big Neighbour involved in a secessionist conflict, whose policy is the internationally-acceptable devolutionary one, to make full use of its diplomatic missions in other countries and in regional and international organizations to propagate it. This could have a marked influence upon a recalcitrant central regime in the affected state.

On the diplomatic front the Big Neighbour by definition enjoys a stronger position: its world wide diplomatic network and its relations with other large countries could become a powerful propaganda machine directed against the central regime. The destructive social effects of the regime's militaristic policies, the plight of refugees and any accompanying incidents of human rights violations in the secessionist region, would receive world wide attention. Such a diplomatic offensive would be calculated to isolate the affected state in international politics and to render support for it from other states less eligible. It might even lead such external supporters of the central regime to persuade their client to opt for participation in the political mediations sponsored by the Big Neighbour.

Such a diplomatic offensive might have a special effect on the super powers whose ideological goals are often associated with humanistic and democratic ideals. A well co-ordinated campaign by the Big Neighbour in the international scene giving prominence to the human dimensions of the conflict might influence these super powers to dissociate themselves altogether from the militaristic policies of the affected state, to protect their wider global interests. It is therefore vital that the Big Neighbour's policy makers succeed in convincing the super powers and other great powers about the real intention of their involvement in the secessionist conflict. If this is accomplished, the Big Neighbour may either get the support of these great powers for its mediatory efforts, or worst offset on the propaganda level the activities of any of them in the secessionist conflict.

Of course if the involvement of the Big Neighbour, especially when it is using the secessionists as a proxy military force, is in reality directed to gaining strategic objectives against hostile regional or extra-regional powers (including great powers), the Big Neighbour will not always be successful in so convincing them to the purity of its motives. This would also inhibit its efforts to find a peaceful settlement to the secessionist conflict.

Diplomatic activity is not out of the question when it is the secessionists who are the intransigent party. The Big Neighbour can use its diplomatic resources against any external supporters providing the financial and military assistance to the secessionist movement which backs their intransigence. Since its diplomatic activities are directed to winning the support of the international community for its efforts to find a political settlement to the conflict, the Big Neighbour can as easily arouse international public opinion against such ill-disposed third parties, and make international pariahs of the secessionist movement, as it can a central regime.

In illustrating the Big Neighbour's use of diplomatic and political resources as instruments of pressure we have many instances from the secession conflicts in East Pakistan, Sri Lanka and Cyprus. The Indian policy-makers developed much expertise in this regard from their experience in the East Pakistan secession conflict. They used every domestic and international platform, such as meetings of the national legislature, press conferences, meetings of the UN security council, and India's diplomatic representations in the major capitals, etc., to make known their views and policies towards the conflict in Pakistan, while providing first hand information to the world public about the plight of the displaced Bengali people. There is no doubt that these Indian efforts immensely contributed to the process of internationalization of the conflict in East Pakistan, and to the international isolation of the Pakistan central regime. The main objectives of these efforts were to block possible external assistance to that regime and to influence friendly states to apply pressure on the military regime to find a negotiated settlement, or in case the need arose for direct military intervention in East Pakistan, to use such an international isolation to gain the advantage over Pakistan.

As part of this overall exercise the then Indian Prime Minister, Mrs Indira Gandhi, personally participated in the Indian diplomatic campaign. The leadership role she played is alone sufficient to illustrate our theme. In October 1971 she visited six western capitals, namely Brussels, Vienna, London, Paris, Bonn and Washington, after having visited the Soviet capital just a month before, to brief the leaders of these countries regarding the situation developing on India's eastern frontier (Keesing's 1971:24991,249993). As well as explaining to the governmental leaders of these countries her government's policy towards the East Pakistan conflict and its spillover effects upon Indo-Pakistan relations, she attended many public meetings, press conferences, Radio and Television interviews to win public opinion in these countries in favour of Indian policy towards the conflict in East Pakistan, and to counteract the propaganda currently put out by the regime in Pakistan.

For example on one such occasion she '...told the French people that she was prepared to meet President Yahya Khan to discuss all the problems between India and Pakistan...' (Keesing's 1971:24993) but maintained that that could not help to resolve the East Pakistan conflict, because it was a problem between West Pakistan and the Bengalis, not between India and Pakistan (Keesing's 1971:24993). This was a clear attempt on the part of the Indian leader to get international acceptance for the secessionist leadership of the Bengali community, and to strengthen their hands in future dealings with their central regime. While the central regime in Pakistan was trying to discredit the Awami League leadership as an anti-national movement responsible for instigating terrorist violence, Indian strategy was to use international public opinion to bring pressure on Pakistan to treat the Bengali leadership on an equal footing and participate in political negotiations with them. The very same message was conveyed to the Secretary General of the United Nations by the Indian leader. Replying to a letter sent by the UN Secretary General she stated,

> The problem, which involved the rights and the fate of the people of East Bengal, could only be resolved by peaceful negotiations between the military regime and the leaders of East Bengal. Only in this manner could the flow of refugees into India be reversed and the threat to India's security relieved (*Year Book of the United Nations* 1971:45).

These personal attempts by the Indian leader on the international stage were echoed on domestic platforms. The Indian Prime Minister made the following statement to the lower house of the Indian Parliament:

> We are convinced there can be no military solution to the problem of East Bengal. A political solution must be brought about by those who have the power to do so. World opinion is a great force. It can influence even the most powerful. The great powers have special responsibility. If they exercise their power rightly and expeditiously then only can we look forward to a durable peace on our subcontinent. But if they fail ...then this suppression of human rights, uprooting of people and continued homelessness of vast numbers of human beings will threaten peace (Keesing's 1971:24686).

Another successful strategy followed by the Indian policy-makers was to invite foreign observers to the conflict-affected areas in Indian territory and allow them to provide first hand information to the international community. One notable incident involved a visit by the US. Senator Edward Kennedy. His account was a reprimand to the pro-Pakistani policy followed by the then American administration of Richard Nixon and an endorsement of Indian efforts to find a solution to the conflict:

> At no times had any official of our government including the President, condemned a brutal and systematic repression of East Bengal by the Pakistan

Army - a repression carried out in part with American guns and bullets and aircraft. In sharp contrast to our defence of Pakistani sensibilities over these past months of violence in East Pakistan, our national leadership suddenly denounces India. We have made her the scapegoat of our frustration and failures, and after the bankruptcy of our policy towards Pakistan (Keesing's 1972:25069).

Almost a decade later, in respect of the Sri Lanka situation, there were not many differences in Indian behaviour on political and diplomatic platforms. However, this time the mission of the Indian 'spin-doctors' was a more complex one. They had to offset the influence of already-infiltrated foreign powers, supporters of the Sri Lanka government's counter-insurgency campaign, and focus attention on the ongoing Indian mediation. But as India herself was using the secessionists as an instrument of pressure on the central regime, their diplomatic and political manoeuvres were constitutive elements of the 'cold war' tactics already being employed in the conflict in Sri Lanka. The risky 'special relationship' with the secessionist movement had already given the impression to the outside world that India would make a Bangladesh-type direct military intervention against Sri Lanka in the near future (see *The New York Times* 29 April 1984); the Indian policy-makers had the task of convincing the international community of the sincerity of India's search for a negotiated solution - a matter of some urgency, since in some eyes the United States of America was already involved in the conflict through its surrogates (as discussed in Chapter 2).

The shifts of the Sri Lanka regime between political negotiations and military action came not only from its suspicions of Indian intentions but also from its faith in the (friendly) great powers' support in case of an Indian invasion. Since the final outcome in East Pakistan, a strategic victory for India over Western interests in South Asia, was still in mind among the policy-makers of the western powers, Sri Lanka had a basis for expecting their assistance against an Indian invasion, since it could characterize such an action by its Big Neighbour as another potential strategic defeat for them. That measured the size of the Indian policy-makers' responsibility: no less than to reverse the great power's attitudes and prejudices about India's Sri Lanka policy, and make a delusion of Sri Lanka's hope for great power assistance in its counter-insurgency posture.

Therefore, unlike the East Pakistan situation, India's use of diplomatic and political resources as elements in the 'pressure role' it was playing in the Sri Lanka secession conflict, required the exercise of great patience by the Indian policy-makers. Since neither secession nor annexation was considered an acceptable option in the Sri Lanka situation, they couldn't expect as swift a success as they achieved in 1971 in the East Pakistan conflict. Compared with that involvement, they spent years rather than months in pressurising the antagonists in the Sri Lanka conflict. Even with such a long entanglement, they did not change their policy, but only the role played in the conflict. It was a protracted exercise of forbearance intended to keep the process of Indian mediation in Sri Lanka running and unbroken.

Acting within the limits of these political realities, India used its domestic and diplomatic platforms to send messages through the international media to the rivals in the conflict, and to the world powers who had become keen spectators of developments in the Sri Lanka-India theatre. Sometimes Indian criticisms of the militaristic policies of the Sri Lanka government created immense political difficulties for the Sri Lankan leaders and led to open rhetorical warfare between Indian and Sri Lankan leaders (see *Asia Year Book* 1988, Far Eastern Economic Review, Hongkong, p.246). When Indo-Sri Lanka relations deteriorated to such an extent that the leaders of both countries engaged in bitter polemic, and Sri Lanka took refuge in renewed militarism, India successfully influenced the passing of a resolution against the Sri Lanka government in the United Nations Human Rights Commission, requesting the UN Secretary General to report to the United Nations General Assembly on the human rights situation in Sri Lanka (see *Tamil Times* 1987,6(5):10-11; Kodikara 1987:643). The Indian Ambassador told the UN Human Rights Commission,

> The violation of human rights in Sri Lanka are genuine and widespread. The fact that negotiations are going on, is not sufficient ground for tolerating the violence. ...India's position is very clear. There is an ethnic conflict in Sri Lanka which has taken heavy toll of life. It is a problem between two sections in of the Sri Lankan population, not a dispute between Sri Lanka and India. We had offered our mediatory role to keep the process of negotiation going. This process had made sufficient progress till last year ...but has come to a halt because of certain steps taken by the Sri Lanka Government. It is difficult for India to continue the progress as long as violent conditions in Sri Lanka prevail. The violence must end. The Sri Lankan Government must show the will to negotiate (as quoted in *Tamil Times* 1987,6(5):15).

If we move to the Eastern Mediterranean, we can find manoeuvres of Turkish policy-makers of the same kind and for the same purpose in organizations like NATO, the UN, the Islamic Conference and the Regional Co-operation for Development Pact (created in 1964 by Iran, Pakistan and Turkey).

Apart from such political and diplomatic pressures, a Big Neighbour can open an economic front against the central regime in the affected state. The reduction or cancellation of already promised economic assistance to the central regime from the Big Neighbour, or any other source which can be persuaded to co-operate, or even giving of an advance warning of such action, may be a potent mechanism of pressure against the central regime. By intense lobbying the Big Neighbour may be able to influence the world community of states and the international monetary and financial institutions to impose collective sanctions on the central regime, by the reduction or cancellation of already promised economic aid, or by the imposition of trade embargo and the like.

Amongst our ethnic secession situations it was the Australian policy-makers who enjoyed the strongest economic clout in relation to their small neighbour, should they want to use economic pressure on the central regime. Apart from Australia's massive subsidy to PNG's annual budget and aid for the maintenance of its defence system, it could use its influence in the western camp and in world financial institutions for this purpose. The Australian undertaking to supply half of the aid package (US$ 31 million) agreed by the International Monetary Fund (IMF) for the PNG government, to compensate the economic cost of the closure of the Bougainville copper mine in November 1990 (see *News Week* 17 December 1990), demonstrates the extent of their economic power.

What was lacking in the cases of the Indian and Turkish Big Neighbours was this direct access to economic power. As influential actors in regional and international politics, however, and using international media, they were able to generate public reaction against human rights violations in the affected state, and urge governments in the economically affluent states to use 'their' economic leverage to bring pressure upon the central regime.

India's success in influencing western governments to terminate their already agreed military assistance to Pakistan can perhaps be taken as an example (Keesing's 1972:24993; Wilcox 1973:31). In 1986 the Sri Lanka government faced a similar denunciation from its donors, such as the United States, Japan, Saudi Arabia, Sweden, Norway and the World Bank; and in 1987 suffered a reduction of economic aid previously agreed by these sources (see Pfaffenberger 1987:162; Keesing's 1987:35316,35586; Rao 1988:428). There was no direct involvement of the Indian government in these actions. But one cannot leave out of account the world-wide campaign carried out by India against the human rights record of the Sri Lanka government (see Pfaffenberger 1987:156).

The big stick role

For the Big Neighbour, the achievement of a speedy resolution of an intensified secession conflict through playing only a 'pressure role' is not always a realistic hope. Sometimes 'pressure' is not sufficient even to keep the antagonists under its influence and make them more responsive to the mediation process. The conflict may become a running sore, dragging the whole region into instability. Such a situation is often associated with the intransigence of one or both the domestic actors, continually seeking to break the Big Neighbour's grip on the conflict situation. Understandably, this may make the policy-makers of the Big Neighbour lose patience and think about stronger action. But at this stage, direct military intervention to impose its own solution on the conflicting parties is not necessarily the appropriate move for the Big Neighbour. It still has some room to manoeuvre.

Big Neighbour may now move to the 'big stick role', the next step in the progression of four different roles which, we have postulated, feature in a secession conflict. This refers to overtly threatening actions aimed at '...the creation of expectations about (the Big Neighbour's) punitive actions in response to the actions or inaction of (the rivals in the conflict)' (Payne 1970:4, words in brackets added).

This applies just as well to a Big Neighbour already engaged in mediation between the domestic rivals in the conflict. There is, of course, a difference between the role played by a conventional third party mediator and that of the Big Neighbour. The Big Neighbour has a stake in the secession conflict, and therefore, does not always 'stay out of the way of the conflicting parties' (cf. Wall 1981:157). If the conflict is escalating, or the combatants slipping out of its control, the Big Neighbour may decide to escalate its pressure tactics by waving a 'big stick', without abandoning its hope of finding a political settlement to the conflict.

Big Neighbour's waving the 'big stick' may of course reawaken old fears in the central regime or the secessionists about the intentions of the Big Neighbour. Although neither objective is a real option in the Big Neighbour's own national interests, the 'big stick' role may imply secession or annexation as the objective. There is little doubt that either of these outcomes would be anathema to the central regime. However, a signal from the Big Neighbour indicating an intention of annexing the secessionist homeland, though it would free the secessionists from their present state, would not always be acceptable - annexation would deprive them of full independence.

The threat of annexation is not the only minatory action available to the Big Neighbour against an intransigent secessionist movement. A worse threat is that of sending its armed forces in an 'invitational role' (discussed next), assisting the affected state to quell the insurgency movement. To create such expectations in the minds of the secessionists the Big Neighbour may suspend its connections with the secessionist movement: expel the secessionists from their sanctuary in its territory; and withdraw military and other assistance. Further, the Big Neighbour may take military and police actions against secessionist militants in its own territory or on its frontier with the affected state, and patrol along the territorial or maritime boundary between the two states, restricting cross-border movements and the smuggling of arms from external sources.

Thus it is principally the fear of direct military intervention by the Big Neighbour, that may eventually create a *de facto* partition situation, which dominates the interaction between Big Neighbour in the 'big stick' role and the affected state. This is of course, a form of psychological warfare in itself and, like the 'cold war' tactics discussed earlier, it has accompanying risks. Specific actions of the Big Neighbour may be far from peaceable ones: sometimes they may amount to an actual infringement of international law, and invite the attention of other international actors, reluctantly or eagerly getting themselves involved. It may be difficult to avoid the appearance of preparing for an outright invasion of its neighbour. Waving the 'big stick' may involve the mobilization of Big Neighbour's armed forces in the frontier area; naval, air and ground movements by its armed forces towards strategic points within its borders; operational exercises explicitly demonstrating its military clout; perhaps the dispatch of symbolic missions using air, ground or naval forces, marginally violating the affected state's territory, territorial waters or air-space. Needless to say the policy-makers of the Big Neighbour will enhance the appearance of belligerence by accompanying such threatening actions against the affected state's central regime with a barrage of appropriate rhetoric. The risk is that the elaborate bluff may be called by the affected state in a pre-emptive strike, or that the international community may act before the strategy has time to work.

We can bring forward instances from our selected Big Neighbour situations and other relevant situations around the world to illustrate the Big Neighbour's behaviour in the 'big stick' role. But the Turkey-Cyprus and India-Sri Lanka situations are sufficient to illustrate our case. Turkey's threats against the regime in Cyprus first started in December 1963, when the uneasy ethnic balance established by the London and Zurich agreements of 1960 was disturbed by the outbreak of serious communal violence between the Greek and Turkish Cypriot communities, costing more than 200 lives on both sides, following the Makarios regime's arbitrary decision to abolish the minority guarantees provided by the independence settlement (see Keesing's 1964:20113). As violence continued, causing severe damage to the property and the lives of Turkish Cypriots, and as the Greek Cypriot leaders took no action to end the violence and were still expressing their resoluteness on the proposed constitutional change (Keesing's 1964:20113), Turkey decided it had no option but to get out the 'big stick'. First it was a warning from the Turkish Prime Minister, Professor Turhan Feyzioglu:

> the Turkish Cypriots are not an ordinary minority but a separate community with special rights safeguarded by the Cyprus constitution; that the London and Zurich agreements were the result of mutual compromise... if the agreement based on this compromise is broken, the dispute of the past between Turks and Greeks will break out in even more violent form than before (Keesing's 1964:20113).

Within a few days of this statement, the Turkish government mobilized its armed forces and created an invasion scare among the Greek Cypriot community. The Turkish forces stationed in Cyprus took up strategic positions, and jet aircraft belonging to the Turkish air force flew over Nicosia, violating Cyprus airspace. Troop movements in Central Anatolia to the ports of Mersin and Iskenderun, the closest harbours to Cyprus territory, added to the tension, and the Turkish fleet in Istanbul was sent to ports in the Eastern Mediterranean (Keesing's 1964:20114). This led the Cypriot government to submit to the UN Security council a '...formal complaint of Turkish intervention in the internal affairs of Cyprus by the threat and use of force against its territorial integrity and political independence' (Keesing's 1964:20114).

The Turkish 'big stick' thus forced the central regime in Cyprus to seek international mediation. The UN Security Council provided an opportunity to the parties involved in the conflict to present their case in front of the international community. Then came 'shuttle diplomacy' by the NATO powers, especially the US government. A conference was held in London under the aegis of the British government to end the immediate dispute and the violence. It was attended by the leaders of the Greek and Turkish Cypriot communities and their international backers. When the London conference ended without any settlement, the British and American governments proposed a NATO force in Cyprus in a policing role (Keesing's 1964:20115).

When the proposal for a NATO force in Cyprus was rejected by the Cyprus leaders, Turkey again started a fresh invasion scare among the Greek Cypriots (Keesing's 1964:20115). The warring factions resumed their fighting, and Turkish Cypriot leaders announced 'If Turkey does not make an immediate landing in Cyprus the Greeks will massacre all the Cypriot Turks on the Island' (Keesing's 1964:20118). On February 14-15, 1964 there was a 48-hour Turkish naval and air exercise off Iskenderam which created much alarm among the Greek Cypriot community. Even the Greek government put its armed forces on the alert (Keesing's 1964:20118). Three days after this military exercise the Turkish Minister of Information declared,

> if the Security council failed to find a practicable peace-keeping plan the result would almost certainly be full-scale communal war in Cyprus, in which Turkey would be forced to intervene (Keesing's 1964:20118).

Again in March 1964 as fighting broke out all over Cyprus between Greek and Turkish Cypriot communities (even after the UN Security council's decision to establish its own peace-keeping force in the Island) the Turkish government sent a warning note to the Cyprus government calling for an immediate cease-fire and acceptance of certain conditions viz. complete freedom of movement for the Turkish community and the release of hostages by the Cyprus government (Keesing's 1964:201120). In this letter Turkey warned the Cyprus central regime that: 'if these conditions were not observed Turkey would use its right of unilateral intervention' (Keesing's 1964:201120).

Through this exercise, waving the 'big stick' against the central regime in Cyprus, Turkey achieved a greater internationalization of the Cyprus conflict. The governments of the United Kingdom and the United States of America on the one hand, and the North Atlantic Treaty Organization (NATO) and the United Nations on the other sent special envoys to Nicosia, Ankara and Athens for mediation. The failed proposal for a NATO peace-keeping force, followed by the Turkish government's ultimatum to the Cyprus government, as mentioned earlier, led the UN Security council to send its own peace-keeping force (UNFICYP) immediately to the Island to avert the Turkish intervention (Keesing's 1964:20121). However, Turkish policy makers waved the 'big stick' against the Cyprus regime even after the landing of the UNFICYP in Cyprus. In August 1964 when fresh violence broke out in the Island, Turkey sent 64 aircraft to attack Greek Cypriot targets in the North-West of Cyprus for several hours. On this occasion a cease-fire was agreed through the mediation of the United Nations. But an important development was the beginning of UN-mediated inter-communal talks between the Cyprus government and the Turkish Cypriot community (Keesing's 1964:20121).

Turkey took this opportunity to declare that it would prefer a 'federal system of government' as the solution to the ethnic conflict in Cyprus. This was openly stated by the then Turkish Prime Minister after meeting UN mediator Mr Erkin (Keesing's 1964:20121). From then on federalism or partition, became the theme of Turkish threats to the central regime in Cyprus. While the Turkish Prime Minister was pronouncing his government's preference for a federal solution to the Cyprus conflict, the official Ankara Radio announced,

> if a federal system of government is not to be created then partition. This is not just a claim. This will be confirmed by those concerned as a decision already made. …Turkish troops would land in Cyprus and take their place along the Green line that is, on the new Turko-Greek frontier, if the rifle of a single Greek soldier was fired at them Turkey would not be responsible for the consequences (Keesing's 1964:20121).

Between 1964 and 1967 Turkey continuously pressed for a federal solution to the Cyprus conflict while repeating the threat of unilateral intervention. Once in 1965 when public opinion in Turkey expressed its anger through violent demonstrations in Ankara in reaction to a fresh outbreak of anti-Turkish violence in Cyprus, and demanded 'the army to Cyprus' (Keesing's 1965:20627), the then Turkish Prime Minister Mr Inonu declared in his statement to the Turkish Parliament:

> so long as the Cyprus government tried to undo Turkish efforts to find a peaceful solution 'we have the right' to apply military intervention any time (Keesing's 1965:20627).

The Turkish threat held over the Cyprus government was not limited to creating an invasion scare among Greek Cypriots, carrying with it the possibility of partitioning the Island. For example in 1965 when the Cyprus government imposed an economic blockade against Turkish Cypriots living in the Kikkina area, the Turkish government announced its own plans to deliver supplies to the affected areas in Cyprus, saying that it would take appropriate action to meet any resistance from the Greek Cypriot side against its humanitarian mission (Keesing's 1965:20627). Again in 1967 when it received news that the Greek Cypriot government had received an arms shipment from Czechoslovakia, Turkey issued an ultimatum to the Cyprus government saying that unless the arms received were surrendered into UN custody it would send a similar consignment of arms to the Turkish Cypriots (Keesing's 1967:21948).

These incidents in the Turkey-Cyprus theatre in 1967 demonstrate that after nearly three years of UN-sponsored mediation, and of their urging a devolutionary (federal) settlement to the conflict, the Turkish policy-makers were running out of patience with the Cyprus leadership. That year, on the 27th of November, reacting to a fresh outbreak of violence against the Turkish community in Cyprus, the Grand National Assembly of Turkey passed a unanimous resolution empowering the government to send its armed forces outside Turkey (Keesing's 1967:22435). A week after the passing of this resolution the Turkish President sent messages to several heads of states, including the Presidents of the US, France and the Soviet Union, to Queen Elizabeth II, and to the Muslim countries, declaring that his country had decided to 'solve the Cyprus problem once for all' (Keesing's 1967:22436). This announcement was accompanied by the preparation of an invasion fleet in Turkey's Mediterranean ports. This time Turkey's decision to take a decisive initiative was averted by political pressure from the then American President Lyndon B. Johnson, who warned the Turkish leaders of the repercussions of such an action i.e., the possibility of an intervention by the Soviet Union, and the inability of NATO to defend Turkey from such an attack (Markides 1972:29).

However, the Turkish threat was taken so seriously by the Greek Cypriot leadership that they entered into direct negotiation with the Turkish Cypriot leaders. These inter-communal talks continued for the next six years, until April 1974 when they reached deadlock due to the Turkish Cypriot leaders' insistence on a federal solution and the Greek Cypriot leaders' intransigence towards that demand (Souter 1984:663; Keesing's 1971:24398-99).

Then came the anti-Makarios coup of 1974. The new regime in Cyprus was dominated by extremist 'Enosis' campaigners who demanded the abandonment of the inter-communal talks. From Turkey's viewpoint, the situation in Cyprus was going from bad to worse. Realising that the 'big stick' role it was currently playing could no longer cope with the rapidly changing situation, as we shall see in the next section, Turkey moved to the 'interventionist role'.

The India-Sri Lanka situation forms a good parallel to the Cyprus secessionist conflict, except that here, unlike the Turkey-Cyprus situation, both the central regime and the secessionists were to become the targets of the Big Neighbour's 'big stick' role.

During the period 1983-87 Indian mediators achieved considerable progress in improving the devolution package offered by the Sri Lanka government, and successfully influenced the conflicting parties to start direct negotiations. There was an All Party Conference (APC) in Colombo where the moderate Tamil leaders represented by the TULF had extensive negotiations with the Sinhalese leaders and the other influential political parties of the country. In 1986 India successfully organized direct negotiations between the militant secessionist leaders and the Sri Lanka government, bringing them to the capital of the Himalayan kingdom of Bhutan for a round-table conference (see Ram 1989:57,89-90). During the same period several drafts of the Sri Lanka government's proposals for the granting of regional autonomy to the Sri Lanka Tamils were exchanged between the governments of India and Sri Lanka (see *Draft Proposals* - 30.8.85 to 19.12.86, Department of Government Press [Sri Lanka], Colombo, Undated).

However, after more than three years of this mediation, the Indian leaders found that everything they had achieved was still 'on paper'. The rival parties were still in fighting mood, and the conflict was becoming a running sore, dragging India into an unforeseen regional conflict. To their great frustration, there were regular interruptions in the negotiation process due to the intransigence of the domestic rivals, or the escalation of violence in the conflict-affected areas. Indian leaders began to express their disappointment about the poor response of the parties to the conflict (see Ram 1989:60).

In 1985 India served deportation orders on two leading members of the Tamil secessionist movement, one of them being the political advisor to the LTTE leader and the top theoretician of the movement, as a reaction to the Tamil militants' refusal to attend discussions arranged in New Delhi by the Indian government (Keesing's 1986:34359). Again in November 1986 when the Indian Prime Minister Rajiv Gandhi was due to meet the visiting Sri Lankan President J. R. Jayawardane in Bangalore during the summit meeting of the South Asian Association for Regional Cooperation (SAARC), Indian central authorities ordered the Tamil Nadu police to launch a crack-down against the Tamil militants living in the state of Tamil Nadu. They rounded-up more than 1,000 Tamil militants and seized their firearms and communication equipment (Keesing's 1987:34876-77; *The Hindu International Edition* 13 November 1986). Though it was presented as a precautionary measure to ensure the safety of the visiting Sri Lankan head of state, it had all the signs of a trial-run for more strong-arm tactics against the Tamil secessionists. There were warnings from Indian policy-makers to the Tamil secessionists saying that '...there is a limit beyond which India cannot espouse their cause' (*The Hindu International Edition* 1 November 1986).

In December 1986 the Indian government emerged with an improved proposal from the Sri Lanka government, satisfied that it was the maximum bargaining position that could be expected from the Sri Lankan side (Ram 1989:60, *The Hindu International Edition* 27 December 1986). Under this proposal, popularly known as the 'December 19th proposal', Sri Lanka agreed to make the necessary constitutional provision for the merger of the Eastern Province with the Tamil majority Northern Province, but excluding Amparai district where the Sinhalese and the Moors are dominant (see Ram 1989:60). This was a marked concession from the Sri Lanka government, extending the territorial unit of the devolution package in an attempt at compromise between the Tamil demand for the preservation of the integrity of the Tamil homeland and the anxiety shown by the Sinhalese and Moor communities living in the Eastern province about becoming a minority within the Tamil-dominated Provincial administration.

Indian policy makers expected from the Tamil movement at least a willingness to start negotiations on the basis of the new proposals. But the reaction from the Tamil side to the 'December 19th proposal' was an outright rejection. Indian policy-makers regarded the arguments presented by the militant Tamil movement as simply expressions of their intransigence, and of their inclination to violence rather than to the political process of finding a settlement to the conflict. At this stage India decided to use the 'big stick' against the Tamil secessionist movement more decisively. Madras police under orders from the central government arrested in a sudden raid hundreds of Tamil militants living in various parts of Tamil Nadu state, and confiscated a huge amount of weapons, ammunition and radio communication equipment belonging to them. They put several prominent leaders of the Tamil secessionists under house arrest while their followers were in police custody (*Tamil Times* 1986,6(1):1-3). This was clearly a message to the Tamil militants forcing them to accept the Indian-sponsored political settlement or forfeit the support and sanctuary provided by India. Even the Tamil Nadu Chief Minister M. G. Ramachandran, who maintained a close political relationship with the LTTE, had to follow suit. As reported by the Indian press he told the LTTE leader '...to decide whether he wanted a negotiated settlement or not and if it was the latter to continue the warfare from Jaffna' (Ram 1990:61).

Responding to this warning the LTTE decided to withdraw its cadres and equipment leaving only a representative office in Madras (Ram 1990:61). This marked a turning point in the relatively short history of India's relationship with the Tamil secessionist movement in Sri Lanka. The message behind the Indian action was very clear. The Indian leaders were running out of patience with the intransigence of the domestic rivals in the conflict, and were now preparing to take stronger action against them.

If the last days of 1986 were a bitter experience for the Tamil militants vis-a-vis their patron, the Indian central government, the first six months of 1987 were the worst for the Sri Lanka government regarding its relationship with its Big Neighbour. After their withdrawal from India, the LTTE movement created difficulties for the Indian leaders by announcing plans to take over the civil administration in the Jaffna peninsula. Although under Indian pressure they withdrew this plan, the Sri Lanka government used the LTTE's establishment of a parallel administration in the Jaffna peninsula to launch a massive military assault against LTTE positions in the peninsula. This was accompanied by an economic blockade, restricting all essential supplies to the region, and creating severe hardship for the civilian population (see Ram 1989:61). India found that it was going to lose all leverage on the Tamil movement because of the timing of the Sri Lanka government's newest military action - just when India itself was clamping down on the secessionist movement. The Indian policy-makers realized that if India did not act decisively to stop the Sri Lanka government's fresh attempt at a military solution to the conflict, it would lose all its achievements from its long involvement in Sri Lanka's secession conflict.

First India tried diplomatic manoeuvres to change Sri Lanka's mind, but without success. The Indian Premier sent a message to the Sri Lankan President in February 1987 saying that '...it would be very difficult for India to resume its mediatory efforts as long as the military offensive against Tamil civilians continued' (*The Hindu International Edition* 30 May 1987). At one time during this initiative India threatened to withdraw its good offices (*The Hindu International Edition* 21 February 1987). But Sri Lanka's reply was a demand for the cessation of armed operations by the Tamil militants as the condition for stopping its military offensive (*The Hindu International Edition* 28 February 1987).

In April there was a short-lived unilateral cease-fire by the Sri Lanka government in response to Indian pressure, but very soon it resumed its military campaign, which provoked protest in the Indian state of Tamil Nadu due to the heavy civilian casualties reported by the Indian media (see *The Hindu International Edition* 18 April 1987; Ram 1989:61). In June 1987 the Sri Lanka government launched what it called the final offensive against the rebel-controlled Vadamarachi area, from which they could launch a full-scale attack on Jaffna city. In view of this military movement, that was calculated to be very costly in terms of civilian lives (*The Independent* 29 May 1987, Ram 1989:93-4), the Indian leaders were compelled to change their approach towards the conflict. The leading Indian daily *The Hindu* reported,

> India's policy-makers were today confronted with a new challenge as the Sri Lanka security forces stepped up their offensive against the Tamil civilian population of the Jaffna peninsula, causing death and destruction on a large scale. It should be clear in the near future whether the current peripheral exercise by New Delhi became a permanent stance or whether it comes out with a matching response and an effective plan of action (*The Hindu International Edition* 6 June 1987).

According to the Indian media, various forms of direct military intervention in Sri Lanka were considered by the Indian leaders (*The Hindu International Edition* 6 June 1987) before they came out with a plan of action. First came an announcement from the Indian government that it had decided to send humanitarian aid to the Tamil population in Northern Jaffna peninsula, who were under severe hardship due to the six-month-old economic blockade imposed by the Sri Lanka government. But the Indian action was a unilateral one. A flotilla of boats loaded with food, medicines and other essential items sailed under the leadership of an Indian Coast Guard Vessel towards the Sri Lanka coast on 3 June 1987. This mission was abandoned in mid-sea due to the naval blockade imposed by the Sri Lankan navy, and the boats were ordered to return by the Indian government (see *The International Herald Tribune* 4 June 1987; Ram 1989:127).

It was meant as a symbolic exercise to signal Indian resentment at Sri Lanka's disregard of India's concern over developments in Sri Lanka. But the signal from the Indian side was not properly read by the Sri Lankan side. Instead there was euphoria over India's swift withdrawal of its flotilla. Then came the next step in the Indian plan. Within two days India sent a more specific signal. This time it dispatched seven transport planes and four Mirage Jet fighter craft into Sri Lanka's airspace on an air-drop mission, delivering food, medicines and other essential items on the Jaffna peninsula. The four fighters had definite instructions to face up to any resistance, but the action met with no resistance from its small neighbour, which has no air defence system (Ram 1989:127; *The Hindu International Edition* 13 June 1987, 27 June 1987).

Although India characterized its air dropping operation (named 'garland of flowers') as a humanitarian mission, it was undoubtedly a gross violation of Sri Lanka's airspace, with no prior approval from any international or regional organization. It was a Big Neighbour using its military clout against a small neighbour. However, this time the Indian message was very clear. As noted by an Indian commentator, it was,

> ...ostensibly a relief mission, but in actuality intended to show Sri Lanka that India could bomb it into submission with impunity (Ram 1989:61).

Sri Lanka responded promptly and favourably to the Indian move. Though initial reactions from Sri Lankan leaders suggested they would take the matter to the UN Security Council, after assessing international reaction to the Indian action, the Sri Lanka government stopped its military operation and lifted the economic blockade. Furthermore, the Sri Lanka government decided to accept the Indian supplies, and co-operated with the Indian government in finalizing the modalities for the distribution of Indian aid to the Tamil areas (see *Tamil Times* 1987,6(9):14-15). Meanwhile direct diplomatic contacts were resumed between the two governments in fresh rounds of discussions. The outcome of these speedy diplomatic and political manoeuvres soon emerged: in the third week of the following month the two governments announced that they were going to sign an agreement to end the secessionist conflict in Sri Lanka.

The agreement signed on 29 July 1987 by the Indian Prime Minister and the Sri Lanka President is a clear example of a diplomatic achievement by a Big Neighbour using first its 'pressure' role and then its 'big stick' role in imposing its own will upon the rivals in the conflict. The agreement envisaged the settlement of the conflict by Sri Lanka offering regional autonomy to the Tamils on the basis of the improved devolution scheme negotiated during the 1983-86 period (see *Draft Proposals* - 30.8.85 to 19.12.86, Department of Government Press [Sri Lanka], Colombo, Undated). In return India undertook the responsibility of arranging an immediate ceasefire and laying down of arms by the Tamil militants. Further it agreed to send an Indian Peace Keeping Force (IPKF) to Sri Lanka, on invitation from the government there, to monitor the ceasefire and the disarming of the Tamil militants (for the full text of the accord see Ram 1989:140-6; Marasinghe 1988:585-7).

There had been no direct participation by the Tamil militants in the preparation of the Indo-Sri Lanka accord or in the conditions of a ceasefire and laying down of arms. The final arrangements for the settlement of the conflict and the ceasefire were communicated to the Tamil secessionists two days prior to the agreement. From the point of view of the Tamil secessionists, it was all something dictated to them by the Indian government.

However, all the Tamil groups except the LTTE decided to accept the accord and surrender their arms to the Indian Peace Keeping Force (IPKF) which was sent to Sri Lanka on the invitation of the Sri Lanka President within two days of the signing of the accord. The LTTE refused to accept the accord as the permanent solution to the conflict and claimed its provisions were inadequate for the accommodation of Tamil aspirations. But they did agree to co-operate with India and surrender their arms, laying the responsibility of protecting the Tamil population on the Indian government. Explaining its reservation the LTTE leader declared,

> This agreement did not concern only the problem of the Tamils. This is primarily concerned with Indo-Sri Lanka relations. It also contains within itself the principle, the requirements for making Sri Lanka accede to India's strategic sphere of influence. ...When a great power has decided to determine our political fate in a manner that is essentially beyond our control, what are we to do? (Ram 1989:147-8).

All Tamil militant groups did participate in the process of surrendering their arms to the IPKF. However the LTTE did not do so speedily like the others. Soon they found reasons to delay their demilitarization. They started clashes with rival Tamil groups and attacked Sinhalese peasants living in the Eastern province. Then they found numerous reasons to agitate against the presence of the IPKF. Within three months they were back in their armed struggle rejecting all of the undertakings given to the Indian government. In the face of the intransigence of the LTTE movement, the Indian peace-keeping mission was gradually transmuted into a full-scale military campaign against the LTTE movement. By the end of the year India, using an army of 70,000 soldiers (Ram 1989:24), was fighting someone else's war, but on an invitation extended by its small neighbour. The Indian role in Sri Lanka's secession conflict had thus shifted again, from 'big stick' to an 'invitational role'.

The interventionist role

Once the Big Neighbour moves from the 'pressure' role to the 'big stick' role, involving a threat of military action of some kind against one of the internal actors, the policy-makers of the Big Neighbour as we have seen have to prepare the necessary logistics for the implementation of such action if it is to have any credibility. If the conflicting parties arrive at a negotiated settlement while Big Neighbour's 'pressure' and 'big stick' roles are being played out, the preparations can be abandoned and any damage to Big Neighbour's international standing minimized. But this does not always happen. The conflicting parties may continue their military manoeuvres, and resort to actions endangering the national interests of the Big Neighbour. If the internal rivals continue their usual conduct in such a manner, the situation the policy-makers of the Big Neighbour face is certainly an uncomfortable one. Now they have to give serious consideration to carrying out the threats so assiduously implanted in the minds of the conflicting parties.

The problem becomes even more vexing where the Big Neighbour has successfully contained one of the parties to the conflict, and obtained its acceptance of a settlement which would protect the Big Neighbour's national interests; but where the other actor is still showing intransigence, or has resorted to immoderate action contrary to Big Neighbour's interests. At this stage the policy-makers of the Big Neighbour are faced with adopting one of the two alternative military options, namely the 'interventionist' role and the 'invitational' role. Which it is to be depends on which internal actor it is who is most intransigent and needs to be constrained.

Of these two alternatives the 'interventionist' role is more likely to be appropriate where an unyielding central regime has taken or is near to taking some excessive military action in the conflict, endangering the whole process of conflict regulation. As will be discussed in the next section, it is most likely that the Big Neighbour will play the 'invitational' role where the intransigence is on the secessionist side.

The 'interventionist' role thus refers to a direct military operation by the Big Neighbour against the central regime in the affected state. Primarily this is an invasion by the Big Neighbour's military forces of the affected state's territory, usually undertaken to create a 'green line' around an 'ethnic enclave' in the secessionist region. Apart from separating the two warring factions and protecting the minority community from the military onslaught launched by the affected state's security forces, the most significant effect of such action is the partitioning of the affected state, giving an opportunity for the secessionist community to establish separate political, administrative and economic structures in the areas protected by the Big Neighbour.

If the Big Neighbour has undertaken this military action as a joint exercise with other regional states, or with the assistance of other concerned extra-regional states, or, best of all with an internationally-accepted mandate, its 'interventionist' role may provoke little international condemnation or none at all, rather understanding and approbation. But if the Big Neighbour has unilaterally taken its decision to send armed forces against the affected state's central regime, its military occupation becomes a breach of international law, an occasion for the international community to intervene in its turn.

However, before taking any action - by verbal condemnation, by imposing economic sanctions, or even by organizing international military resistance to the invading forces - against such violation of international law, the international community may consider humanitarian arguments for intervention. To a certain extent, international sympathy for the plight of the minority community can moderate its reaction, but the international community cannot condone the Big Neighbour's unlawful action merely because of its effects on the welfare of the minority community, for this would establish a bad precedent for inter-state relations elsewhere. More likely is that the international community will take action not only to resolve the intervention crisis brought on by the Big Neighbour, but also to settle the conflict between the central regime and the secessionist community in the affected state. The most likely reaction to this type of intervention situation is that while deploring the Big Neighbour's intervention and calling for withdrawal of its forces, the international community will take the responsibility of finding a negotiated solution to the conflict into its own hands. If the minority community insist on the continuation of the Big Neighbour's military presence to guarantee their personal safety, international mediation may become the price of the withdrawal of the Big Neighbour's military forces.

In considering the 'interventionist' role, then, the policy-makers of the Big Neighbour will do well to minimize the likelihood of international retaliation, by maximizing in advance the international goodwill generated by its commitment to the conflict resolution process. In this connection it will be useful if its relations with the great powers are generally good. If the Big Neighbour can maintain good working relations with the great powers, it may at least expect their neutrality, and perhaps their support, in international forums debating collective international action against its military 'intervention'. In this 'softening-up' process, the policy-makers of the Big Neighbour will extensively emphasize the humanitarian dimensions of the conflict, e.g. the refugee problem, atrocities against the minority community, allegations of starvation and so on. If then, as postulated earlier, the immediate trigger for the Big Neighbour's intervention was a military campaign by the central regime associated with human rights violations against the minority community, the defence of its launching of an intervention is already in place.

However, the international community may still refuse to accept the legality of the partition situation created by the Big Neighbour. All the parties must come to terms with the fact that an international mediation will be according to the international principles covering the problem of secession and the rights of minorities. The central regime is expected to honour international principles governing minority rights, the secessionists are obliged to pursue political goals which respect the 'territorial integrity and sovereignty of states'. In other words both parties are required to compromise at a point which provides regional autonomy to the minority community, and preserves the territorial integrity of the state. Then an 'interventionist' role which leads to the acceptance of these principles of a solution to the conflict by the conflicting sides can be considered a successful strategy, from Big Neighbour's point of view.

For illustrations of the Big Neighbour's 'interventionist' role our attention has been mainly directed to India's intervention in East Pakistan in 1971, Turkey's intervention in Cyprus in 1974, and the preparations made by Indian policy-makers for a similar action against Sri Lanka in June 1987.

Since the Indian intervention in East Pakistan ended with the dismemberment of Pakistan and the acceptance by the international community of an independent Bangladesh, it might seem a contradiction of what has just been said. It is, perhaps, the exception which proves the rule. As discussed in chapter three, at the time of the Indian intervention in East Pakistan there were indeed no precedents at all, at least since the second world war, for the prompt international acceptance of the dismemberment by force of an existing state. The bloody experience of the secessionist civil wars in Katanga and Biafra had established firm international disapproval for such attempts by secessionist minorities. Therefore at the beginning the Indian intervention in East Pakistan, despite the hidden Indian objective of scoring a strategic victory over Pakistan (as discussed in chapter 2), appeared as a Big Neighbour intervention aimed at the protection of a minority community after the 'pressure' and 'big stick' roles had failed. Until it achieved international acceptance and finally membership of the United Nations, East Bengal remained as an 'ethnic enclave' protected by the Indian military; what we are discussing here as one stage in a Big Neighbour's 'interventionist' role.

By contrast, Turkey's invasion of Cyprus in 1974 provides an illustration of the complete functioning of the Big Neighbour's 'interventionist' role. The Turkish intervention and subsequent occupation in Cyprus created a *de facto* partition in Cyprus, and there has been a separate 'ethnic enclave' in Northern Cyprus since 1974, enabling the Turkish Cypriot community to establish their own separate political, administrative and economic structures, and strengthening their hands in participating in the UN-sponsored negotiation process. The Turkish invasion received immediate international disapproval but provoked no collective international action. The United Nations passed a resolution requiring the withdrawal of all foreign forces from Cyprus, and since then has taken the full responsibility for finding a settlement to the conflict through negotiation between the domestic rivals.

Certainly the long agitation of the minority community for a just solution and Turkey's uninterrupted commitment to the protection of their rights, the poor record of the new regime which came to power in Cyprus in 1974, and Turkey's strategic position and close relationship with the NATO powers (especially with the United States), can be counted among the factors which contributed to the softening of the international reaction towards the Turkish intervention in Cyprus.

The intervention in Cyprus in 1974 followed closely on the Greek inspired pro-Enosis coup in 1974, whose leaders demanded a plebiscite and the abandonment of inter-communal talks (Keesing's 1973:25578). Widespread fighting within the Greek-Cypriot community, in which more than 2,000 pro-Makarios activists died, created anxiety among the Turkish Cypriot community about their own safety (see Denktash 1982:64-7), and together with the support given by the Greek military regime to the 'Enosis' aims of the new regime in Cyprus (see McDonald 1989:17-18), made the Turkish leaders fear that time was running out.

However, the long-threatened Turkish intervention was not just an arbitrary decision by a Big Neighbour. Before making its unilateral intervention Turkey had approached the British government to participate in a joint military exercise to restore order in Cyprus. But the British government, the other guarantor power of the Cyprus constitution, turned down the request for a joint peace-keeping mission, whereupon Turkey, whose national interest was immediately endangered by the new situation, acted on its own. Although there were claims (mainly from the Greek Cypriot side) that the real intention of the Turkish intervention was to achieve the long-held ambition of *Taksim*, the then Turkish Prime Minister Mr Ecevit denied this interpretation:

> The objectives of the new military action was not to destroy the state of Cyprus but to contribute to its rebuilding on a sounder basis, ensure its territorial integrity and bring peace, freedom, sanity to the Island. We intended to establish a balanced society which will enable Turk and Greek to co-operate and prosper under equitable conditions (Keesing's 1974:29710).

Whatever the arguments raised by the Greek Cypriot side, so far the main effect of the Turkish occupation in Northern Cyprus has been the physical separation between the two warring factions in Cyprus, compelling the domestic rivals to engage in negotiation under the auspices of the United Nations. But perhaps even more significantly, the Turkish intervention caused the Greek Cypriot leaders and their 'national centre', Greece, to abandon their long held ideal of 'Enosis' (see Keesing's 1982:31602). The Greek Cypriots recognized the geopolitical reality of a Big Neighbour with strategic and ethnic interests in their Island society, which in the immediate aftermath of the Turkish invasion led them to accept 'bi-communal' federation as the political solution to the conflict.

In July 1975 the then acting President of Cyprus Mr Glafkos Clerides, in full agreement with the ousted Cypriot President Makarios (who was due to return to Cyprus within a few days as the President of Cyprus), declared:

> The Turkish stand will insist on a bizonal system of some kind. Under present circumstances it would be impossible to find an agreed solution based on the unitary state we have had in the past. Therefore geographical federation is the only thing that can come out of negotiations with Turkey. We will have to accept evetually some federal solution on a geographical basis, and therefore we shall come to some form of cantonal state (Keesing's 1975:26886).

On the other hand the prompt international disapproval of the Turkish intervention and the world community's repeated rejection of the secession of Northern Cyprus persuaded the Turkish Cypriot leaders of the impracticability of their attempted secession. Though they took further steps to establish separate political and administrative structures in Northern Cyprus, declaring a 'Turkish Federated State of Northern Cyprus' in 1977 and then in 1983 the Unilateral Declaration of Independence, an international pronouncement on the legality of these moves led the Turkish Cypriot leadership to come to terms with economic realities (see Keesing's 1984:32638-40, 1990:37517), and to declare all of their actions taken after the 1974 invasion as measures aimed at a future bi-communal federation. In February 1990 the leader of the Turkish Cypriot community Mr Rauf R. Denktash stated:

> We want to become good neighbours and partners in a new political association... We have had no common institution and virtually no ties at any level for the past 20 years. This is a very long time. We have now two clear alternatives. We can either reach agreement to move towards a federal relationship or we can peacefully coexist as binary states (as quoted in Ertekun 1990:66).

The Turkish invasion of Cyprus facilitated the transformation of the secessionist conflict in Cyprus into an international matter which was then subjected to intense international mediation. It was later seen as a precedent for other Big Neighbours. For example the policy-makers of India considered military intervention against the central regime in Sri Lanka on several occasions during their involvement in Sri Lanka's secession conflict (see Ram 1989:122-3; Austin & Gupta 1988:12), the last time being in 1987 in connection with the 'air-dropping mission' into the Jaffna peninsula (discussed in the previous section). According to a newspaper account, they studied:

> an Indian military intervention on the ground through a combined arms operation involving a two-pronged thrust, one point near Mannar and another from a point near Trincomalee and cutting the Sri Lanka army's main force in

the North providing protection to the Tamil minority (*The Hindu International Edition* 6 June 1987).

Since the central regime in Sri Lanka responded promptly to the message sent through the 'air dropping mission' by entering into direct negotiation with the Indian central government, and in the end signing the Indo-Sri Lanka accord of 1987, Indian policy makers did not face the dilemma of playing the 'interventionist' role in the secession conflict in Sri Lanka.

The invitational role

As noted in the previous section, the 'invitational' role primarily refers to the Big Neighbour's participation in military action in the affected state's territory against an intransigent secessionist group, by invitation of the central regime. We have already cited India's engagement in military confrontation with the intransigent LTTE secessionists in Sri Lanka during the period 1987-90 as an example of the Big Neighbour's 'invitational' role.

However, the 'invitational' role usually embraces more than military confrontation. The 'invitational' functions assigned to the Big Neighbour may entail peace-keeping in the conflict-affected areas and policing a ceasefire agreement, as originally envisaged by the signatories to the Indo-Sri Lanka accord. In the Australia-PNG situation, Australia was accepted as one of the contributors to the Multinational Supervisory Team (MST) stipulated by the *Honiara Declaration* of January 1991, to oversee the ceasefire agreement signed by the Bougainville secessionist movement and the PNG government (see *Far Eastern Economic Review* 7 February 1991).

Military confrontation with the secessionists comes about as the Big Neighbour's peace-keeping forces go after secessionist groups who persistently refuse to co-operate, or who resort to violence to disrupt the peace-keeping exercise - especially if this involves the responsibility of disarming the secessionist groups.

However, Big Neighbour's participation in military actions against an intransigent secessionist movement may not always start that way. Sometimes, the central regime's invitation may not be accompanied by any peace-keeping function. The Big Neighbour may 'offer' to send its armed forces merely to assist the security forces of the affected state in their efforts to quell the insurgency. For example, in 1985, some two years before the signing of the Indo-Sri Lanka accord, the Indian Prime Minister Rajiv Gandhi stated that his government was prepared to provide military assistance to assist the Sri Lanka government in its efforts to quell the Tamil insurgency, if requested (see *The New York Times* 15 July 1985). Though it did not materialize at that time, for the Indian policy-makers this was not a new phenomenon. A case in point was the Indian government's prompt response to Sri Lanka's request to send air and naval support to protect Sri Lanka's maritime boundary and main international airport during the 1971 youth uprising in Sri Lanka (though it was not a secessionist rebellion: see Ram 1989:119). The strategic-tie Big Neighbour situation, where the Big Neighbour and the affected state share common strategic interests (as in the PNG-Australia situation), has great potential in producing this type of 'invitational' role.

As an interesting illustration of the 'invitational' role, we can use Syria's military involvement since 1975 in the protracted civil war in Lebanon. As the Lebanese Big Neighbour, the Syrian policy-makers have long supported a power sharing compromise within a unitary form of government, to preserve the territorial integrity of Lebanon, rather than any scheme of territorial devolution to the various ethnic and religious groups;[2] and it is not primarily a secessionist conflict situation. Nevertheless, there are parallels: the civil war in Lebanon had created a *de facto* partition of Lebanon, and a political vacuum, enabling the various ethnic and military factions to declare their own separate administrations in the areas under their control (see Haddad 1985:31-5); and matching other Big Neighbours' rejection of secession, were Syria's vehement opposition to partition solutions whether proposed by Muslim or Christian factions (see Keesing's 1976:27769, Meo 1977:115-22), and its firm commitment to the territorial integrity of its small neighbour on its 'strategic flank' (Keesing's 1983:32409).

Having been involved in mediating several unsuccessful ceasefires between the various factions in Lebanon since the beginning of the civil war in mid-April 1975 (for a brief discussion of Syrian role in Lebanon, see Everon 1987:34-42), Syria undertook more active participation in the Lebanese conflict in January 1976 by accepting two places in the 'Higher Military Committee' appointed by the Lebanese President to oversee the most recent ceasefire brokered by the Syrian government. At this juncture Syria sent a small military contingent, comprising some 50 officers, into Lebanese territory to undertake monitoring responsibilities (Keesing's 1976:27770). But very soon Syria was compelled to engage in military confrontation with the Lebanese factions to maintain the authority of the Lebanese government and the territorial integrity of the Lebanese state.

This Syrian involvement, because of its legal unimpeachability and Syria's known commitment to the territorial integrity of Lebanon, received acclaim from the

---

2. In the past Syria rejected any kind of regional devolution because of the partition demands made by the parties to the Lebanese conflict. It treated regional autonomy as a stepping stone to the partition of Lebanon and the undoing of Lebanon's Arab character. As noted by some analysts, since there is a long held irredentist claim from the Syrian leaders over Lebanese territory considering it as a part of the pre-colonial 'Greater Syria' entity, they may want to keep Lebanon as an undivided territory until such objective is attained (see Haddad 1985:48,59; Everon 1987:19-23; Saliba 1988:147-8, 156-7).

Secretary General of the United Nations, who explained the possible dangers of the Lebanese crisis (such as partition, the involvement of neighbours etc.) to the Security Council (Keesing's 1976:27772). But Syrian involvement in Lebanon did not receive unqualified support from the Arab world. When Syria became fully involved in a military campaign against Muslim forces in Lebanon, Libya, Iraq and Egypt, for different reasons, voiced their opposition, persuading the Arab League to take the matter to an Arab summit meeting. However, Syria managed to turn the tables, settled its outstanding problems with other Arab countries, especially with Egypt, and got their support for its involvement in Lebanon. The summit meetings of the Arab League held in Ryadh and Cairo in October 1976 established a peace plan for Lebanon, and provided further legitimacy for Syrian military involvement in Lebanon by converting its mission into a pan-Arabian initiative (Keesing's 1976:28118,28122-23).

The Arab League issued a mandate, forming an Arab Deterrent Force (ADF) under the authority of the Lebanese President to implement the Arab League's peace plan, and accepting the Syrian forces already stationed in Lebanon as Syria's contribution to the ADF. But in fact, the ADF was composed largely of Syrian soldiers (nearly 80 percent), and the contribution of other Arab League members in the ADF was limited to a representative force. Therefore, in actual practice the Syrian military command in Lebanon took the important decisions regarding operations of the ADF, though it was formally under the authority of the Lebanese President (Haddad 1985:56-7). After 1979 when the other Arab countries decided to withdraw their military contingents, the ADF became completely a Syrian undertaking (Keesing's 1979:30005). In this way, receiving an Arab League mandate for its 'invitational' role, Syria carried out its mission until September 1982.

During the period 1976-82, Syria waged military campaigns against both Muslim and Christian militias whenever they took arms against the ceasefire settlement, or made efforts to impose a partition solution. In November 1976 Syria successfully implemented the Arab peace plan, and brought the fighting to an end (see Haddad 1985:57; Everon 1987:60). But by 1978, it had again to become involved in a full-scale military exercise, this time against the Christian (Phalangist) militias who had been its collaborators in 1976 against the leftist Muslim and Palestine forces (Everon 1987:46,66-8), following Syria's refusal to accept the partition plan proposed by the Christian groups (see Keesing's 1977:30005). It was during this fighting with the Israel-backed Christian forces, that Syria eventually mixed its peace-keeping mission with the wider Arab-Israel conflict, and lost its support base in the Lebanese government, leading to its its withdrawal in 1982, and replacement by a mainly western multinational force (see Keesing's 1983:31919; Haddad 1985:79,85, Everon 1987:94-102).

Although the Syrian government's 'invitational' role ended in 1982 with inconclusive results, it furthered its Lebanon policy by playing the same 'invitational' role again in 1989, by invitation of the Lebanese President, and under a fresh mandate from the Arab League. After several unsuccessful Lebanese initiatives to find a peaceful settlement to the Lebanese conflict - inviting the US-led multinational peace-keeping force in 1982, negotiating an agreement with Israel in 1983, and so on (see Haddad 1985:79,92), the Arab League prepared a new peace plan for Lebanon. Its summit meeting held in Taif, Saudi Arabia, in October 1989 established a new constitutional settlement with the participation of the Lebanese Parliament, refurbishing the existing power-sharing formula in the constitution. Under this new peace-plan the Arab League got the consent of the Lebanese government to admitting Syrian forces into Lebanese territory to guarantee the implementation of the Taif plan within two years (see Keesing's 36986).

This time Syria succeeded in its Lebanese policy, i.e., preservation of the territorial integrity of Lebanon and establishing the authority of the Lebanese government. In October 1990 it carried out a joint military expedition with the Lebanese Army against General Michel Aoun's[3] Christian militia and removed the last stumbling block for the implementation of the Taif plan. This action of Syria's drew no objection whatever from any of the great powers, mainly perhaps because of Syria's newly-acquired international stature from its participation in the allied military campaign against Iraq's annexation of Kuwait. According to reports, this time the US government had given Syria '...a free hand to curb the rebellion of General Aoun in Lebanon' (Keesing's 1991:38069). Finally all the military factions in Lebanon, except the South Lebanese Army in Israel occupied areas in South Lebanon, responded favourably to the Lebanese government's deadline for the disbanding of their militias. As a result, the Lebanese government had successfully established its authority throughout the country, at the end of 1991.

As witnessed by these cases the task assumed by the Big Neighbour under the 'invitational' role is not the same as that under the 'interventionist' role. In the first instance it may take the form of military involvement by the Big Neighbour in assisting the central regime to quell the insurgency, or of peace-keeping and policing the conflict-affected areas, but may be extended to a military campaign against the intransigent secessionist groups. In contrast to the 'interventionist' role, the 'invitational' role primarily gives more weight to the ending of insurgency or disarming of the secessionist groups as a prerequisite for conflict resolution, and can be successful without introducing international mediation.

However, once there is an agreed peace settlement, and if the secessionists are offering their co-operation in the implementation of that agreement, the Big Neighbour may take on the responsibility of monitoring the implementation of the

---

3. The self-proclaimed Prime Minister of the separate administration functioning in the Christian sector of East Beirut since 1989 (see Keesing's 1989: 36986, 1990:37792).

reconciliation settlement and the policing of the conflict-affected areas without any further military designs. These monitoring exercises could include, supervising the surrendering of arms by the secessionist groups and demilitarization of the secessionist homeland by the government security forces, helping the central government and the regional groups in the establishment of an interim administration, providing expertise to the central regime for the setting up of the constitutional and legal framework of the devolutionary package envisaged in the peace settlement, and overseeing elections and other procedures for the establishment of a new regional administration etc. These functions were undertaken not only by the Syrian policy-makers but also the Indian Peace Keeping Force (IPKF) during the early phase of their 'invitational' role in Sri Lanka. The Big Neighbour's 'invitational' role appears to be implicitly biased against the secessionist movement even though it carries such peace-keeping functions. What is abundantly clear is that the Big Neighbour's very involvement in invitational functions symbolizes its willingness to commit itself openly and completely to the territorial integrity of the affected state, vis-a-vis secession. Under modern international customary law this practice, i.e., sending military forces into another state 'by invitation of the government' (Doswald-Beck 1988:189-92), has been accepted as legal by the international community, most prominently by the United Nations, though there are reservations in the literature regarding the validity of such actions in saving unpopular or illegally installed regimes (Doswald-Beck 1988:251-2).

For example, at the beginning the Indo-Sri Lanka accord and the subsequent Indian military involvement in Sri Lanka received wide international acceptance, though they had followed a period of pressures and threats by a Big Neighbour on a small state. The two Super Powers, the Commonwealth and the United Nations saw it as a good precedent for resolving regional conflict through bilateral negotiations (see Parasher 1987:111; *The Hindu International Edition* 10 October 1987, 19 December 1987).

If the Big Neighbour's 'invitational role' was initiated as a contribution to a joint exercise organized by other states or on a mandate given by a regional or international Inter-Governmental Organization, like the Syrian 'invitational' role, it would be accorded an even higher degree of legitimacy on the international front, though the world may be well aware of the Big Neighbour's national interests in getting involved in the conflict in the first place.

Whatever the legal validity and the international acceptance of its 'invitational' role, the Big Neighbour's involvement in policing and peace-keeping in the affected state or disarming the rebel movement is not always a popular one. It is likely to face counter strategies from the parties to the conflict as well as from other regional actors wary of Big Neighbour's success. There will always be some interested states ready to accuse the Big Neighbour of interfering in the internal affairs of its small neighbour for strategic gains. Indeed, as clearly manifested by the Indo-Sri

Lanka accord of July 1987 (see next page), and most recently, the treaty of co-operation signed by the Syrian and Lebanese governments on 22 May 1991 (see *The Times* 23 May 1991), the Big Neighbour may actually have extracted strategic concessions from its small neighbour in return for its commitment to the territorial integrity of the affected state, seemingly justifying the characterizing of its achievement in resolving the conflict as a grand design aimed at seizing strategic resources in the affected state's territory. If another neighbouring state or a great power has its eyes on these same resources, the Big Neighbour will certainly face such a challenge.

For example in the Syrian-Lebanese situation, the Israel government was prompt in expressing its disapproval of the Syrian government's getting legal status for its control of Lebanon's domestic and foreign affairs through the treaty of co-operation signed on 22 May 1991 (see *The Guardian* 24 May 1991). Later Israel mounted air raids into Southern Lebanon, ostensibly targeting the Palestine guerrilla camps in southern Lebanon but indirectly aimed at the disruption of the Syrian peace-making initiative. This was a repetition of Israel actions in the past, raiding the Palestine camps and giving assistance to the Christian militias in East Beirut and to the 'Independent Free Lebanese' state in southern Lebanon, actions which finally disrupted Syria's work in Lebanon during the 1978-82 period (see Keesing's 1980:30094; Haddad 1985:79-85).

The same is true of the Indian involvement in Sri Lanka. Here, Pakistan and China, India's main rivals in the South Asian region, openly declared their disapproval of the Indo-Sri Lanka accord; characterizing it as Indian meddling in the internal affairs of Sri Lanka by manipulating Sri Lanka's ethnic conflict. Although the official policy of the United States was acceptance of India's 'invitational' role in Sri Lanka, the Indo-Sri Lanka accord of 1987 did not receive whole hearted support from US strategists because of the strategic concessions received by the Indian side. For example the right-wing Heritage Foundation of Washington, one of the major think tanks of the American foreign policy-making process, openly declared its disapproval of the American Government's welcome for India's 'invitational' role in Sri Lanka. It described India's achievement in Sri Lanka as a gain for the Soviet Union. Considering the Soviet influence in the South Asian region, already '...enhanced by cosy Moscow-New Delhi ties...', to use its own wording, 'it expressed the fear that Soviet access to the strategic deep-water port of Trincomalee in Eastern Sri Lanka could lead to the establishment of a massive naval and air base' (*The Hindu* 1 August 1987).

This led some Indian commentators not only to defend the Indian role in Sri Lanka but also to characterize American objectives in the South Asian region as inherently challenging Indian interests (see Parasher 1987). India's Chief of Naval Staff, Admiral J.G. Nadkarni's statement may have been directed at these criticisms:

(Trincomalee) is a harbour of Sri Lanka. Indeed our ships have been visiting it in the past. We have no grand design. ...We must not look upon the Indo-Sri Lanka agreement as a grand design of acquiring the Trincomalee harbour. In our strategic environment, we want to ensure that this harbour is not utilized by any other power which will place India at a disadvantage. The agreement was arrived at mainly to ensure the aspirations of the Tamil people of Sri Lanka are met within the boundaries of the agreement (*The Hindu International Edition* 26 December 1987).

Whatever the Indian interpretation of the Indo-Sri Lanka accord, there is no doubt that the Sri Lanka government's undertakings included in the documents annexed to the Indo-Sri Lanka accord, such as reviewing Sri Lanka's agreements with foreign broadcasting organizations, establishing a joint venture between India and Sri Lanka for restoring the Trincomalee oil tank complex, and agreement not to offer its Trincomalee or any other ports in Sri Lanka to any country for military use in a manner prejudicial to India's interests etc., (see *Indo-Sri Lanka agreement*, Annexture; Ram 1989:143-6; Rao 1988:434) emanated directly from the very suspicions held by the Indian policy-makers about American involvement in Sri Lanka (also see Jooshi 1990:9). As such it is not strange for American strategists to count India's achievement to their disadvantage.

This type of suspicion or disagreement among interested parties may encourage intransigent rebel groups to seek assistance from those unhappy international actors. If they succeed, the rebel movement may try to transform the Big Neighbour's peace-keeping mission into a protracted counter-insurgency operation, with all the natural evils of such a military operation viz., civilian casualties, excesses of its military forces, destruction of property etc. Then the peace-keeping mission of the Big Neighbour becomes a partisan war carried out for the sake of its own national interest.

Almost certainly this would lose Big Neighbour the international acclaim received for its commitment to finding a peaceful settlement to the conflict, at the very beginning. The Syrian policy-makers faced the above situation while they were engaging in military confrontation with the Lebanese factions in 1976. Iraq, Libya and Israel had become the external backers of Syria's opponents in the Lebanese conflict mainly because of their strategic concerns over the growing Syrian influence in the region.

However, the Syrian peace-keeping mission achieved a limited success in November 1976 in containing the leftist Muslim and Palestine forces, because Syria settled its outstanding problems with its Arab neighbours. But it couldn't achieve the same result during the period 1978-82, when it was fighting against the Christian militias backed by Israel. Then the Syrian peace-keeping mission was transformed into a partisan war, which even extended to creating a proxy military force (nick-named 'Pink Panthers', see Keesing's 1983:31922), to maintain its influence in Lebanon in the event of its having to withdraw.   These partisan actions, as we have seen, eventually led to the loss of its support base in the Lebanese government.

In the Sri Lanka theatre, India did not find substantial evidence of such external involvement.   But when their mission changed into a protracted military engagement against the militants of the LTTE movement, Indian commentators found reason to speculate about covert foreign involvement behind the military capabilities of the LTTE movement.   One of India's influential newspapers, *The Hindu*, commented,

> The presence of the IPKF does not seem to have stopped the endless flow of arms and ammunition into the LTTE's camp, and on a scale that has given it substantial combative ability.   It is an outside power (not India, for sure) that must be behind such supplies, which thus acquire more than ordinary significance (*The Hindu International Edition* 23 December 1989).

However, the other Tamil militant groups which supported the Indo-Sri Lanka accord were more open in spotting the external backers of their rival, the LTTE. A spokesmen of the Eelam People's Revolutionary Front (EPRLF) once said that '...the Liberation Tigers of Tamil Eelam (LTTE) was being externally manipulated by certain forces having direct links with the dispensation in Washington... (thus) ...not an internal phenomenon nor is it a patriotic force...' (*The Hindu International Edition* 6 December 1987).

The secessionists' attempt to drag the Big Neighbour into a protracted military conflict in another's territory was not to the Big Neighbour's benefit.   Any protracted war by a state in a foreign land, and most significantly against a rebel movement which has become a representative organ of an ethnic group, would very soon become unpopular.   First it comes to the surface as a popular unrest among the minority population which once warmly welcomed its arrival as a peace-maker.   The situation provides grounds for the intransigent secessionist movement to characterize the Big Neighbour's military as 'an occupying force'.

Further, the continuous presence of the Big Neighbour's military in the affected state territory, and its failure in implementing the task assigned by the central regime, may influence the dominant community to press the central regime to withdraw its invitation.   The opponents of the central regime may then characterize its action in inviting the Big Neighbour into its territory as a sellout of the country's national sovereignty.   In view of such protests and the failure of the Big Neighbour to fulfil its mission in time the central regime may change its mind and ask for the withdrawal of the Big Neighbour's military forces.

The chances are very remote (whatever the central regime may expect) of a prompt withdrawal by the Big Neighbour which has already become involved militarily in the conflict.   This may lead to a disagreement between the policy-makers of the Big Neighbour and the central regime.   If the Big Neighbour and the central regime reach a point of disagreement regarding the withdrawal of the

Big Neighbour's military from the affected state territory both parties come to a new stage of their relationship. Sometimes, the Big Neighbour may try to keep its forces in the affected state territory, threatening to transform its 'invitational' role into an 'interventionist' role.

In this situation one possible development would be that the central regime and the intransigent secessionist movement would come to an understanding as a price for the withdrawal of the Big Neighbour. Looking at their Big Neighbour as an external threat and a common enemy by the domestic actors may further influence them to settle their discord within the limits of their territorial boundary. Thus, to a certain extent this is a positive development in the direction of the resolution of the conflict, even though caused by the withdrawal of the Big Neighbour's military.

However, this is not always the case. The withdrawal of the Big Neighbour alone cannot guarantee the resolution of the conflict. Unless the conflicting parties make genuine efforts to resolve the real issues relating to such a negotiated settlement i.e. the degree of the devolution of power, the territorial unit of devolution, and the basic framework of the power sharing arrangement and so on, they cannot reach a lasting settlement to the conflict on the departure of the Big Neighbour. If they fail to come to a compromise within a reasonable period the parties will lose this valuable opportunity for settling the conflict. In this situation it is the central regime which suffers most. As the Big Neighbour's withdrawal has taken place amidst disagreement with the central regime it has removed by its own action an important external actor that is vital to the management of the secessionist conflict.

Empirical evidence from the Lebanese and Sri Lankan situations can be brought in here. The political atmosphere which led to the Syrian military withdrawal in 1982 and that of the Indian Peace Keeping Force in March 1990 had other similarities. At the time of their departure the Syrian forces had spent nearly six years on their mission in Lebanon while the Indian Peace Keeping Force spent nearly three years. Both the Big Neighbours' 'invitational' roles ended without achieving the immediate objectives set out by their original invitation. When their presence and the military campaign against the intransigent domestic actors were transformed into protracted partisan conflicts, the very same central regimes which brought them into their territory requested the withdrawal. The failure of both the Syrian ADF and the IPKF to fulfil their mandate in time hardened public opinion against their long presence.

The continuous presence of the Syrian forces re-awakened the fears that existed in the minds of the Lebanese people regarding Syrian irredentism over Lebanese territory. Even the Maronite leadership in Lebanon (which once treated the Syrian presence as an essential requirement for maintaining peace in Lebanon) expressed their dissatisfaction regarding the continuation of Syrian involvement in the Lebanese conflict. They alleged that Syrian actions in Lebanon were directed at the achievement of their long held objective of annexation of the Lebanon into their 'Greater Syria' entity (Haddad 1985:59).

In Sri Lanka, opponents of the Indo-Sri Lanka accord among the majority community used the presence of the IPKF in Sri Lanka territory as a political issue to revive the majority community's old fears about 'Indian expansionism'. Using this very slogan, the *Janatha Vimukthi Peramuna* (the People's Liberation Front) which organized the ill-fated youth insurrection of 1971, launched an unprecedentedly violent campaign, protesting at the presence of the IPKF in Sri Lanka's territory (see *India Today* 30 September 1989; *The Guardian* 22 June 1989).

This violent situation finally led the Sri Lanka government, then under a new leadership, to request the Indian government to withdraw their forces from Sri Lanka, giving its own deadline. This created a row between the governments of India and Sri Lanka. India refused to follow the Sri Lanka government's timetable, and stated its own conditions for withdrawal (see *The Economist* 10-16 June 1989; *India Today* 30 June 1990). At this juncture some observers suspected that India was about to transform Sri Lanka's Northern and Eastern provinces into a Cyprus-like situation (see *The Times* 18 July 1989), with some grounds. For example the EPRLF, the pro-Indian Tamil militant group which was controlling the provincial administration established under the Indo-Sri Lanka accord, announced 'UDI' in the midst of this withdrawal controversy, demanding that the Sri Lanka government call off its request for the withdrawal of the IPKF (Keesing's 1990:37317).

At the same time the IPKF created a proxy military force called the 'Tamil National Army' (TNA) under the EPRLF-controlled North-eastern Provincial Council,[4] to fight the LTTE movement (Keesing's 1990:37353). Finally, the withdrawal of IPKF took place in March 1990 under a timetable set out by both governments, but after the electoral defeat of Rajiv Gandhi, one of the two signatories to the Indo-Sri Lanka accord (the Sri Lankan signatory, President J. R. Jayawardane retired from active politics and was replaced by his party's nominee, President R. Premadasa, elected at the Presidential election held in November 1988).

As the withdrawal of the IPKF became a point of disagreement between two governments, the Sri Lanka government started negotiations with the LTTE using their common stand against the presence of the IPKF in Sri Lanka, and successfully reached a ceasefire agreement in June 1989, making the mission of the IPKF unneeded. This ceasefire agreement created a peaceful atmosphere in the troubled Northern and Eastern provinces for nearly a year, creating hope for a peaceful settlement to the conflict. But the withdrawal of the Big Neighbour did not bring the long awaited negotiated settlement to the ethnic conflict in Sri Lanka, which would at least have given some satisfaction to the Indian policy-makers that the role

---

4. Established under the Indo-Sri Lanka accord of 1987.

that they played in Sri Lanka had made this possible.[5] The conflicting parties did not even wait to celebrate the first anniversary of their longest cease-fire since the secessionist violence intensified in 1983. In June 1990 the conflict again came full circle, and still continues at the time of writing.

But this time the LTTE seem to have accepted the geopolitical realities attached to its secession ideal, especially India's opposition to that demand and the strategic concerns attached to it. Though the 'invitational' role played by Sri Lanka's Big Neighbour ended without apparent success, it persuaded the LTTE leadership to change their goal from 'secession' to 'devolution'. The LTTE declared that they would like to compromise with the Sri Lanka government for a 'federal' system of government. Anton Balasingham, the top theoretician of the LTTE stated:

> We are prepared to negotiate for more regional autonomy if Sri Lanka proposes a federal system (*Tamil Times* 1990,9(9):6).

The Sri Lankan President (Mr R. Premadasa) too has reacted positively, insisting that everything is negotiable except 'Eelam' (see *Tamil Times* 1991,10(6):3,the editorial). In his policy statement to the Parliament in April 1991 he declared,

> We are determined to break away from the past and cut through years of prejudices and suspicion. We are ready to make the necessary accommodation and compromises. There is no other road towards prosperity. There is no road towards united Sri Lanka. Foreign forces came to the North and East because of our disunity. However, we were able to send them away (*Tamil Times* 1991,10(6):6).

Putting together these conciliatory approaches of the LTTE and the Sri Lanka government, the London based *Tamil Times*, once very outspoken about its support for the Sri Lanka Tamil's demand for a 'separate state', commented,

> If the President is serious about being ready to discuss everything else except a separate state, then the time has come for government to announce a federal structure in which the Tamil people of the north-east will enjoy a high degree of autonomy acceptable to them (*Tamil Times* 1991,10(6):3, the editorial).

---

5. To understand the Indian perception regarding the Tamil-Sinhala detente which existed after this ceasefire agreement it is worth quoting an Indian commentator: '...In the present circumstances India has no alternative but to sit back and watch which way things go... However, from the Indian point of view, if the LTTE is willing to live within a united Sri Lanka, the crucial Indian national aim will have been met' (Joshi 1990:09).

In the light of these developments the only available explanation for the continuation of the conflict in Sri Lanka is that both the adversaries are now fighting an unwinnable war just to achieve the highest bargaining position in their future negotiations, or to keep the emotions of their respective ethnic groups alive.

It is not only Sri Lanka that missed the opportunity of resolving the conflict with the withdrawal of the Big Neighbour's military. The withdrawal of the Syrian ADF in 1982 and its replacement by a multinational peace-keeping force did not bring peace and stability to Lebanon. Despite various initiatives to find a settlement, the civil war in Lebanon continued for another nine years before coming to the conclusion which we are witnessing at the time of writing. This time the central regime in Lebanon, as we have seen, succeeded in its objective by extending a fresh invitation to its Big Neighbour, asking it to repeat the 'invitational' role that it played during the period 1976-82. If Sri Lanka fails to achieve its elusive peace within a reasonable period of time, this type of repetition cannot be ruled out altogether there also. The continuation of India's devolutionary policy towards Sri Lanka, despite the change of government leadership twice after the election defeat of Rajiv Gandhi in 1989, suggests that the conflict in Sri Lanka will continue as a running sore and de-stabilizing factor in Indian domestic politics (as has now been further illustrated by the alleged involvement of the LTTE movement in the assassination of the former Indian Prime Minister Rajiv Gandhi). In these circumstances repetition of the Indian role in Sri Lanka, through 'pressure', 'big stick', 'interventionist' and 'invitational' phases is not so remote a possibility.

Conclusion

It seems fairly clear that the theoretical framework presented in chapter one, explaining 'alternative modes of action' available to a Big Neighbour in an ethnic secessionist situation, works well, and is rationale enough to explain the 'Big Neighbour syndrome' in real politics, especially Big Neighbour/affected state relations in a perspective of secessionist conflict management.

The findings are quite straightforward. The evidence presented in the analysis shows that the four Big Neighbour roles identified in the model are available to any Big Neighbour with strong commitment towards a 'devolutionary' settlement. A committed participation by a Big Neighbour state in the secession conflict through one or more of these roles facilitates the reception of devolution of government by the conflicting parties, influencing them, one way or another, to abandon their extreme stances in the conflict, viz. 'secession' or 'repression'.

As we saw, some of our historical Big Neighbours did not play all the roles predicted in the model. This doesn't mean that we were selective in choosing evidence or that the model is flawed. The point is that these Big Neighbours were not provoked by their respective secessionist situations, or by recalcitrance in the internal actors, to play all the roles available. Of course these variations are to be expected. The model has connected each of the four roles available to the Big Neighbour with the level of conflict-escalation and of intransigence found in either of the conflicting parties.

Moreover it is worth noting that none of the Big Neighbours in our historical situations played a role not allowed for in the theoretical model. Thus the model provides a workable framework to understand the behaviour of a Big Neighbour state whose national interests have been threatened by an ethnic secessionist conflict in a neighbouring state. How it might react to such a conflict situation, moving from one role to another, and the way in which the internal actors become receptive to a 'devolutionary' settlement in this process, have been illustrated by the evidence collected from our selected secessionist situations. From the analysis some new understandings emerged as well. One sheds light on the termination or prolongation of the 'interventionist' or 'invitational' roles by the Big Neighbour with inconclusive results. Another is the possibility of the repetition of such roles by the Big Neighbour at a future stage of the conflict.

Furthermore, the evidence showed that the Big Neighbours which prefer 'secession' or 'annexation' may also play some of the roles predicted in the model, keeping the 'devolution' option open. As such, the model can be generally applied to any secessionist conflict situation where a Big Neighbour has made its presence felt, whatever the final policy objective preferred by its policy makers. However, we must note that the model is best equipped to explain the 'Big Neighbour syndrome' in respect of the management of ethnic secessionist conflict through devolution of government, as the 'invitational role' cannot normally be expected in other Big Neighbour situations.

In the next chapter, to complete our discussion of the model we will examine the remaining external factors and internal conditions (other than the existence of a Big Neighbour) predicted in our theoretical model, with a part to play in the reception of 'devolution of government' by the conflicting parties in an ethnic secession situation.

5 The Reception of a Devolutionary Settlement

Introduction

In the previous two chapters we have been investigating 'the role of the Big Neighbour' and the implication of the various Big Neighbour roles in the adoption of a devolutionary settlement by the main adversaries in the secessionist conflict. To try to come closer to an exhaustive understanding of the conditions of the reception of a devolutionary settlement in an ethnic secessionist conflict, we will in this chapter look at the evidence already exhibited from another point of view.

We will look in two directions: first, more widely, at the influence of the world beyond the Big Neighbour and the small affected state; and second, more finely, at conditions within the affected state. First, then, a section on the external dimension of Big Neighbour/affected state relations.

The external dimension of Big Neighbour relations

In chapter one, we identified the salience of international pressure (including launching of conflict management initiatives by Inter-Governmental Organizations (IGOs) or other third party states) as generally supportive of the Big Neighbour's efforts in the containment of the secessionist conflict.

As we have seen, other members of the international community often have specific reasons to get themselves involved in the secessionist situation. By 'other members of the international community' we mean mainly the United Nations (UN) system and its member states, other international and regional Inter-Governmental Organizations, international aid institutions and donor countries, Non-Governmental Organizations (NGOs), and the world's media. In the foregoing analysis of the role of the Big Neighbour, we came across many such illustrations of the involvement of Great Powers, regional neighbours other than the Big Neighbour, and these other international actors. This is perhaps inherent in any Big Neighbour/secessionist situation that has reached the stage of organized violence; it is liable to create humanitarian issues of international concern, and to spill across other international borders in one way or another.

But the roles of each of these other members of the international community in the conflict may differ from each other, and do not necessarily complement the Big Neighbour's efforts towards the containment of the secession conflict.

The UN and other IGOs as organizations of states, are legally and politically obliged to support such efforts by the Big Neighbour, and if necessary, to launch their own conflict management initiatives. Such international efforts will normally be organized when the conflict itself becomes an international matter, endangering international peace.

However, given the central significance of the Big Neighbour's strategic and ethnic ties with the conflict, the policy approaches available to the the UN and other international and regional IGOs in a secessionist conflict of this kind are constrained. They are effectively prevented from 'non-intervention' (standing by while the central regime crushes the rebellion as in the case of the Biafra secession in 1962) or 'military intervention on invitation of the government' (against the secession movement, as in the case of the Katanga secession in 1960), because of the Big Neighbour's prior involvement. They can therefore wield most influence by taking conflict management initiatives', offering 'good offices', mediation, conciliation and peace keeping (see Bilder 1989:481-2), or by the exertion of direct economic or diplomatic pressures on the conflicting parties to go for political negotiation. This was clearly illustrated by the already cited UN involvement in East Pakistan, Cyprus and Lebanon, by the role played by regional IGOs such as the North Atlantic Treaty Organization in the Cyprus situation or the Arab League in the Lebanese conflict, and by the good offices of Britain and the US in the Cyprus conflict in the 1960s or of New Zealand and the Solomon Islands in the Bougainville secession conflict in Papua New Guinea.

Such conflict management exercises not only register the international community's commitment to the territorial integrity of the affected state and disapproval of any military suppression of the secessionist community but become a virtual directive to member states in their individual foreign policy decisions. The UN and the IGOs become forums for organizing an international consensus in pressurizing the conflicting parties, also signalling to economically affluent states and the international aid agencies, such as World Bank and International Monetary Fund, to use economic aid as an instrument of pressure upon the central regime, the party with which they have relations.

The role of NGOs and the world media, it seems, is to mobilize international public opinion about the humanitarian and human rights aspects of a secession conflict. While inter-governmental organizations and their member states are mainly concerned with the 'principle of territorial integrity of states', the NGOs and the media, in the context of global awareness of the international ethic, appear to have assumed a quasi-independent role on behalf of aggrieved ethnic minorities. Perhaps for this reason, some have named NGOs as supporters of the secessionist minorities (see Heraclides 1990:347).

The conflict management initiatives organized by the individual states, the UN and other IGOs, and the roles played by the NGOs and the world media in organizing international public opinion, not only put pressure on the conflicting parties to resolve their enmity politically, they also greatly enhance the Big Neighbour's public commitment towards the territorial integrity of the affected state. The current UN mediation in Cyprus provides a good example. Although the presence of the UN in Cyprus has inhibited the pursuit of an 'annexation' policy by the policy-makers of Turkey, the intercommunal talks undertaken by the UN has so far contributed greatly in developing the idea of bi-zonal federation put forward by the Turkish leaders. In this regard the UN Secretary General has even submitted his own draft on the implementation of a bi-zonal federal system which has been accepted by both sides in principle (see Reddawa:1987).

However, individual Great Powers and regional neighbours do not always acquiesce in this drive by the international and regional IGOs or the Big Neighbour to contain the secession conflict. A Great Power's policy towards the secessionist conflict will conform to its global political strategies. For it the foremost consideration is always its own self-interest, and how that may be affected by the involvement of the Big Neighbour, or by the escalation (or de-escalation) of the secession conflict. If some Great Power interests are threatened by the policies of the Big Neighbour, or by the central regime in the affected state, it may not be conflict management, but its exacerbation, that results; the adversaries being used as pawns in the game, each perhaps receiving covert or overt assistance from different Great Powers, and perhaps other interested neighbours being encouraged to make their presence felt.

The absence of total commitment on the part of some Great Powers and regional neighbours may also weaken UN and IGO international efforts in the containment of the secession conflict. A clear illustration of this is the conflict in East Pakistan, where the UN lost momentum in finding a political settlement due to Great Power rivalry and antipathy towards any settlement short of full independence for East Bengalis.

On the other hand Great Power non-commitment towards the conflict management may help the internal actors to defy the Big Neighbour, even after it has reached the stage of playing an 'interventionist' or 'invitational' role. As happened in Sri Lanka in 1990 and Lebanon in 1982, the Big Neighbour may then be compelled to end its involvement role with inconclusive results, or else settle for a prolonged engagement, undermining its international image - as in the case of the Turkey-Cyprus situation where the Big Neighbour maintained an 'interventionist role' for more than twenty years.

As we saw, our historical Big Neighbour situations are not devoid of Great Power participation complementary to the Big Neighbour's efforts to contain the ethnic conflict, or in international conflict management, finding community of interests at the UN level. The deployment of UN (peace-keeping) forces in Cyprus (UNFICYP) in 1964 and in Lebanon (UNFIL) in 1978, and the continuing UN mediation in the Cyprus conflict illustrate such occasions where the rival Great Powers have found an equilibrium in their individual interests, to make international conflict management possible. In Cyprus the US and British governments wanted to avoid a military confrontation between two friendly NATO powers, and to keep their dominance over the strategic resources in the island, while the Soviet Union wanted to support its friendly regime in Cyprus in its efforts to avoid further involvement by the NATO powers (Black 1977:45). In 1978 when the UN Security Council passed a resolution to send UNFIL to Lebanon, it was apparent that the US objective was to avoid a major confrontation between Israel and Syria in order to preserve its newly developing rapprochement with Syrian leaders (Everon 1987:77-8; Meo 1977:119-20). The Soviet Union was already acquiescent in this move in the Security Council as the friendly Great Power of Syria.

The already cited US approbation of the Indo-Sri Lanka accord and the subsequent Indian 'invitational role' in Sri Lanka, and also, of the Syrian 'invitational role' in Lebanon, provide good instances of complementary initiatives taken by a Great Power once identified by the Big Neighbour as an opponent of its policy towards the ethnic conflict in the affected state.

In the Sri Lanka situation, while the Indian leaders had their suspicions about an American hand behind the scenes (as discussed in chapter 2), the US policy-makers too had their suspicions over India's true intention in Sri Lanka. Thus during the period between 1983 and 1987 the American policy was to avoid total international isolation for the pro-western government of the United National Party (UNP) in Sri Lanka, which might have freed India to give decisive support to the secessionists in their bid for total independence. But it was fairly clear during this time that the American policy-makers remained critical of human rights violations in Sri Lanka (see Rao 1989:90). Sometimes they openly advised the Sri Lanka government to withdraw its forces from the troubled areas in order to find a political settlement to the conflict (see *Asia Year Book* 1986, Far Eastern Economic Review, Hongkong, p.238).

When once they realized that Indian policy towards Sri Lanka was *not* essentially directed at the accomplishment of secession or annexation (as expressed by Deputy Assistant Secretary of State Robert Peck in March 1987: '...we have been gratified in the last year or two that our policies and the policies of India on Sri Lanka are very much running parallel...', quoted in Rao 1988:425), the American policy-makers co-operated with Indian policy-makers in their efforts to manage the conflict (Rao 1988:425). From the end of 1986 when India began to play the 'big stick' role in Sri Lanka's secession conflict, the US government advised Sri Lanka, as later disclosed by the Sri Lankan leaders, to settle things with India. The Sri Lanka President, J. R. Jayawardana, after the signing of the Indo-Sri Lanka agreement of 1987, stated that,

> ...the whole world accepts India's pre-eminence in this part and India is a big-power in the region. The US will not lift a finger to help me without first consulting India (*The Hindu International Edition* 19 September 1987).

Given international sympathy with the plight of the Tamil minority in Sri Lanka, coupled with the growing international pressure on the central regime in Sri Lanka, such a policy helped to make the signing of the Indo-Sri Lanka agreement of 1987 possible.

This situation, of the Big Neighbour receiving diplomatic and political approval from a Great Power which had been identified as a possible obstacle in its efforts to contain the conflict, is almost replicated in the US policy towards the Syrian 'invitational role' in Lebanon. In 1976 when Syrian policy-makers sent its military forces into Lebanon in support of the Lebanese government, the then American President Gerald Ford openly praised '...Syrian policy towards Lebanon as constructive' (Keesing's 1976:27773), although the US had disapproved of any external involvement in Lebanon at the outset of the civil war (Keesing's 1976:27770). When Syrian forces advanced towards Southern Lebanon to disband the Palestine guerrillas, the US government even used its influence to persuade Israel to allow the Syrians to accomplish their objective (Keesing's 1976:27773, 28124).

The American strategy in the Lebanese situation was quite apparent. The US government backed the Syrians in the interests of its own strategy towards the settlement of the wider Arab-Israel conflict (see Meo 1977:112-13). Perhaps the American policy-makers were using Lebanon as a bargaining chip to win over the Syrians to their Middle East policy, and as a meeting place between the main rivals in the Arab-Israel conflict (Haddad 1985:90). This became more open during 1982-83 when Israel moved to undermine the Syrian 'invitational role'. By that time Syria had become a leading opponent of the American-sponsored 'peace agreement' between Israel and Egypt, and the Israeli action in Lebanon with the tacit approval of the US government seemed to be a way of punishing Syria for its resistance to the American peace initiatives (see Schiff 1988:161-2).

In 1990 when the Syrians completed their second 'invitational role' in Lebanon, in disbanding most of the Lebanese and non-Lebanese militias and establishing peace in Lebanon, winning the approval of the US administration, this same strategy was repeated by the American 'spin-doctors'. The change of American heart is not just a result of Syria's participation in the Gulf war in 1991, but relates to a new-found co-operation between Syria and the US administration in making international efforts to settle the wider Arab-Israel conflict (see Keesing's 1991:38069).

These instances show not only the Great Power stand-off picking sides in these Big Neighbour/secessionist situations but its working in favour of international conflict management and of the role played by the Big Neighbour. However, united Great Power approbation of this kind depends not so much on the strategy being followed by the Big Neighbour, as on the emergence of an accommodation between the different interests pursued by the Great Powers in regional politics, including the developments within the affected state. As we saw, many of these Great Power involvements are often pre-emptive actions, to prevent their enemies getting some strategic benefit.

The involvement of the US and Chinese governments in supplying arms and political and diplomatic support to the central regime in Pakistan during the secessionist crisis in East Pakistan, the US and British role at one stage against the central regime in Cyprus, the alleged involvement of the US and UK governments in Sri Lanka via Israel, Pakistan and South Africa, or the role played by Israel with the tacit approval of the United States in sabotaging the Syrian initiatives in Lebanon (1982), are illustrations.

Correspondingly any reduction of Great Power interest in the conflict in the affected state, because of a new-found understanding between the Big Neighbour and a concerned Great Power, or because the rival Great Powers have reached tacit agreement to reduce global competition, or simply because the Great Powers have diverted their attention to another area, may have certain negative consequences for other international efforts to contain the conflict. As the Great Powers lose their interest in the internal ethnic conflict of the affected state, the internal actors may sometimes assume a freedom to ignore international pressure now weakened by the uninterest of the Great Powers, and reopen the conflict or settle into a new intransigence.

The foregoing may serve to clarify the nature of the external dimension of the Big Neighbour/affected state relations. Now we must look at some more specific factors (other than the humanitarian and human rights aspects), which generate international interest and work in favour of international action in the conflict situation. We have discerned two such factors: (a) the affected state's or the secessionist region's location in a highly sensitive geostrategic spot, and (b) high dependence of the affected state on the international economic and political system. The following two sub-sections analyse these two dimensions with relevant illustrations from our selected Big Neighbour situations.

The location of the affected state

The central argument in this section is that the international community's involvement in the secessionist conflict, taking conflict management initiatives and wielding pressure on conflicting parties, becomes almost inevitable if the affected state is in a highly sensitive geostrategic location. Such international interest in the ethnic conflict in the affected state, especially after it reaches the stage of outright violence, may arise from various points. If the affected state is situated in a region where victorious secessionist upheavals or intervention by a neighbour state may set off a chain reaction of such events, stability in the affected state becomes a matter of international importance as jeopardizing the peace and security of the whole region - all the more so if the region is already unstable from other regional disputes of international concern, when the resolution or management of the conflict in the affected state might be a precedent or a prerequisite for settling other conflicts in the region. Alternatively the affected state may lie in an area where the Great Powers are already active, working competitively towards the advancement of their several economic, trading, political and military gains, each having a special interest in the affected state's strategic resources.

Thus a relatively small conflict may achieve great significance in international politics, either as a potential powder-keg likely to send the entire region into turmoil, tempting more states in the region to further inflame the conflict as supporters of the conflicting parties; or as a snare in which the Great Powers may become enmeshed, their rival interests in the region, or in the affected state's strategic resources, drawing them into conflict between themselves at further hazard to international peace. Either of these political imperatives, arising from the geostrategic location of the affected state, might eventually bring the international community and their IGOs to see the urgent necessity of managing the conflict.

In this regard the most suitable illustration is the secessionist conflict in Cyprus. Apart from the various perspectives which we have already identified as reasons for Great Power involvement, such as the US interest in avoiding a military conflict between Greece and Turkey, and retaining NATO's dominance over the strategic resources of the Island, it was the location of Cyprus which generated not only the interest of these Great Powers but also their rivals in international politics and the United Nations. The strategic situation of Cyprus in the Eastern Mediterranean, straddling Europe and the Middle East, has always been recognized as the major cause attracting outside powers into the Cyprus conflict. As noted by an analyst:

> ...because of its location in the Middle East on the one side and Europe on the other the island is too important to too many powers. Not only Greece and Turkey claim a stake in Cyprus, but also the Russians, the Americans, the British, the Israelis and the Arabs (Markides 1977:79).

Such discussions are very familiar in the literature (for example see Souter 1984:657-60; Birand 1988:173-8). Many have argued that the conflict in Cyprus is an international problem not an internal one. Some see the conflict as a left over of the 'Eastern Question' of earlier days, linked to its strategic location:

> Whenever Cyprus has captured the attention of students of politics, it has done

so as an international problem, an element in the strategy and power relations in the eastern Mediterranean. What has come to be known as the *Cyprus question*, essentially a left over of the Eastern question of old, has involved the issue of control over a strategically located island at the threshold of the Near East' (Kitromilides & Couloumbis 1976:189-90, emphasis added).

Since the current conflict in Cyprus brought the ancient rivalry between Greeks and Turks into the arena of the Eastern Mediterranean, that unstable situation has become a problem for Europe itself, apart from its implications for the middle East. The European Community (EC) has received formal applications from both Cyprus and Turkey to become members. Greece has made its protest against Turkey's entry into the community because of its occupation of Northern Cyprus while some other members of the community have protested that the unresolved Cyprus conflict would become a burden.

According to reports, the US and British governments have given high priority to a resolution of the Cyprus conflict after their experiences in the Gulf War against Iraq. They want to establish a NATO Rapid Reaction Force to face such challenges in the future, but for that they need joint participation from Greece and Turkey, the two NATO powers with closest access to the Eastern Mediterranean and to the Middle East (see *The Daily Telegraph* 15 August 1991). And of course it was the strategic location of Cyprus that enabled the British bases in the island to play a part in the war in the Gulf.

Whatever the concerns of the Great Powers or the states in Europe, the international community cannot ignore the problem in Cyprus. The end of the Cold War and the collapse of Soviet Communism has not reduced the UN responsibility for resolving the Cyprus conflict. It still haunts the international community because of its highly sensitive location in the Near East, once more a region of powder kegs. Now its resolution has become a test case for the international community, a necessary step in dealing with the wider regional problems of the area. This was clearly explained by Xavier Perez de Cuellar, the then Secretary General of the United Nations:

> ...Cyprus is in both Europe and Asia. A solution to the Cyprus problem is part of the stability in the Middle East (*NewSpot* 11 July 1991)

It was reported in 1991 that the UN mediators, with the UN Secretary General himself (Mr Xavier Perez de Cuellar) making a visit to Ankara, Athens and Nicosia for the purpose, were preparing for a peace conference on Cyprus with the approval of the US government (see *NewSpot* 4 July 1991).

In this regard all our other Big Neighbour situations are contrasts. As we have seen, the conflict in Papua New Guinea is the only secessionist situation where no Great Power involvement is found, and the Big Neighbour has been given a relatively free hand because of the absence of Great Power involvement. Thus the conflicts in East Pakistan, Sri Lanka and Lebanon differ from the conflict in PNG, as they received Great Power attention when their respective Big Neighbours made their presence felt in the conflict. But these conflicts did not become so internationalized or receive so much international attention as the Cyprus conflict. If we take the prevalent conflicts in Sri Lanka and Lebanon (excluding more historical East Pakistan, and PNG where no Great Power involvement is found), we can see that the Great Power interest in these situations rapidly decreased once their respective Big Neighbours received Great Power approval for their role in the conflict, and even more clearly, since the end of the Cold War.

The international interest in pressurizing the conflicting parties has also declined. For example, before 1990 there was a great deal of attention and activity on the part of NGOs and the international media devoted to the conflict in Sri Lanka, though there was no UN participation in conflict management. In this context the conflicts in Sri Lanka, Lebanon and PNG are all now of the same kind: all of them are regarded as internal affairs of the respective affected states, susceptible only to Big Neighbour pressures and further involvement. (The presence of UNFIL in Lebanon is the exception; but that force went there to create a Green line between Israel and the Palestine forces in South Lebanon, not between internal warring factions.) If any of these affected states again finds itself in a strategically sensitive area, as is Cyprus, the situation may change, and it may again be the focus of international attention towards the management of its internal conflict.

The dependence of the affected state

Our cases however, have shown that it is the response of the internal actors to external pressures which matters most for the success of international efforts to resolve their conflict. International involvement even with total commitment from the Great Powers cannot be successful without an appropriate response from the internal parties to the conflict.

One of the reasons why an 'appropriate' response from the conflicting parties might not be forthcoming, however, is if the political economy of the affected state afforded them the necessary clout to ignore international pressure. So we need to examine the place of the affected state's economy in the world market, and above all the extent of the central regime's reliance on international financial assistance for the management of its domestic economy. Apart from a moral commitment to the international political order, these are the couplings which connect states into the international political and economic system. For a small state (which by definition all states with Big Neighbours are), the quality of these exchanges (the degree of self-reliance) is crucial for its very existence in the international system.

When the affected state is highly dependent on the international economic system, in both trade and aid terms, even mild economic pressure would be a most powerful weapon. If mild economic pressure does not force the internal actors to the negotiation table, the reduction or suspension of economic aid, or the imposition of total economic sanctions, may be applied by the international community - with severe effects on the standard of living of the domestic public, affecting their attitudes towards their political leadership and the cost of their military activities. These actions have particular impact on the central regime, weakening its support base among the majority community. If, however, the state has a more self-reliant economy, the central regime has a freer hand.

The implications of economic dependence are illustrated by the international atmosphere surrounding Sri Lanka's ethnic conflict. In 1987 when Sri Lanka's Big Neighbour was formally invited by the central regime to undertake a policing task, the country had become '...on a per capita basis, one of the most heavily-aided nations in the world' (Moore 1990:354), leading some others to call it '...the best beggar in the world' (Singer 1989:23). Being a small state, like other affected states named here, the country was already within the purview of the international monetary system. But this time there was a particular reason for Sri Lanka to become one of the third world countries most highly reliant on international aid.

In 1987 the country completed its first decade of implementing a new economic policy intended to dismantle the government-regulated closed economic system which had prevailed in the country for nearly twenty years, and to create a more market-oriented open economic system (see Levy 1989; Moore 1990). But for various reasons the country did not attract private foreign capital for the establishment of new manufacturing capacity to replace the declining plantation sector's foreign exchange earnings, on its road to economic liberalization. However, the central regime in Sri Lanka overcame this difficulty in the late seventies by attracting much attention and support from the World Bank, as one of its first test cases of a liberalizing regime in the third world (see Moore 1990:349-57). In channelling a huge flow of foreign aid, it helped Sri Lanka's economic policy and development priorities. The result was, as noted by an analyst:

> In the absence of major new sources of foreign exchange earnings, the economy has become structurally dependent on continuous net foreign aid inflows (Moore 1990:354-5).

The country's external public debt increased from $317 million in 1970 to $1,013 million in 1978 at the beginning of this new economic policy, and reached $3,448 million in 1986 (*World Development Report* 1980, The World Bank, Washington, D.C., p.138; *World Development Report* 1988, The World Bank, New York, p.252).

This further strengthening of the dependence relationship had the expected effect on the ethnic conflict. As Marshall R. Singer puts it, it had '...given the donor countries a certain amount of leverage, i.e., they can threaten to withdraw their support unless there is a peaceful solution' (Singer 1989:24).

This became reality when the US government cut half its aid commitment to Sri Lanka in the beginning of 1987 (Rao 1988:428; Pfaffenberger 1987:157). Before 1987, when the US and British governments were providing indirect assistance to Sri Lanka to tackle Tamil secessionism, as we have seen, and were reluctant to use economic leverage decisively on the central regime in Sri Lanka, countries like Canada, Norway and Sweden used it very effectively - 'potent small powers and ineffective Big Powers' (Egeland 1984) - probably in response to pressures from various NGOs and world media in sympathy with the plight of the minority community in Sri Lanka. Even the World Bank and the IMF were drawn into this international effort because of the alarming increase in the defence budget of the Sri Lanka government (see *Asia Year Book* 1987, Far Eastern Economic Review, Hong Kong p.239). The then Finance Minister of Sri Lanka Mr Ronnie de Mel, responding to the pressure exerted by the World Bank and Sri Lanka's main donors, urged his government to find an immediate solution to the conflict:

> (W)e cannot create employment without development and we cannot allocate enough money for development by spending so much on defence and security... Otherwise, let me tell you frankly that Sri Lanka faces disaster (*Asia Year Book* 1986, Far Eastern Economic Review, Hong Kong, p.241).

During this time there was a strong lobby in America and Europe, pressing Sri Lanka's donors to use aid as a weapon to put pressure on the regime in Sri Lanka. In the end the US policy-makers bowed to the pressure from the pro-Tamil lobby in America and as we saw reduced its aid commitment by half at the beginning of 1987. Thus the decision taken by the Indian policy-makers to wave the 'big stick' against Sri Lanka in May 1987 took place at a time when Sri Lanka's dependence relationship in the international system was successfully working against the militaristic policies pursued by its central regime. With all its hopes for possible assistance from the West crumbling, and in face of the pressure from the international community, the regime realized that they had no choice but to accept India's terms for the management of its secessionist conflict. However, the dependence of the affected state on the international system is not always linked only to the *economic* relationship between the international community and the affected state. There are political dimensions also. The intensification of the secessionist conflict itself may create a political atmosphere which would induce one or other of the conflicting parties to align themselves with the international system. The most important political dimension, of course, is the pressure created by the involvement of the Big Neighbour and the Great Powers in the conflict, which might certainly drive one of the conflicting parties to seek international mediation for the management of the conflict.

Efforts made by the conflicting parties to find external military assistance, paradoxically, may increase the chances of a mediation initiative by the international community. It is true the immediate result could be the emergence of international patrons for one or other of the conflicting parties, leading to the exacerbation of the conflict. But the presence of such international patrons would produce intermediaries through whom the international community could reach the internal actors: and if these patrons were themselves amenable to reason or to international pressure, at a certain stage of the conflict, they might be brought to assist as agents of the international community in pressurizing the conflicting parties to settle the conflict through negotiations. Once the conflicting parties became dependent on the support of these international patrons, their pressure could not be ignored.

These political dimensions are seen in the Cyprus, Lebanon and Sri Lanka situations. The Turkey-Cyprus situation was a clear example of a central regime seeking international mediation in its secession conflict in response to the involvement of the Big Neighbour and the Great Powers in the conflict. When Turkey flexed its military muscles for the first time against the central regime in Cyprus in December 1964, Cyprus raised the issue at the UN Security council branding it '...intervention in the internal affairs of Cyprus by threat and use of force against territorial integrity and political independence' (Keesing's 1964:20114).

The Sri Lanka situation illustrates the impact of the conflicting parties' reliance on external supporters in the presentation of the secession conflict. While the Tamil secessionists were strengthening their reliance on India for their material and moral support, the central regime relied on the West for military assistance (even if it was channelled through surrogate powers). As explained in the previous section when the western powers instructed Sri Lanka to settle things with India, Sri Lanka responded promptly mainly because of its dependence on the West for its economic survival. There were official promises from the World Bank and donors that they would come to the help of Sri Lanka's post-civil rehabilitation programmes if only it could find a peaceful settlement to the conflict (*Asia Year Book* 1987, Far Eastern Economic Review, Hong Kong, p.239). As the international patrons of the conflicting parties, in this case US and India, came to a closer understanding on their policy towards Sri Lanka's secession conflict (discussed in the previous section), the conflicting parties in Sri Lanka had no alternative but to go for a negotiated settlement on the insistence of their international supporters.

The internal dimension of the reception of a devolutionary settlement

In the second half of this chapter we turn away from the external world again - Big Neighbours, Great Powers, United Nations, and so on - and return to the purely internal conditions of the reception of a devolutionary settlement, the factors which will bring the internal actors to abandon military solutions, or secession aims, and approach each other for a negotiated settlement. An ethnic secessionist conflict that has reached the stage of outright violence, and persisted with some severity for a considerable period, inevitably creates new issues which to a degree replace the original causes of the conflict. Most frequently these new issues change the shape of the original conflict and create further animosities among the internal actors, hardening their resolution.

However, the continuation of such a violent situation may create an internal environment so intolerable as to cause the conflicting parties and their respective ethnic groups to re-examine their position. In this frame of mind they may respond favourably to the Big Neighbour's and others' efforts towards the containment of the conflict, and be prepared to consider a devolutionary settlement. In Chapter One we postulated that this juncture arrives under the following three conditions.

(a) a substantive breakdown of central control over the secessionist region accompanied by strong and widespread popular nationalism among the secessionist community;

(b) a relative decline in the capabilities of the antagonists, following a long period of warfare that brings home the destructive impact of the conflict;

(c) the emergence of an auspicious conjunction such as the inauguration of a new constitution, a change of leadership of the government or the secession movement or both.

The breakdown of central control over the secessionist region

The situation that emerged in East Pakistan after the Pakistan army's 'genocide' action in March 1971 was an ideal one to exemplify the breakdown of central control over the secessionist region. The indicators include: the loss by the central regime of its authority over the civil administration in the secessionist region: the flight of a considerable proportion of the population in the secessionist region to refuge in neighbouring countries; the refusal of all the political parties representing the interest of the secessionist community to negotiate with the government; and the establishment by the secessionist movement of a government-in-exile.

From the secessionist conflicts in Cyprus, Sri Lanka, and Papua New Guinea, and the civil war in Lebanon, we can identify many similar indicators which characterize the substantial breakdown of central control over the secessionist region. The central government's inability to exert effective administrative control over the secessionist community (e.g. Cyprus, Sri Lanka and Papua New Guinea): the withdrawal of the military forces of the central government from the secessionist region (Papua New Guinea in March 1990): the disruption of normal political activities in the region, i.e. of the functioning of political parties, local governmental institutions and representation in the central legislature and so on, which gives greater scope to extremist groups in the secessionist movement (Sri Lanka after 1983): and the unwillingness of secessionist leaders (both moderate and extremist) to participate in direct negotiations with the centre (Sri Lanka prior to the Indian intervention in 1987): these are some of the notable features of the breakdown of central control, in these secessionist conflict situations. The establishment of parallel civil administrations (Cyprus since 1965, Lebanon after 1976 and Sri Lanka after 1986), collecting taxes and other levies in the secessionist region (Sri Lanka since 1986, Lebanon since 1982), or the achievement of substantive military control of the secessionist region by the secessionist movement (Sri Lanka after 1986, PNG after March 1990), would reflect a higher level and greater extent of breakdown of central control.

There is no doubt that this last group of indicators portrays one of the worst scenarios which could be faced by a central regime in a secessionist conflict situation. It would place the secessionists in a very advantageous position vis-a-vis the central regime in advancing their cause in the international sphere and seeking external friends. Although this could give them a high bargaining position at the negotiation table, it is more likely that secessionists in this state of rebellion will prefer to move to the next stage of their struggle to achieve complete independence.

Life becomes very uncomfortable for the central regime. Especially among the majority community, there may be strong reaction to the central regime's failure to maintain the territorial integrity of the state, and to uphold the majority community's nationalistic claim to the whole territory. The centre's loss of political support among the majority community may be increased by the economic costs arising from this 'breakdown' situation. The government loses the income deriving from the secessionist region, but it is still obligated to maintain essential services in the secessionist territory, namely, supply of food, medicine, fuel and other basic necessities such as health care, the functioning of the communications system, water and electricity etc. As the mainstream political institutions, such as the political parties, representation in the national legislature, and local government institutions, have ceased to function in the secessionist region, the central regime loses all its political means of communication with the secessionist community. In that community, the political moderates in the secessionist movement tend to be neutralized or overwhelmed by the exultant extremist sections, which seek further militarization of the conflict, the requisite for their own aggrandizement.

Therefore, weakened by the collapse of its authority in the secessionist region, facing threats to its own political support base in the internal society, and above all, losing its political communications with the secessionist leaders, the central regime faces two options: namely, either to find outside mediators for the arrangement of negotiations with the secessionists, or to take ever stronger military and repressive action against the secessionist movement.

Experience shows that the most likely immediate reaction of central regimes in a secessionist situation is to take the military option, not to go for mediation. For example, what notoriously happened in the case of East Pakistan, the resort to uninhibited military force against the secessionist region, ignoring possible violations of international humanitarian principles by the security forces, was also the immediate reaction of the central regimes in Cyprus, Sri Lanka and Papua New

Guinea to breakdown of control in their respective secessionist situations.

In Cyprus, when the Turkish Cypriot leaders declared a 'transitional administration' for their community in December 1967, the Cyprus central regime (using Greek Cypriot irregular forces as well as its own security forces) simply increased their military and other repressive measures against the Turkish Cypriot community. This is what triggered the policy-makers of the Turkish mainland to get out their 'big stick' (discussed in chapter 4).

The Sri Lanka government's reaction to LTTE's decision to establish a parallel administration in the Jaffna peninsula, which was to launch a military offensive to capture Jaffna city in April 1987, ended in a similar experience. It was the drive on Jaffna that resulted in India sending its fighters in 'an air-dropping mission' to Jaffna peninsula in June 1987 (discussed in chapter 4). The establishment of a parallel administration was not a sudden elevation for the LTTE movement: for some time the secessionist region had been virtually under its control. The government had abandoned all police stations in the region at the beginning of 1986, because of its inability to defend them from armed attacks organized by the militant secessionist groups. The functions of civil administration had been restricted to the maintenance of essential services, the LTTE enjoying the vandal role of disrupting those services at will. Thus the LTTE's announcement of the establishment of a parallel administration in Jaffna peninsula was taken at a time when the central government's power in the region was virtually limited to military manoeuvres.

The PNG government's military adventure (sending its military forces to Bougainville island in September 1989) faced stiff resistance from the Bougainville Revolutionary Army (BRA) which enjoyed the overwhelming support of the Bougainville population, and ended amidst international protest over human rights violations by the PNGDF. The immediate outcome was the PNG government's withdrawal of all its security forces and civil administration from the island. Then came the imposition of an economic and communications blockade on Bougainville Island in March 1990.

As the repressive actions taken by the central regimes in Cyprus, Sri Lanka and PNG show, the desperate reaction of the central regimes to the breakdown of their control over the secessionist region - so oppressively militaristic and in disregard of international humanitarian principles - represents nothing else but their frustration at the apparent success of the secessionists. Thus, the underlying reality of such desperation is the central regime's coming to recognize the failure of its policy towards the secessionist community, and its vulnerability to external and internal forces opposed to its repressive policies. This is not difficult to illustrate from the common experiences of the secessionist conflicts in East Pakistan, Cyprus, Sri Lanka and PNG - the centre's failure subsequently to achieve substantial victory over the secessionists, even after strong military and repressive measures. What they achieved was further deterioration of their relationship with the secessionist community, international condemnation over the atrocities committed against the civilian community by their security forces, and the resolve of their Big Neighbours to act quickly to stop spillovers from their latest action. The implicit lesson of the Cyprus and Sri Lanka situations was that the Big Neighbour was presented with a political atmosphere conducive to a military intervention, playing the 'big stick' or the 'interventionist' role, as a last resort to bring the central regime to the negotiation table.

The breakdown of central control over the secessionist region itself pays further dividends for the Big Neighbour. The situation shows not just military and administrative failure on the part of the central regime; it reflects how badly the central regime has become alienated from the minority community. The assumption by the secessionists of political, administrative or military control over the secessionist region relies mainly on the strength of national feeling among the members of their community, and reflects the material, moral and psychological support it has extended to the activists. No secessionist group can achieve substantial control over the affairs of their own community, or create a breakdown in central control in the secessionist region, without the substantial backing of the secessionist community. Evidence from the conflict in East Pakistan to the continuing secessionist conflicts in Cyprus, Sri Lanka and Papua New Guinea bears this out.

All these secessionist situations entered the stage of the breakdown of central control showing passionate nationalistic fervour within the secessionist community, and the repressive actions of the central regime merely further exposed its inability to retain its grip over the secessionist region. The developments in Bougainville Island are very illuminating. While in the case of Sri Lanka and Cyprus the respective Big Neighbours appeared in the conflict theatre as the protector of the rights of the secessionist community, the Bougainville secessionist movement resisted the military assault from its central regime without any external assistance. There is no doubt of the fierceness of their resistance by a small group of secessionists, armed only with light shot guns and some weapons abandoned in the island during the second world war, against a well equipped army which received logistic support from its Big Neighbour. Their success in repelling the PNGDF reflected less their military strength than the total support they enjoyed from the population in Bougainville Island. The comment of the PNG Attorney General, Bernard Narokobi, '...we probably made the wrong diagnosis and approached the problem as a law and order problem' (Bullock 1991:17), was clearly a reference to the strength of nationalist sentiment prevailing in the island's community.

The further developments in Bougainville Island suggest that, the secessionist region having come to such a stand-off, the central regime is likely to soften its intransigence towards political negotiations. The PNG government decided to request some other neighbours (Solomon Islands and New Zealand) to act as mediators between the PNG government and the secessionists, and accepted most of the immediate demands of the secessionist leaders, namely, the immediate removal of the economic and communications blockade, the restoration of essential services, the inviting of a Multinational Supervisory Team (MST), and the return to barracks of the PNGDF, well away from the island (for more details of the accord see *Far Eastern Review* 7 February 1991).

The 1974 Cyprus and 1987 Sri Lanka cases are also evidence that the central regime's loss of its grip on the secessionist region helps the Big Neighbour and the international community to get the central regime to the negotiation table. Once the central regime has ignored the Big Neighbour's call for restraint in repressive action against the secessionist community, the international community is less concerned at the Big Neighbour's threat of military intervention; and the central regime's loss of control over the secessionist region is a further count against it, leading to a call to give careful consideration to the peace-keeping proposals made by the Big Neighbour.

The existence of a long period of warfare

The prolongation of ethnic struggle in a society, with no end in sight, may lead to profound changes in environment that would influence the participants to seek a political settlement. These changes relate to the economic, social and psychological implications of continuous military conflict, making life intolerable for ordinary people, weakening the social and economic structure, and thereby depleting the capabilities of the antagonists.

A long period of warfare affects the lives of ordinary people in many ways. They have to face material destruction, economic hardship, and social and psychological breakdown spreading throughout society. The effects of war may extend to the disruption of civic functions in the society. The more the conflict is prolonged, the more is the daily disruption of social and individual life likely to cause a gradual erosion of civic society.

It has been argued that the buoyancy of the affected state's economy is a determining factor in sustaining such a protracted military situation, and underpinning the intransigence of the main adversaries of the conflict: there is a direct relationship between the economic progress of the country and the viable duration of the conflict. The argument is that a comfortable economic prosperity allows the society to acclimatize to the developing military situation: as long as this lasts, the central regime and the secessionists can ignore political methods of conflict resolution.

Discussing the economic background of the Lebanese civil war, Salim Nasr found four major economic factors maintaining the conflict system and legitimizing its continuation, namely, (1) Lebanon possessed considerable economic reserves (per capita income $1,415 in 1974, and more than $4 billion surplus in its balance of payments in 1975); (2) the transfers and remittances ($910 million in 1975 and $2,254 in 1980) made by Lebanese migrant workers (as a proportion of the national work force, 13 percent in 1975 and 34.6 percent in 1980) working in the Arab states of the Persian Gulf; (3) the existence of a substantial Palestinian economy within the country (which generated more than 15 percent of the gross domestic product from all of Lebanon); and (4) the 'political money' (an estimated $300 million a year) that came into the country as grants and transfers received by the various militias from their external backers (see Nasr 1990:5-6).

In his *Rise and Fall of the Cyprus Republic* (1977), Kyriacos C. Markides has characterized economic prosperity as one of the factors which held back efforts to find a political settlement to the Cyprus conflict during the 1968-74 period. Identifying the favourable state of the Cyprus economy as a '...factor that strengthened the determination of the Makarios government to insist on an independent unitary state...' (Markides 1977:146), as against the Turkish Cypriots' demand for a federal system of government, he noted that,

> ...the condition of the Turkish Community was not desperate enough to prompt a strong sense of urgency for solving the problem quickly. The island as a whole was prospering and a portion of that prosperity was reaching ...the Turkish villages and Turkish quarters of the towns... (Markides 1977:144).

He further claimed that the Cyprus society as a whole had earned considerable economic wealth from the involvement of various external parties in its affairs since the 1950s. First the British government brought large foreign revenues to the island during the time of the Suez crisis in 1956, and the local emergency of 1955-59 as emergency military expenditure. Then after the breakdown of constitutional order in 1963, the Turkish, Greek, British and UN forces stationed in the Island brought considerable amounts of foreign exchange to the country through their local expenditures. The existence of British sovereign bases in the island (which employed 6,215 Cypriots in 1963 - equal to one fourth of the total employed in the Cyprus civil service during the same period) has also been identified as a plentiful source of foreign exchange for the Cyprus economy in these early days. In the end he argued,

> The economy of course was thriving for reasons other than the perpetuation of local and international conflict. The point made here is that conflict far from being an impediment to economic growth, seemed to aid it (Markides 1977:145).

Although specific investigations are lacking for the Sri Lanka situation, it is not difficult to identify a similar social and economic background to the dragging on of Sri Lanka's civil strife for more than eight years (since the eruption of ethnic violence in 1983). The economic data available for this period testify that the liberalizing policies which had been introduced in 1977, together with the economic assistance programme undertaken by donor countries and the World Bank, had created an economic situation in the country comfortable enough to be able to afford such a civil war. The country achieved economic growth at an average annual rate of 6.2 percent from 1977 to 1982 while unemployment was cut by half and inflation reached zero (Pfaffenberger 1987:145). All sectors of the economy received a huge boost from the new economic polices. Internal and external trade, banking, and the tourist industry showed tremendous improvement. There was a massive flow of foreign goods into the domestic market. During this period, as the entrepreneur classes gained confidence from the new liberalization policies, the country was conscious of accelerating economic activity, leading to widespread interest in acquiring material possessions (see Moore 1990:372).

All of this provided the material and social base, if not exactly the incentive, for the central regime and the secessionists to take the society into a violent confrontation. Two points are worth mentioning. First, the revival of economic enthusiasm in the society for new investments and profit-making, and the sound performance displayed by the economy itself, distracted the attention of the population from any long-term implications of the conflict. Second, as most of the basic needs were satisfied, and individual members of the society looked for a greater share of the benefits deriving from this economic upturn, the ethno-nationalist aspirations of each community inevitably came to the surface of politics (see Moore 1990:372-3).

There is perhaps no need to say that economic prosperity and a continuous internal military conflict cannot for long go together. Persistent military conflict eventually produces economic and social costs which may become unbearable burdens for the active antagonists and ordinary masses alike, causing ordinary people to think twice about their actual interests in the never-ending conflict. Prolonged ethnic warfare between the central forces and the secessionists, or infighting among different ethnic factions, may add new elements to the social culture. The society, especially in the secessionist region, becomes militarized, forcing its members to live with continuous bombardment, killing, outbreaks of communal violence, retaliations, curfews, searches, internments, destruction of roads and buildings, disruption of essential services, and shortage of foods, medicines and so on. The war becomes a way of life for the people; they have no alternative but to come to terms with the emerging militarization process. Sometimes, this is exacerbated, as the most committed factions in the conflict try to keep the ordinary people under their political and military influence, not only by the methods of political propaganda but also by military intimidation. Added to this turmoil is the indiscriminate retribution undertaken by the government security forces in secessionist areas.

Against this political and psychological background, the continuation of ethnic struggle might well receive the tacit approval of the ordinary people. Such a militarization of the community may allow the main actors in the conflict to maintain their intransigence towards all conciliatory efforts made by the Big Neighbour (or the international community).

But this cannot become a permanent quality of any society. Continuous warfare, violence, disruption of social and economic activities of the people, and material destruction eventually prohibit stable life in the society, even at a very low level. As they see their genuine ethno-nationalist inspirations giving way to a self-referring 'gun toting' culture which now impoverishes their own way of life, the ordinary people may lose their acquiescence in the ongoing military adventure. The prolongation of conflict, with no end in sight, makes ordinary people war weary (see Malarkey 1988).

A visitor (during March 1992) to the rebel controlled Jaffna peninsula noted,

> Living conditions for people in the North Sri Lanka can only be described as a total breakdown of any normal life. ...People don't talk much about their fate, but most of them emphasize that they are more than fed up with the current living conditions. They feel caught between both sides... Whatever happens in the near future, people are quite conscious about the fact of having no way to escape. Apart from the physical injuries people have to sustain in the course of bombing raids by Sri Lankan air force, many inhabitants suffer from psychic problems caused by the these incidents (Morgenstern 1992:10)

Since they cannot end it, the ordinary people may try to evade the situation by becoming refugees in neighbouring countries or in their own land (as displaced persons). People who can afford to may go to other parts of the world. The people who stay behind can only hope for a superior power to intervene in the situation. As one member of the Lebanese Druze community put it,

> We Lebanese would have gone on slaughtering each other for ever: we needed someone harder, crueler than ourselves to keep us from each other's throats (Hirst 1991).

This is further illustrated by the initial welcome given to the Indian Peace Keeping Forces by the ordinary Tamil people, on their arrival in Sri Lanka's troubled Northern and Eastern provinces in July 1987 (see *India Today* 15 September 1987).

In the long run no conflicting party can ignore the sufferings of the masses, who become the relatively-innocent victims of the vicious circle of retaliation perpetuated by the central regime and the secessionist factions. As Joseph Kaibui, a leading member of the Bougainville Revolutionary Army (BRA), explains:

> Our eyes are not blind, we've seen blood spilled, so much suffering... I would say 1000 deaths is not an exaggerated figure for lives lost as a result of clashes

between BRA and PNG's security forces and people dying from epidemics and lack of medical supplies (*The Australian* 4 February 1991).

Another secessionist leader (of the LTTE) explaining the reasons for their decision to declare a unilateral cease-fire in Northern and Eastern Sri Lanka in January 1991 said,

> It was the plight of the people of the Eastern Province, particularly the plight of the Tamils there that compelled us to take this decision. Their predicament is most pitiable. They have been chased away from their villages, are suffering as refugees... Many are living in the jungles. There is no medicine or medical help... Two hundred and one people have died there due to lack of medical attention and starvation... It is different when people die as a direct result of war. But they are dying because of this situation. It is a duty by us to help these people (*Tamil Times* 1991,10(2):11, an interview with the then LTTE deputy leader, Sathasivam Krisnakumar).

The fading away of the economic capabilities which initially provided the economic support base to run the conflict system also plays a big role in creating the politico-social environment in which a negotiated settlement becomes thinkable. The sharp and sustained rise in the government's defence budget starts to take its toll of the economy, diverting government funds from development and public welfare, and creating uneasiness among the country's donors. Finally the war bill means the central regime begins to face even the problem of maintaining minimum living standards.

We can use for illustration the economic situation faced by the central regime in Sri Lanka just before the signing of the Indo-Sri Lanka accord of 1987. Within three years of the outbreak of communal violence in 1983 the central regime in Sri Lanka realized that it could no longer rely on its post-liberalization economic resilience to pay for its civil conflict. In 1986 Sri Lanka's finance minister announced that his actual defence expenditure for 1985 (estimated at 5.7 percent of the 1985 budget, an increase from 4.5 percent in 1984 and 3.5 percent in 1983) turned out to be 10 percent of the total budget, and would continue at 10 percent for the next financial year. But by the end of 1986, it had actually risen to 15 percent of the government budget. One of the direct results of this high defence bill was the growing deficit in the government budget, which was estimated at Rs 27 billion out of a total budget of Rs 66 billion for 1986 (Ross & Samaranayake 1986:1241,1242) - directly inflationary as Sri Lanka doesn't possess its own defence industrial sector (Ross & Samaranayake 1986:1242).

A special area in the economy which had already suffered from the continuing ethnic warfare was the tourist industry, which provided $108 million gross earnings, and nearly 60,000 employment opportunities in 1984. Tourist arrivals for 1984 were 22 percent below the 1982 figures; in 1985 they were 19 percent down on 1984 (Ross & Samaranayake 1986:1245,1246).

The continuous ethnic violence had also been identified as the reason for the government's failure to realize its high expectations in the field of foreign investment. Some development programmes aided by foreign governments for the Northern and Eastern provinces were abandoned. The violence in these provinces contributed to the decline of rice and fish production (see Seabright 1986:79-80; Ross & Samaranayake 1986:1249,1251), so that the country was compelled to continue its dependence on the traditional plantation sector (Ross & Samaranayake 1986:1255) considered by the authors of the liberalization policies as an unstable source of foreign income (Moore 1990:355).

This is how Mr Ronnie de Mel the then Finance Minister of Sri Lanka explained his reasons for the signing of the Indo-Sri Lanka accord in August 1987:

> I can tell you that if this war lasted for another six months, import controls would have been imposed and the people would have had to suffer shortages, scarcities, queues and even mass starvation. In similar situations of civil war in Biafra and Ethiopia, millions died of starvation. We were able to prevent this for years... but would not have been able to do this for long... In another year, more people may have died of starvation in Sri Lanka than by the war itself if the peace accord had not been signed (Chakravartty 1987:117).

The situation in Lebanon prior to the latest Syrian 'invitational' role was more or less the same as that of Sri Lanka in 1987. The economic prosperity that fuelled the Lebanese conflict system began to evaporate after the Israeli intervention in 1982. According to Salim Nasr the number of Lebanese migrant workers in the Middle East dropped from 210,000 in 1980 to 65,000 in 1987, causing a decline in remittances from $2,254 million in 1980 to $300 million in 1977. The 'Palestinian economy', because of the departure of the PLO and their 'political money' due to the change of external backers, collapsed and was completely lost to the Lebanese economy (Nasr 1990:7). The persistent civil war with an average annual cost of $900 million (Nasr 1990:6) started to take its toll of the economy and society after 1982.

Since *de facto* 'states' in different parts of the country were collecting the central government's revenues for themselves, the Lebanese government faced a budget deficit of 90 percent in 1986, with an accumulated public debt of 147 billion Lebanese pounds by 1987. Once considered one of the soundest economies in the Third World, the Lebanese economy in 1987 produced hyperinflation of 425 percent. The minimum monthly wage in 1977 equalled in real terms only 35 percent of the average monthly wage in 1974, while unemployment rose to 35 percent in 1989, from 5.4 percent in 1970 (Nasr 1990:7-8). Thus, concluding his investigation Salim Nasr declared:

The bill for 14 years of internal wars (was) finally rendered, and when it had to be settled, it led to virtual bankruptcy... In the space of few years, brutally and drastically, Lebanon has been thrown from the most privileged upper layer of Third World countries down to some of the lowest layers... If the Ta'if agreement can be supplemented to win support or acquiescence from the major parties, then a momentum towards reconciliation is possible (Nasr 1990:8).

For the central regime in PNG there were strong economic fundamentals to be reckoned with before counting the economic cost of its year-long military exercise against the Bougainville secessionist movement. The emergence of secessionist violence in Bougainville Island itself ensured economic gloom for the PNG government because of the BRA's action to completely disrupt the working of the Panguna mine (discussed in chapter 2). Measures taken by the PNG government in January 1990 - viz. a 10 percent devaluation of PNG's currency (the Kina), introduction of wage restraint, the reduction of government budget expenditure, and applications for a US $50 million structural adjustment loan from the World Bank and another of US $70-80 million from the IMF (Thompson 1991:81) - reflected the extent of the damage that it expected from the persistence of secessionist violence in Bougainville Island. It was estimated that the closure of Panguna mine would cause a 7 percent decline in real income to the economy, and a decline in government reserves amounting to about Kina 271 million (Weisman 1990:47, 49). When their strategy against the secessionists - making life difficult for the Bougainvilleans in order to arouse their anger against the BRA - backfired (Bullock 1991:15) the PNG leaders found that the conflict threatened economic disaster for the whole country. They tried to deal with local opposition to the Panguna mine by negotiating a new mining agreement with the land owners (Bullock 1991:15), but that did not work either.

Prolongation of a conflict has economic consequences for secessionist movements also. First, they have to guarantee a continuous flow of arms and money from their external backers, if they are not to run out of equipment and ammunition at some crucial time. Second they have the burden of maintaining social and economic order, and sometimes basic services, in the areas where they have effective control.

With the central regime deliberately acting to cut economic supply lines to the secessionist region, as happened in Sri Lanka's Northern province in 1987, and in Bougainville Island in March 1990, the secessionist movement has to devise its own plans for self reliance. But they can hardly avert the frustration of the local population, as the conflict drags on with no apparent sign of victory, with such low living standards.

It can be argued that the emigration of the affluent classes, professionals and intellectuals, to avoid this collapse of living standards, would help the hard-core secessionists in continuing the war, as the community would be left with only the ordinary people who are less capable of organizing opposition to it, and who can more easily adapt to the situation because of their meagre life style and social value system (see Malakey 1988:298-300). But in any case, another effect of the long-term militarization of the secessionist community is the collapse or disruption of the existing social class structure. The militants who are only too willing to take on the responsibilities of military command, also perforce take the lead in the political arena. The orderly way of life of the society is replaced by intense military and paramilitary activities for which the class and social hierarchical structure, and also the religious and cultural norms formerly dominant in the regional society, are irrelevant. But the secessionist militias may not have it all their own way, for the traditional elites may seek to revive factional politics and hence to re-establish their authority, by encouraging opposition to the 'war lords' on what sometimes appears as a social class basis. Such political and social divisions may strengthen the hands of the central regime, which may be ready to offer political concessions to these moderate secessionist leaders. If the prolonged conflict also results in the militants splitting into rival armed groups, 'realists' against 'intransigents', the hands of a Big Neighbour assigned the 'invitational' role are also strengthened.

This was well illustrated by the political divisions among the secessionist Tamil community in Sri Lanka, between the LTTE movement and other Tamil groups such as TULF, PLOTE, EPRLF and TELO. These political divisions were recognized as a reflection of conflicting social interests emerging from the disrupted traditional social caste and class structure and of regional divisions among the Tamil community in Sri Lanka (see Pfaffenberger 1987:143). How the Indian policy-makers used these political divisions during the pre-accord period to counter LTTE intransigence has already been discussed in Chapter four. Their signing of the Indo-Sri Lanka accord without consultation with the LTTE leadership counted on the unequivocal support of these other Tamil groups for the Indian role in Sri Lanka's ethnic conflict.

For example, the TULF was the party of the traditional elite and high caste society in the Jaffna peninsula, and the EPRLF among the Tamils in the Eastern Province, as against the low caste origin of the LTTE leadership and its high concentration in the Jaffna peninsula (see Pfeffenberger 1984:20-1). The LTTE's initial participation in the ceasefire agreement stipulated by the Indo-Sri Lanka accord was attributed to the ordinary people's anxiety to revive their normal social life, in the relatively peaceful atmosphere created by the arrival of IPKF to replace government security forces (Pfaffenberger 1987:137-8; *India Today* 15 September 1987). Later the IPKF openly armed these rival Tamil groups against the LTTE movement (Keesing's 1990:37353). Their participation in the peace process helped the Sri Lanka and Indian governments to go ahead with their plans to hold Provincial Council elections in the Northern and Eastern Provinces in 1988, disregarding the intimidation by the LTTE movement of the ordinary population (see *India Today* 15 December 1988).

This process did not stop after the withdrawal of the IPKF in March 1990. Since then the Sri Lanka government has received military support from some of the anti-LTTE Tamil groups in its drive against the LTTE in the Northern and Eastern Provinces (see *Tamil Times* 1990,10(1):4; 1990,10(2):6). The government convened an all party conference with the participation of the other Tamil groups and the moderate TULF in March 1991. These political groups later arrived at an understanding with the main political parties regarding further improvements in the existing system of devolution of government i.e., the Provincial Council system (*Tamil Times* 1990,10(1):5-6), and co-operated with the Parliamentary select committee which was appointed in 1991 to investigate new proposals to find a political settlement.

The emergence of an auspicious conjunction

This refers to the arrival of an opportune moment or event which may break a deadlock, or change the atmosphere, so as to enable the main adversaries to overcome pride, or otherwise put the past aside, and go to the negotiation table; or having got there, to accept a devolutionary settlement without fear of disowning by their client population.

Here, we point to two particular kinds of events: (a) a structural transformation in the affected state's constitutional framework e.g. the establishment of a new constitution, a new governmental structure, or constitutional amendments which presage important changes in the governmental structure; and (b) a change in leadership in either of the conflicting camps.

There is, of course, a purely 'technical' relationship between the existing constitutional and governmental structure of the affected state, and political efforts to devolve governmental power as a settlement of the secession conflict. If the current arrangements do not envisage or make provision for devolution, then the constitution or governmental structure or both must be changed so that they do, before a political initiative directed at a devolutionary settlement can have effect. Conversely, an explicit move by the government to alter the constitution and/or government structures to facilitate devolution is demonstration of their willingness to concede autonomy to a regional community. But a devolutionary settlement thrashed out at the negotiating table between the two sets of leaders still has to be 'ratified' on both sides, and it may be no easier for the central regime to deliver a constitutional change than it is for the 'moderate' secessionists to shackle their intransigent militants. Changes to the constitution and/or the governmental structure have to be approved by the legislative organs of the government, and are likely to become issues of public concern. Ethnic emotions among the majority community may be aroused by opposition politicians in order to block the central regime's efforts to devolve government power: there may be ethnic demonstrations and backbench revolts.

Against this background a central government is stronger, and hence a devolutionary settlement more likely to be actually implemented, if it already has powers enabling it to by-pass such legislative difficulties, perhaps acquired quite independently of the ethnic conflict.

The present constitution of Sri Lanka provides an illustration. Donald J. Horowitz identified the making of this constitution in 1978 as the creation of an auspicious setting for the establishment of the District Development Council system in 1981 (hereafter the DDC system or DDCs), the first legislative initiative of its kind in Sri Lanka to devolve powers to the regions. This legislative devolution package emerged as a result of negotiations held between the leaders of the government and the TULF (see Wilson 1982:58-62). The agreement was to establish an elected DDC for each of the districts, and merge the DDCs into the District Minister System introduced in 1978. The leadership of the moderate Tamil United Liberation Front decided to participate in the DDC system, ignoring the 'boycott' call raised by the emerging Tamil militant movement, which refused to accept it as satisfying Tamil national aspirations. Unlike the previous attempts in 1957 (see Kearney 1967:86, 117-19) and 1967 (see Jupp 1978:235) by the central regime in Sri Lanka to establish similar devolutions, this particular legislative exercise did not face nationalist opposition from the Sinhalese majority. Given their long opposition to any regional power sharing concessions to the minority Tamils, the establishment of this new system of local government was recognized even by the Tamil leaders as a political breakthrough in Sri Lanka politics (see Tiruchelvam 1984:196). It was the centralization of executive power under an executive Presidency in the 1978 constitution, and the subordination of Parliament to that executive leadership (see Wilson 1980), which enabled the central regime to go ahead with its plans to establish the DDCs without any backtracking in the Parliament. Although the ruling United National Party by their own political error missed this historical opportunity of compromise with the moderate Tamil leaders, this scheme later provided the basic framework for the 'Provincial Council System' that evolved from the negotiations undertaken by the Indian mediators prior to the Indo-Sri Lanka agreement of August 1987.

The District Minister system itself came into being in 1978 by virtue of new powers vested in the executive President to appoint non-cabinet ministers from among the members of the Parliament. Another innovation in the 1978 constitution with useful effect on the devolution scheme was noted by Donald L. Horowitz:

> The Sri Lanka scheme might not have been possible without changes in the structure of the central government. Previous attempts to devolve power on Tamil authorities had failed because Sinhalese opposition had produced back-bench revolts. Since 1978, however, Sri Lanka has had a presidential system and constitutional provision that prevents legislators... from crossing the aisle without risking their seats (Horowitz 1985:625).

The importance of governmental changes in regulating the secessionist conflict was again manifested in 1987 when Sri Lanka President J. R. Jayawardana and Indian Prime Minister Rajiv Gandhi signed the Indo-Sri Lanka agreement. The signing of such a controversial treaty would not have been conceivable under the previous system of government, under which such actions by the head of government were subject to Parliamentary approval. Under the constitution of 1978 the President is entrusted with the powers '...to declare war and peace...' (*The Constitution of the Democratic Socialist Republic of Sri Lanka*, clause 33-e), without the consent of Parliament: and the Indo-Sri Lanka accord of August 1987 never came up for discussion in Parliament. The government then duly presented in November 1987 the 13th amendment to the constitution, to give effect to the devolutionary settlement stipulated in the Indo-Sri Lanka accord, receiving the support of more than two-thirds of the Members of Parliament.

In the context of the violent protest which erupted in Colombo, the capital city, and other major cities in the Southern parts of Sri Lanka against the signing of the Indo-Sri Lanka agreement, and especially of the campaign carried out by the *Janatha Vimukthi Peramuna* (JVP), killing members of the ruling United National Party and supporters of the agreement (discussed in chapter 4), this constitutional change got through Parliament mainly by the single-minded exercise of the centralist powers enjoyed by the executive Presidency. There were occasions when the President himself got involved in political manoeuvres, putting pressure upon members of the government Parliamentary group, threatening to use his presidential powers to remove ministers from the cabinet or to dissolve Parliament, and as the leader of the ruling UNP, the powers entrusted to the political parties to remove MPs from the parliament.[1]

However, even constitutional changes as draconian as these do not always give a completely free hand to the central regime to offer devolutionary concessions to the minority community.

For example, although the central regime in Sri Lanka was able to implement the DDC system, and later in 1987 the 'Provincial Councils', the present constitution still imposes restraints. Parliament alone cannot pass certain amendments to the constitution even on a two-thirds majority. Constitutional amendments to the provisions which declare the unitary nature of the Sri Lanka state, the sovereign rights enjoyed by the people, the duration of Parliament and the term of office of the President need to be subsequently approved by the people at a Referendum. The

---

1. It is worth noting at this point that the then President Mr J. R. Jayawardana had obtained undated resignation letters from all the MPs of the ruling party after the inauguration of the new constitution. Later these letters were used whenever the ruling party wanted to remove one of their sitting MPs from the Parliament, sending the letter signed by the sitting MP to the speaker of the Parliament.

effect of this constitutional requirement limited the central regime's political capacity to accommodate a devolutionary scheme acceptable to the secessionist minority. Holding a referendum would have been disastrous: it would have allowed the intransigent sections to work on the feelings of the majority community and block any constitutional amendment intended to devolve the power of the government. Therefore, the central regime in Sri Lanka had to be extremely careful about the drafting of the necessary constitutional and legislative schemes for the implementation of a devolutionary settlement agreed upon at the negotiating table.

The draft proposals submitted by the Sri Lanka government in negotiations during the 1983-87 period clearly exemplify the efforts made by the the Sri Lankan and Indian constitutional experts to avoid such an outcome (see Marasinghe 1988:373-583). They were compelled to limit the extent of the devolution to avoid the final constitutional amendment (as mentioned above) triggering a judicial directive to hold a referendum. This constitutional barrier still remains as a structural obstacle to meeting the Tamils' demand for more powers for the 'Provincial Council', the objective of Tamil groups which accept the basic framework of the Indo-Sri Lanka agreement, or for the establishment of a 'federal system', as now being promoted by the LTTE leadership.

The other 'auspicious conjunction' thrown up by the case studies was 'change of leadership'. Change of leader in either of the conflicting camps may make a direct impact upon both the antagonists and their clientele ethnic population, nullifying the existing power equation between the antagonists, and creating an opening for a fresh start to the negotiations, or for the abandonment of intransigence towards an already proposed settlement.

In a secessionist conflict situation the leaders are usually all-important in the maintenance of the conflict system. They are often both charismatic personalities and cunning strategists, not only personifying their respective ethnic group's conflicting interests but also determining the policies, stratagems and organizational structures in the day-to-day running of the political and military campaigns, and through all providing the necessary inspiration to the ordinary members of the community. It is natural for an ethnic group in the grip of nationalistic passion to lean towards leaders who are most committed to the cause, and there are always extremists in the group on the look-out for 'backsliding' in the leadership. As such, there is a tendency in most secessionist situations for the leaders to become more and more inward-looking and intransigent as the conflict continues.

Once external mediators enter the scene, it is these very same leaders who have to participate in negotiations to find a political settlement to the conflict. Not only the running of the conflict system and the gaining of military advantage but also the resolution of the conflict thus depend on the personal abilities and characters of the leaders

However, before entering this final stage, the leaders of the conflicting camps have to determine that they should genuinely commit themselves to the peace process. Such a commitment by the leaders is essential for the implementation of any devolutionary agreement, to have any hope of overcoming the less-schooled emotions of the ordinary masses. In this connection, the personal characteristics of the leaders, their preconceptions, their shrewdness in grasping the political realities of the continuance of the conflict in changing domestic and international circumstances, their social class background, and even their age, are all significant.

For example, in an assessment of the Cyprus conflict Robert McDonald identified Rauf Denktash, the leader of the Turkish Cypriot community, as the main obstacle to the resolution of the conflict:

> The principal stumbling block to a settlement is Denktash. His thinking is set in the mould of three decades ago. He professes to believe that the Greek-Cypriots still seek Enosis and, while he pays lip-service to the idea of confederation, basically remains the separatist he was when he helped found TMT in the 1950s (McDonald 1989:76).

Similar concern has been raised regarding the leadership of the LTTE movement in the Tamil secessionist struggle. One of the features of this movement is its members' absolute allegiance to its leader, V. Prabhakaran, amounting to a personality cult among LTTE cadres (see Oberst 1988:193-4, 198-9). On the other hand, the same leader of the LTTE has been characterized as military minded, unfamiliar with political manoeuvres, and thus unwilling to accept the emergence of any type of democratic political framework by which he would lose his authority over the Tamil community (see Hellmann-Rajanayagam 1989:617-19). But the purely military nature of the LTTE movement and its leadership's attempts to retain its military authority over the Tamil community have created the impression that the leadership of the LTTE, and the LTTE movement itself, may be appropriate in a military situation but is quite unsuited for a political process requiring peaceful democratic activities. One of the implications, some argue, is that peace cannot be made with the Tamils unless the negotiators can find a political framework which would allow the LTTE movement to be integrated into political life with their arms and military structure intact.

The efforts (during September and October 1991) made by Mr S. Thondaman, the leader of the Ceylon Workers Congress to mediate a settlement between the LTTE and the Sri Lanka government were characterized as a '...final peace initiative under which the LTTE was given an option to come to a settlement *without laying down arms*' (emphasis added, *Tamil Times* 1991,10(11):5). Explaining his emphasis on 'without laying down arms', he said:

> Prabhakaran depends entirely on his weapons. The moment he lays down arms, he becomes zero. If we cannot meet his demands, we must at least go part of his way. He will now know what the Tamils want and it is up to him

to make a positive response (*Tamil Times* 1991,10(11):5).

This is a not uncommon phenomenon in a secessionist conflict situation, where any settlement which required secessionist leaders to participate in competitive politics in order to retain their dominance might be an unbearable thought for powerful people, who expect the continuation of their unchallenged status as a reward for their years of struggle against the central state. The LTTE movement's constant refusal to lay down their arms as required by a condition of the political settlement, and their insistence on the acceptance of the LTTE as the sole representative of the Sri Lanka Tamil community, are further indicators of their reluctance to relinquish the dominant position which they have enjoyed in the secessionist region. It is not perhaps surprising that the LTTE leader once explained his plans for the future political system in 'Tamil Eelam' in the following words:

It would be a socialist state of Tamil Eelam. And there would be a single political party supported by the people. I am opposed to the multi-party democracy. It is through the one-party rule that we can develop the Eelam faster (*India Today* 30 June 1986).

Prabhakaran's expectations of a totalitarian future for 'Tamil Eelam' have a direct relation to the personal power he enjoys as LTTE leader. Such also is Robert McDonald's impression about Rauf Denktash's reluctance to accept a 'federal' settlement to the Cyprus conflict:

There is no evidence that he has derived any personal advantage from his activities but he must be prey to the psychological factor that he has nothing to gain from a settlement. Unless the notion of an alternating Presidency is resurrected, there is no likelihood that he would ever be elected head of state, and he would be reduced from the status of 'President' of the independent TRNC to that of leader of a constituent part of the new sovereign entity (McDonald 1989:76).

It is easy to see, then, that the departure of the present leaders and the arrival of new leaders in the secessionist movement can make a substantial difference in the secessionist situation. The departure of a secessionist leader who has become a rallying point for a fighting guerrilla movement, such as the LTTE, would be likely tocause general demoralization among the ordinary members of the secessionist organization, which might change the power equation between the conflicting forces. That in turn may influence the new leaders to enter political negotiations in order to avoid further demoralization among the secessionist cadres; or it may provide other rival groups, willing to participate in political negotiations, with an opportunity to take over the dominance of the secessionist movement.

Once the leader of the secessionist movement has been identified by the central regime, or any of the outside mediators, as an obstacle to settlement to the conflict, the departure of such a leader from the conflict scene may start calculations about the possibility of entering an agreement with new leaders. Sometimes, the leaders may come from a younger generation, perhaps more capable of understanding the domestic and international realities of the conflict than the veterans.

Although a change of leadership in the central regime may create a similar new juncture in the secessionist conflict, the way in which such changes come to the surface of politics is different. In a secessionist conflict, it is good propaganda for the secessionist movement to identify all the atrocities done by the security forces and the repressive policies imposed by the central regime with the name of the leader of the ruling party, and put all the blame for the escalation of military violence upon the leader of the government. Then they can use their mistrust of him as an excuse for their refusal to participate in negotiations.

So it was with the refusal of the Tamil secessionist movement (both moderate and militant leaders) to go to the negotiation table during the mid-1980s. The militant organizations openly declared their distrust of the leader of the ruling party:

> Sri Lanka President J.R. Jayawardana (JRJ) will come to the negotiating table only if he has been able to gain some military advantage. Till then, he will only be continuing the military option. ...JRJ may think that he can find a military solution to the ethnic problem. But he can only succeed in bring about genocide on a large scale... (*India Today* 30 June 1986).

To a certain extent this is similar to the Turkish Cypriots distrust of Makarios and his successor, Spyros Kyprianou, identifying both as the committed adherents of 'Enosis', not genuinely in the inter-communal talks to find a negotiated settlement to the conflict. According to the Turkish-Cypriot leader, Rauf Denktash, Archbishop Makarios once took a secret oath as a member of an underground organization committed to 'Enosis' and was later involved in violence against Turkish Cypriots (Denktash 1982:22). These feelings among the Turkish-Cypriot leaders were so strong that they didn't see any major difference between Makarios and his opponents who organized the 1974 coup in Cyprus (see Denktash 1982:62). These perceptions from the Turkish Cypriot side continued despite the death of Makarios. One Turkish-Cypriot writer even went to the extent of representing the arrival of Spyros Kyprianou as President of the Republic as '...continuation of the spirit of the EOKA movement and attachment to Greece' (Nedjatigil 1981:53).

Thus, understandably, the change of leadership of the central regime may induce the more moderate leaders of secessionist organizations to try out the new leadership, seeking a political settlement to the conflict. For example when President Jayawardana was replaced by the President Mr R. Premadasa in 1989, the LTTE leadership sent their emissaries from their jungle hide-outs to the negotiating table. Although this action of the LTTE leadership in participating in peace negotiations with the Sri Lanka government ended without substantial achievement towards peace, it points to the contribution which can be made by a change of leadership of the central regime towards the conflict resolution process. The new President's critical approach towards the Indo-Sri Lanka agreement, describing it as an act against the sovereignty of Sri Lanka, and the election promise given to the country on sending back the Indian Peace Keeping Force, had certainly influenced the LTTE to make such a move. One LTTE leader declared: 'Premadasa appears to be a man we can deal with' (see *The Times* 3 April 1990). In this case the change of central regime leadership in Sri Lanka led the secessionists to seize the change to move against the Big Neighbour's 'invitational' role (discussed in chapter 4). But we have illustrations of such changes which rather strengthened the hands of the Big Neighbour and other international actors interested in the management of the ethnic conflict in the affected state.

A case in point was the appointment of Mr Elias Hrawi as the new Lebanese President in 1989, breaking the long deadlock created by the Lebanese Parliament's inability to elect a new President at the end of the Presidential term of Mr Amin Gemayel in 1988. Mr Hrawi, himself involved in negotiating the Tai'f accord of 1989, and compared with the former President Gemayel, had good relations with the Syrian leadership (see Keesing's 1989:37029). Thus his appointment as the President of Lebanon strengthened Syria's hand in the continuation of its 'invitational' role in Lebanon.

A change of the central regime's leadership which occurred in Cyprus in 1988 with the election of George Vassiliou as President of the Cyprus Republic, was also seen as favourable for the resolution of the Cyprus conflict. Compared with Makarios and his successor Kyprianou, who took 'an unproductive hard-line approach' (McDonald 1989:40), Vassiliou has so far established a conciliatory policy towards the Turkish-Cypriots. His attitude, according to Robert McDonald, '...is that a settlement is desirable - though not any price. Every thing is negotiable, but concessions to the Turkish-Cypriots will have to be matched by flexibility on their part towards Greek-Cypriot sensitivities' (McDonald 1989:40).

The main contribution made by the arrival of Vassiliou to the Greek Cypriot leadership was the removal of the rift between US and Cyprus leaders regarding the role of NATO powers in the resolution of the Cyprus conflict. President Vassiliou successfully kept Cyprus out of the cold-war conflict between the two Super Powers, while accepting the concerns of the US towards Turkey as a friendly power in the Middle East vis-a-vis the Soviet Union. By doing this he anticipated a US involvement in the resolution of the Cyprus conflict in the future once the global tensions between two super powers are reduced (McDonald 1989:41). Probably this occasion has arrived, after the war in the Gulf (against Iraq) and the dissolution of the Soviet Union. The US involvement in helping the UN to bring the conflicting parties to a peace-conference (discussed in chapter 4) has demonstrated that the change of leadership in Cyprus has strengthened the hands of the US government in the making of such efforts to find a settlement.

Conclusion

In the chapter we have looked at certain independent variables which do not depend on the understanding we have gained of the Big Neighbour syndrome: at the positive and negative roles played by major international actors other than a Big Neighbour in the process of secessionist conflict management, and at internal conditions which work in favour of resolving the conflict by political means. Some such international conflict management initiatives organized by the UN and other IGOs complement the role of the Big Neighbour; but other such efforts dissipate momentum towards a settlement because of Great Power rivalry and non-commitment. In this external dimension of Big Neighbour/affected state relations, we focused on two factors leading to international conflict management initiatives: location of the affected state in a highly sensitive geostrategic spot, and its high dependence on the international economic and political system. The evidence showed that these factors, by drawing the international community into conflict management, or strengthening its hand in pressurizing the conflicting parties, can enhance the Big Neighbour's efforts to contain the conflict.

In our examination of the internal dimension of the reception of devolution of government, we examined the way in which the presence of certain internal conditions might dispose the conflicting parties and their clientele populations to respond favourably to the Big Neighbour's and others' efforts to contain the conflict, or provide an opportune moment to implement a devolutionary settlement.

However, our evidence suggests that these external factors and internal conditions do not always coincide with the Big Neighbour's intervention in the conflict. Indeed their influence must be expected even without the presence of a Big Neighbour, although we have limited this investigation to considering the implications of these external and internal dimensions in relation to the role of the Big Neighbour.

Our investigation further suggests that these external factors and internal conditions might persuade leaders and masses on both sides of the ethnic divide to emerge from their closed social and psychological world of conflict, and seek national reconciliation, even after the termination of the Big Neighbour's intervention in the conflict - particularly in the stalemate created by the 'prolongation' or 'premature termination' by the Big Neighbour of its 'interventionist' or 'invitational' roles. In such a situation it is the leaders of both camps who are entrusted with the responsibility of finding the way to a national reconciliation, and the working of these external factors and the favourability of these internal conditions may strengthen their hands in overcoming opposition in the internal society to a devolutionary settlement.

This chapter has made it clearer than ever that our analysis points to the immensity of the external and internal restraints faced by the Big Neighbour in an ethnic secessionist conflict situation, suggesting that we should expect conflict management, not complete resolution, to result from the roles played by the Big Neighbour in an ethnic conflict situation.

The next is the concluding chapter. Here, we shall integrate all our major findings and appraise the validity of our theoretical model in practical politics, while identifying areas where further research is required.

6 Conclusion

The broad goal of this study was to develop a model of the conditions under which the devolution of government may be the preferred settlement to an ethnic secessionist conflict in a modern state. To narrow the scope of this broad objective somewhat, however, the study selected the existence of a Big Neighbour as the central focus of its investigation. Thus, the model of conditions developed in the study is centred around the role played by the Big Neighbour in the secessionist situation and the implications of such a Big Neighbour role in the reception of devolution of government by the conflicting parties in the secessionist situation.

The overall findings of the study have proved that the theoretical model which we developed in the earlier part of this study was robust enough to delineate the role of a Big Neighbour state in the management of secessionist conflict and the obtaining of the reception of 'devolution of government' by the conflicting parties, over several different case studies in various parts of the world. Many of the findings in the study, it is submitted, have provided clearer insights into these Big Neighbour situations, giving our theoretical model a practical validity. A breakdown of the findings of the study will demonstrate how the original theoretical model, in its various stages, was modified so as to improve its validity in practical politics.

To begin with, we noted on the basis of the exploratory investigations we made into our selected case studies that the Big Neighbour secessionist situations fell into one or both of two main types, viz. (a) ethnic-tie situations, (b) strategic-tie situations. Further, we explored the several different roots of Big Neighbour involvement in those secessionist situations, and categorized them as (i) those that emerge from the escalation of the conflict, and (ii) those that have an intrinsic relationship with the Big Neighbour's national interest.

This was by way of simplification of our original hypothetical framework for Big Neighbour involvement in a secessionist conflict situation. In the analytical model we predicted that where the Big Neighbour shared (or wanted to share) with the affected state (i) common strategic resources, (ii) a common security zone, (iii) a common territorial boundary, and above all, (iv) ethnic ties, its involvement in the secessionist conflict was virtually unavoidable. All these factors, indeed, did appear in our case studies of secessionist situations. But we identified the first three as components of the 'strategic' dimension, and the fourth as the 'ethnic' dimension of the Big Neighbour's national interests attaching to its small neighbour's internal conflict.

Our identification of the indispensability of the 'strategic dimension' in deciding the way in which the Big Neighbour gets involved in the secessionist situation confirms that Big Neighbour states have no 'natural propensity' to intervene in a secessionist conflict on behalf of their ethnic-kin. Certainly, as the study's findings have shown, an ethnic secessionist movement can expect diplomatic and political support from their ethnic-kin Big Neighbour, to protect their rights as a threatened ethnic minority. But we found that a secessionist movement cannot always expect an intervention from such a Big Neighbour that would be decisive for the success of its secessionist ideal. It is not this ethnic relationship between the Big Neighbour's people and the secessionist community alone, but the immediate strategic threats perceived by its policy-makers, that would determine the course of action taken by the Big Neighbour. Then, if the policy-makers of the Big Neighbour were convinced that the events unfolding in the conflict situation were endangering its strategic interests, we established (as we stated in the first chapter) that international principles like 'non-intervention', 'territorial integrity', and 'national sovereignty' may have little practical validity in halting an intervention from the Big Neighbour.

According to the theoretical model, the Big Neighbour has four alternative policy options, viz. repression, annexation, secession and devolution. We have seen that the Big Neighbours in our historical Big Neighbour situations all preferred either 'secession' or 'annexation' or 'devolution', according to their own strategic interests towards the affected state and its secessionist conflict: no Big Neighbour preferred 'repression', or wanted to support the affected state's central regime in achieving a military solution to the conflict.

Further, by investigating the policy objectives preferred by the Big Neighbour states that were involved in the case study secessionist situations, we identified reasons which had influenced their policy-makers to take an active part in the containment of the secessionist conflict, and to influence the conflicting parties to settle the conflict through political negotiations. On the basis of these observations we concluded that the containment of the secessionist conflict through devolution, or within some other power-sharing arrangement, would become the preferred option of the Big Neighbour, not only because other options become more risky for its own security and stability, or unattainable in current international conditions, but because to maintain the territorial integrity of the affected state was of crucial importance to Big Neighbour's own national interest.

The theoretical model then predicted four possible roles for the Big Neighbour in the secessionist situation, towards the containment of the secession conflict: viz. (i) the pressure role, (ii) the big stick role, (iii) the interventionist role, and (iv) the invitational role. We did, indeed, find our respective Big Neighbours playing these roles at different stages of their involvement in the secessionist situation, moving from one role to another depending on the response of the most intransigent actor in the conflict situation. In this connection our prediction from the theoretical model of a 'cycle of Big Neighbour roles' gained a strong practical validation, except for our findings about the termination of 'invitational' and 'interventionist' roles by our actual Big Neighbours without apparent result, or their prolongation, thus raising the likelihood of 'repetition' of such roles by the Big Neighbour.

However, our investigation of the different roles played by the different Big Neighbours showed that even the Big Neighbours which preferred 'secession' or 'annexation' as their final policy objective towards the secessionist situation, also played some of the other roles, keeping the 'devolution' option open. We identified this as a possibility, because of our finding that international acceptance is vital to the realization of these other objectives, viz. 'secession' or 'annexation' by a Big Neighbour state. Therefore, we concluded that where this international acceptance is withheld, pressure from other states, mediation, and finally, the giving of specific guarantees of the Big Neighbour's strategic interests in the affected state, can reverse such policy objectives, making even those Big Neighbours amenable to a 'devolutionary' settlement.

In this connection however we found that all the case study Big Neighbours, one way or another, playing those different roles in the conflict, established a firm stand against either 'secession' or 'repression' or both, thus influencing the main adversaries to abandon their intransigence towards 'devolution' (or some other power sharing settlement) which might bring a political solution to the conflict.

However, even if those Big Neighbours once succeeded in obtaining the reception of 'devolution' of government by the conflicting parties, there was still a possibility of a continuation of the conflict between the recalcitrants in the two parties. We noted that this depended on what further external support they could achieve, enabling them to ignore the Big Neighbour's role, or in some cases on the sheer intensity of the conflicting social and psychological dimensions of the secession conflict. In this connection the theoretical model predicted that the removal of the difficulties arising from these external and internal dimensions might be possible, depending on the availability of international pressure and conflict management, and one or more of certain internal conditions. They were: (1) a substantial breakdown of central control over the secessionist region; (2) a relative decline in the capabilities of the antagonists, accompanied by a long period of warfare to bring home its destructive impact; and (3) the emergence of an auspicious conjunction such as the inauguration of a new constitution, a regime change or a leadership change in the secessionist movement.

Indeed, we found that these external factors and internal conditions played a vital role in each of the case study Big Neighbour's efforts to contain the secession conflict. The availability of these conditions had important implications as they influenced the conflicting parties (both leaders and masses) to come out from their closed social and psychological world of perpetual conflict and respond positively to the efforts made by the Big Neighbour, the international community or other third party mediators to contain and even end the secession conflict.

However, as happened in some of the case study Big Neighbour situations, we found that the occurrence of these external factors and internal conditions did not always coincide with the period of their respective Big Neighbour's intervention. There was evidence to suggest that they take time and need the conflict to persist for a lengthy period before they obtain in the secessionist situation. Also, we gathered that in a 'protracted' secessionist conflict situation, the antagonists needed time to find a way towards national reconciliation, even after the stabilization of the conflict's external system by the intervention of the Big Neighbour. This is understandable. There are no 'quick fixes' for the internal actors to settle their internal divisions and remove their misconceptions, as the origins of these conflicts have their own historical evolution, and are closely knitted into the deep social and psychological differences between the conflicting ethnic groups and their perceptions of each other's territorial and political claims.

We argued that the conflicting parties cannot simply overlook the Big Neighbour's stance against 'secession' or 'repression', even if the conflict persists after the intervention of the Big Neighbour, because the 'repetition of Big Neighbour roles' remains a possibility in a future stage of the conflict. Therefore in this regard, our conclusion was that the way cleared by the Big Neighbour's intervention in obtaining the reception of 'devolution' or another power sharing settlement, will remain as the political directive of any national reconciliation settlement negotiated by the conflicting parties or by any neutral third party mediators, in these unresolved secessionist conflict situations.

The model developed here emphasizes that the management of secessionist conflict in small states is always in the context of the natural power relationships in the regional political environment. In this context, a Big Neighbour has been identified as the main stabilizing force of the external system of the conflict, though the conflicting parties, one way or another, may tend to resist its involvement in the process of conflict management. Its role in the conflict can bring about not only '...a reduction of the means of conflict from violent to normal political and diplomatic means...' (what some analysts recognize as '...the goals of conflict management...' see Zartman:1990:9) but also the reception of a devolutionary or some other power sharing settlement by the conflicting parties.

Further, the study has proved that success by the Big Neighbour in cutting the external supply channels of the adversaries, and in obtaining the approval of the international community for its efforts to preserve the territorial integrity of the affected state, increased the prospects of managing the secessionist conflict through devolution of government.

The absence of prospective external supporters, or their withdrawal, we found, was the major factor in influencing the conflicting parties to give up their extremist stance and violence, and to go on trying for political negotiations towards national reconciliation. Further, the lessening of outside opposition to its role in the secessionist conflict increased the Big Neighbour's capability to impose a settlement upon the conflicting parties. Thus, the negative international approach towards the forcible break-up of existing states through 'secessionist self-determination', and the decisive effects which can be produced by the removal of external supporters of the conflicting parties upon the conflict system, have become two important pillars in the development of our central thesis.

As such, within the broad aim of extending the understanding of devolution of government as a method of managing ethnic secessionist conflict, the study, as anticipated, has also perhaps made a contribution to the field of conflict management in divided societies. The study has explored how certain Big Neighbour states, by making their presence felt in the conflict, eventually connect the conflict's external system to the geopolitical realities of the regional political environment, and pressurize any external actors that had already become involved in the conflict to rethink their position in relation to the Big Neighbour's interests in the region. We found that once the Big Neighbour had obtained the upper hand in the conflict system, influencing other external parties to withdraw from the conflict and thus achieving dominance in the external system of the conflict, the conflicts were isolated from the danger of external parties acting as the supporters of either of the conflicting parties. Then the opponents were left alone to settle their differences within their own social and psychological environment under the influence of their Big Neighbour or with the assistance of neutral third parties, but giving due weight to the wider geostrategic interest of the Big Neighbour. The other major effect of Big Neighbour involvement was to clear the way for conflict management initiatives taken by international or regional inter-governmental organizations and great powers, by treating the conflict as an international dispute. Such initiatives did take place in our case studies where the Big Neighbour's 'interventionist' or 'invitational' role became a prolonged exercise, because of the conflicting parties' unwillingness to settle the conflict under the influence of the Big Neighbour, or if despite the efforts made by the Big Neighbour towards its containment, the dragging on of the conflict became a potential threat to international peace.

We are concluding this study at a time when the world community is emerging from the bipolar system that dominated its political environment for more than forty years. When the study began, it was within that bipolar world system, and we made our investigations of the case study Big Neighbour secessionist situations taking global and ideological conflict between the two Super Powers as given. Are there any major implications for the model that has been developed in this study from this changing international situation ?

The collapse of Soviet communism has given rise to some new Big Neighbour situations in Eastern Europe and in the territories of the former Soviet Union. There are plenty of reasons to believe that the emerging new independent states of former Soviet republics may in the near future provide several Big Neighbour secessionist situations, as the states that are emerging on the territory of the former Soviet Union themselves comprise some ethno-regional groups that have already declared independence from their emerging new states. Perhaps the secessionist civil wars in the former Yugoslavian Republics provides a precedent. The role played by Germany in pressurizing the European Community (EC) countries to recognize Slovenian and Croatian independence, and by Greece to deny recognition to Macedonia, has strengthened the basic argument developed in the study, regarding the role of the Big Neighbour in an ethnic secessionist conflict situation. Germany's role in influencing the EC countries to change their earlier approach towards the secessionist conflict in Croatia points to the role of a determined Big Neighbour able to use its economic and political clout through a regional IGO to advance its secessionist policy.

The EC's involvement in implementing the political will of the Big Neighbours of the Yugoslavian republics is not a new experience. But, certainly, it has some new dimensions. For example Germany, which has been barred by its own constitution from sending its military forces beyond its borders, has achieved its objectives by only flexing its economic and political muscles within the EC. The actual involvement in the conflict was done by the EC as an regional inter-governmental organization; but in the end all of those efforts have served Germany's own political interest. Interestingly, during its involvement in the Yugoslav crisis the European Community, while organizing its own mediation and brokering several ceasefires, has played different roles similar to these we assigned to the Big Neighbour. Is this a case of a Big Neighbour achieving its policy towards its small neighbour's secessionist conflict using a regional organization ?

Certainly, the Yugoslav situation warrants closer observation to grasp its implications for the improvement of the model developed in the study. However, it has proved that the collapse of a bi-polar world or the emergence of a 'multi-power world' (see *The Economist* 23 December 1991 - 3 January 1992, pp.65-7) has not eliminated the role of Big Neighbour states in secessionist conflicts beyond their frontiers.

There are reasons to argue that the emergence of a 'multi-power world' may create some favourable conditions for the management of secessionist conflicts that have reached the stage of outright violence. First, it may confine secessionist situations to their own internal and regional environment, excluding undue involvement by outside parties as an extension of global or ideological conflict between great powers. Second, against this new background, regional or extra-regional states may take a more cautious approach to becoming involved in such an internal conflict in order to achieve international political gains. Third, regional and international organizations may take on greater responsibility in the management of such conflicts, in order to stop their spilling over into the regional political environment. Fourth, this may furnish closer co-operation between great and regional powers for the maintenance of stability in the international system.

All of these developments suggest that in the emerging 'multi-power world' a Big Neighbour may enjoy more space for manoeuvre in the containment of a secessionist conflict that threatens its national interest. The isolation of regional and internal conflicts from great power conflict has strengthened the Big Neighbour's role in different ways. One of the important outcomes would be the relative autonomy which may be acquired by the Big Neighbour in its regional environment (cf. Thornton 1991:133). As national interest becomes the first priority of states in the absence of global and ideological conflict between super powers, the Big Neighbour as the economically, politically or militarily dominant state in the regional environment may secure a greater say in the management of secessionist conflict of its small neighbours.

Therefore, the model developed here appears to be equally valid in both bipolar and multi-power world systems. The growing importance of the United Nations and of regional inter-governmental organizations as 'little United Nations' (Zartman 1991:10) in the containment of regional and international disputes would strengthen 'the role of the Big Neighbour', as a regional power which may be expected to take the initiative in implementing the decisions taken by such organizations. It is also true that this would enhance the Big Neighbour's ability, if it is determined to act contrary to international acceptability, to go ahead with its own policy towards the secessionist conflict, especially against a central regime which is intransigent and repressive towards an ethnic-kin secessionist minority. But this doesn't mean that the Big Neighbour would continue to receive silent international approval for all its actions, especially those taken in breach of international customary law, for example the playing of 'the interventionist role'. Then, as happened in the past, the conflict may become an international dispute which awaits international conflict management initiatives.

Thus, the role of the Big Neighbour in the containment of secessionist conflict within its small neighbour's territory, and the four roles available to its policy-makers to implement a devolutionary policy, will remain to be used at its discretion even in the changing international environment.

However, these are not definite conclusions but hypotheses regarding the model's applicability in the emerging international environment. It needs further empirical observations in the changing international situation. The idea of a multi-power world is still an untidy one. The emerging world situation and its governing rules are not yet clear. It's too early to suggest whether the changing situation is creating a 'new world order' with a multi-power world, or 'the older order in the clothes of the new' (Hamilton 1992), or as some have argued, merely a 'disorder' (Zartman 1991:8).

Bibliography

Aguado, Laura Donnadie (1990), 'The National Liberation Movement of the Kurds in the Middle East', in Ralph R. Premdas et al. (eds), *Secessionist Movements in Comparative Perspective*, Pinter Publishers, London.

Alford, Jonathan (1984), 'Security Dilemmas of Small States', *The World Today*, 40(8-9):363-9.

Ali, Ameer (1990), 'The Muslim Predicament', *Tamil Times*, 9(11):14-16.

Anderson, Benadict (1987), *Imagined Communities, Reflections on the Origin and Spread of Nationalism*, Verso, London.

Apter, David E. (1961), *The Political Kingdom in Uganda, A Study in Bureaucratic Nationalism*, Princeton University Press, Princeton.

Arasaratnam, S. (1964), *Ceylon*, Prentice-Hall Inc., Englewood Cliffs.

Austin, Dennis & Gupta, Anirudha (1988), *Lions and Tigers, The Crisis in Sri Lanka*, (Conflict Studies No.211), The Centre for Security and Conflict Studies, London.

Australian Broadcasting Corporation (1991), *Blood on Bougainville*, (Transcript typed from a documentary film broadcast on 24-06-91), Australian Broadcasting Corporation, Canberra.

Ayoob, Mohammed & Subramanyam, K. (1972), *The Liberation War*, S. Chand & Co., New Delhi.

Babbage, Ross (1987), 'Australia and the Defence of Papua New Guinea (PNG)', *Australian Outlook*, 41(2):87-93.

Bacho, Peter (1987), 'The Muslim Secessionist Movement', *The Journal of International Affairs*, 41(1):153-64.

Baldwin, George B. (1978), *Papua New Guinea, Its Economic Situation and Prospects for Development*, The World Bank, Washington, D.C.

Baral, Lok Raj (1985), 'Nation Building and Region Building in South Asia', *Asia Pacific Community*, 28(Spring):54-73.

Bhalla, R. S. (1991), 'The Right of Self-Determination in International Law', in William Twining (ed.), *Issues of Self-Determination*, Aberdeen University Press, Aberdeen, (91-101).

Bilder, Richard B. (1989), 'International Third Party Dispute Settlement', *Denver Journal of International Law and Policy*, 17(3):471-503.

Birand, Mehmet Ali (1988), 'A Turkish View of Greek-Turkish Relations', *Journal of Political and Military Sociology*, 16(2):173-83.

Birch, Anthony (197aw, 'Minority Nationalist Movements and Theories of Political Integration', *World Politics*, 30(3):325-44.

Black, Naomi (1977), 'The Cyprus Conflict', in (Suhrke & Noble 1977:43-71).

Bogdanor, Vernon (1979), *Devolution*, Oxford University Press, Oxford.

Boynton, G.R. and Kwon, W.H. (1978), 'An Analysis of Consociational Democracy', *Legislative Studies*, 3(1):11-25.

Bromley, Julian and Kozlov, Viktor (1989), 'The Theories of Ethnos and Ethnic Process in Soviet Social Sciences', *Comparative Studies in Society and History*, 31(3):425-38.

Brown, David (1988), 'From Peripheral Communities to Ethnic Nations: Separatism in Southeast Asia', *Pacific Affairs*, 61(1):51-77.

Buchheit, Lee C. (1978), *Secession, The Legitimacy of Self-Determination*, Yale University Press, New Haven.

Bull, Hedlley (1974), 'Australia's Involvement in Independent Papua-New Guinea', *World Review*, 13(1):3-18.

Bullock, Katherine (1991), *Australia and Papua New Guinea: Foreign and Defence Relations since 1975*, (Working Paper No. 227), The Strategic Defence Studies Centre, The Research School of Pacific Studies, The Australian National University, Canberra.

Chadda, Maya (1987), 'Domestic Determinants of India's Foreign Policy in the 1980s: The Role of Sikh and Tamil Nationalism', *Journal of South Asian and Middle Eastern Studies*, 11(1-2):21-35.

Chakravartty, Sumit (1987), 'Prospect after Accord', *Mainstream*, 25(annual):115-29.

Choudhury, G. W. (1974), *The Last Days of United Pakistan*, C Hurst & Company, London.

Cloete, Fanie (1988), 'Decentralisation: Instrument for Constitutional Development in South Africa', *Politikon*, 15(1):16-30.

Cohen, Stephen & Arnone, Hariet C. (1988), 'Conflict Resolution as the Alternative to Terrorism', *Journal of Social Issues*, 44(2):175-89.

Coomaraswamy, Radhika (1984), 'Through the Looking Glass Darkly, the Politics of Ethnicity', in Committee for Regional Development (ed.), *Sri Lanka - The Ethnic Conflict, Myths, Realities and Perspectives*, Navarang, New Delhi.

_____ (1986), 'Nationalism: Sinhala and Tamil Myths', *South Asia Bulletin*, 5(2):21-26.

Coomaraswamy, Radhika (1987), 'Myths without Conscience, Tamil and Sinhala Nationalist Writings of the 1980s', in Newton Gunasinghe (ed.), *Facets of Ethnicity in Sri Lanka,* Social Scientists' Association, *Colombo,* (72-99).

Connor, Walker (1972), 'Nation-Building or Nation-Destroying', *World Politics,* 24(3):319-55.

_____ (1977), 'Ethnonationalism in the First World: the Present in Historical Perspective', in Milton J. Esman (ed.), *Ethnic Conflict in the Western World,* Cornell University Press, Ithaca.

_____ (1978) 'A Nation is a Nation, is a State, is an Ethnic Group, is a...', *Ethnic and Racial Studies,* 1(4):377-400.

Crawshaw, Nancy (1978), *The Cyprus Revolt,* George A. Allen, London.

Crouch, Harold (1986), 'Indonesia and the Security of Australia and Papua New Guinea', *Australian Outlook,* 40(3):167-74.

Daalder, Hans (1974), 'The Consociational Democracy Theory', *World Politics,* 24(4):604-21.

Davis, Horace B. (1978), *Towards a Marxist Theory of Nationalism,* Monthly Review Press, New York.

Denktash, R.R. (1982), *The Cyprus Triangle,* George Allen & Unwin, London.

Department of Census and Statistics (1984), *Statistical Pocket Book of the Democratic Socialist Republic of Sri Lanka,* Department of Census and Statistics, Colombo.

Deutsch, Karl (1963), 'Nation-Building and National Development: Some Issues for Political Research', in Karl Deutsch & William J. Foltz (eds), *Nation-Building,* Atherton Press, New York, (1-16).

Dinstein, Yoram (ed.), (1981), *Models of Autonomy,* Transaction Books, New Brunswick.

_____ (1981), 'Autonomy', in (Dinstein 1981:291-303).

Dommen. Arthur J. (1967), 'Separatist Tendencies in Eastern India', *Asian Survey,* 7(10):726-39.

Donaghy, Peter J. & Newton, Michael J. (1987), *Spain, A Guide to Political and Economic Institutions,* Cambridge University Press, Cambridge.

Doswald-Beck, Louise (1985), 'The Legal Validity of Military Intervention by Invitation of the Government', *British Year Book of the International Law,* 56:189-252.

Duff, Ernest A. & McCament, John F. (1976), *Violence and Repression in Latin America,* The Free Press, New York.

Egeland, Jan (1984), 'Focus on: Human Rights - Ineffective Big States, Potent Small States', *Journal of Peace Research,* 21(3):207-13.

Elazar, Danial J. (ed.), (1979), *Federalism and Political Integration,* Turtledove Publishing, Tel Aviv.

_____ (1979-a), 'The Role of Federalism', in (Elazar 1979:13-57).

_____ (1979-b), 'A Preliminary Inventory', in (Elazar 1979:215-31).

Elliot, R. S. P. (1971), *Ulster, A Case Study in Conflict Theory*, Longman, London.

Enloe, Cynthia L. (1973), *Ethnic Conflict and Political Development*, Little Brown and Company, Boston.

_____ (1975), 'Central Government Strategies for Coping with Separatist Movements', in (Institute of Commonwealth Studies:1975:79-84).

Eradman, Howard L. (1979), 'Autonomy Movements in India', in (Hall 1979:379-408).

Ertekun, Necati Munnir (1990), 'A Tale of Two Peoples Inhabiting an Island', *Turkish Review Quarterly Digest*, 4(21):45-68.

Esman, Milton J. (1973),'The Management of Communal Conflict', *Public Policy*, 21(1):49-78.

_____(1977), 'Perspective on Ethnic Conflict in Industrial Societies', in Milton J. Esman (ed.), *Ethnic Conflict in the Western World*, Cornell University Press, Ithaca.

_____ (1985), 'Two Dimensions of Ethnic Politics: Defence of Homelands, Immigrant Rights', *Ethnic and Racial Studies*, 8(3):438-40.

Esterbauer, Fried (1979), 'Austrian Experiences in Utilising Federation to Conciliate Ethnic Minorities', in (Elazar 1979:145-54).

Evans, Gareth (1986), 'Australia-PNG-Indonesia Relationship' [speech], *Australian Foreign Affairs Record*, 57(3):154-5.

_____ (1990), 'Australian Assistance to PNG' [statement], *Australian Foreign Affairs Record*, 61(1):28-30.

Everon, Yaiz (1987), *War and Intervention in Lebanon*, Croom Helm, London.

Farberov, N. P. (1975), 'Self-Determination in the Soviet Union', in William F. Mackey and Albert Verdoodt (eds), *The Multinational Society*, Newbury House Publishers Inc., Massachusetts, (173-85).

Fernando, Tissa (1982), 'Political and Economic Development in Sri Lanka', *Current History*, 81(475):211-14, 226-28.

Filer, Colin (1990), 'The Bougainville Rebellion, the Mining Industry and the Process of Social Disintegration', in (May & Spriggs 1990:73-112).

Franda, Marcus & Rahman, Ataur (1985), 'India, Bangladesh and the Superpowers', in Paul Wallace (ed.), *Region and Nation in India*, American Institute of Indian Studies, New Delhi.

Furnival, J. S. (1948), *Colonial Policy and Practice*, Cambridge University Press, Cambridge.

Geertz, Clifford (1963), 'The Integrative Revolution, Primordial Sentiments and Civil Politics in the New States', in Clifford Geertz (ed.), *Old Societies and New States, The Quest for Modernity in Asia and Africa*, The Free Press of Glencoe, New York, (105-57).

Gellner, E. (1964), *Thought and Change*, Weidenfeld & Nicolson, London.

_____ (1973), 'Scale and Nation', *Philosophy of the Social Science*, 3:1-17.

Ghai, K. K. & Sharma, B. B. (1987), 'Regional Politics in India - Case Study of DMK and AIADMK in Tamil Nadu', *Journal of Political Studies*, 20(2):56-72.

Ghazi, Abidullah (1972), 'Muslim Bengal: A Crisis of Identity', in Barbara Thomas and Spencer Lavan (eds), *West Bengal and Bangladesh, Perspective from 1972*, (Occasional Paper No. 21), Asian Studies Centre, Michigan State University, Michigan, (147-61).

Ghosh, Partha S. (1985), *Ethnic and Religious Conflicts in South Asia*, (Conflict Studies Report No. 178), The Institute for Study of Conflict, London.

Gitelman, Zvi (1979), 'Federalism and Multiculturalism in Soviet Systems', in (Elazar 1979:157-69).

Goldman, Robert B. & Wilson, A. Jeyaratnam (eds), (1984) *From Independence to Statehood, Managing Ethnic Conflict in Five African and Asian States*, Frances Pinter, London.

Greenwood, Christopher (1991), 'Iraq's Invasion of Kuwait: Some Legal Issues', *World Today*, 47(3):39-43.

Griffin, James (1990), 'Bougainville is a Special Case', in (May & Spriggs 1990:01-15).

Guha, Ashoka Sanjay (1971), 'Bangladesh and Indian Self-Interest', *Economic and Political Weekly*, 6(20):983-85.

Gunter, Micheal M. (1985), 'Transitional Sources of Support for Armenian Terrorism', *Conflict Quarterly*, 5(4):31-52.

Gurr, Ted (1970), *Why Men Rebel*, Princeton University Press, Princeton.

Haddad, Wadi D. (1985), *Lebanon, The Revolving Doors*, Praeger Publishers, New York.

Hall, Raymond L. (ed.), (1979), *Ethnic Autonomy-Comparative Dynamics, The Americas, Europe and the Developing World*, Pergamon Press, New York.

_____ (1979). 'Introduction', in (Hall 1979:xvii:xxxii).

Hamilton, Adrian (1992), 'America at Loss as Middle East Finds a New Place', *The Sunday Observer* (London), 12 January 1992.

Hannum, Hurst & Lillich, Richard B. (1981), 'The Concept of Autonomy in International Law', in (Dinstein 1981:215-54).

Harris, George S. (1977), 'The Kurdish Conflict in Iraq', in (Suhrke & Noble 1977:68-92).

Havini, Moss (1990), 'Human Rights Violations and Community Disruption', in (May & Spriggs 1990:31-37).

Hayden, Bill (1985), 'Papua New Guinea and Australia: Ten Years On', [speech], *Australian Foreign Affairs Record*, 56(9):812-17.

Hechter, Michael (1975), *Internal Colonialism, The Celtic Fringe in British National Development 1536-1966*, Routledge and Kegan Paul, New York.

Hechter, Michael and Levi, Margaret (1979), 'The Comparative Analysis of Ethnoregional Movements', *Ethnic and Racial Studies*, 2(1):260-73.

Hegarty, David (1988), 'South Pacific Security Issues: An Australian Perspective',

Conflict, 8(4):311-26.

Hellmann-Rajanayagam, Dagmar (1989), 'The Tamil Militants - Before the Accord and After', *Pacific Affairs*, 61(4):603-19.

Heraclides, Alexis (1985), *The International Dimension of Secessionist Movements*, Unpublished Ph. D. Thesis, University of Kent at Canterbury.

——————— (1990), 'Secessionist Movements and External Involvement', *International Organisation*, 44(3):341-78.

Herz, John H. (1978), 'Legitimacy, Can We Retrieve it?', *Comparative Politics*, 10(3):317-43.

Holloway, John (1985), 'Australia-Indonesia: Managing the Relationship', *Australian Foreign Affairs Record*, 56(6):512-16.

Horiwitz, Donald L. (1981), 'Patterns of Ethnic Separatism', *Comparative Studies in Society and History*, 23(2):165-95.

——————— (1985), *Ethnic Groups in Conflict*, University of California Press, Berkeley.

——————— (1990), 'Ethnic Conflict Management for Policy Makers', in (Montville 1990:115-30).

Hossain, Ishtiaq (1981), 'Bangladesh-India Relations: Issues and Problems', *Asian Survey*, 21(11):1115-128.

Hough, William J. H. (1985), 'The Annexation of the Baltic States and its Effect on the Development of Law Prohibiting Forcible Seizure of Territory', *New York Law School Journal of International and Comparative Law*, 6(2):301-533.

Hirst, David (1991), 'Pax Syriana, Lex Lebanon', *The Guardian*, 17 July 1991.

Huntington, Samuel P. (1972), 'Forward', in (Nordlinger 1972).

Idiz, Dundar E. (1975), 'The Cyprus Situation', *Pakistan Horizon*, 28(2l):5-23.

International Commission of Jurists, (1972), 'East Pakistan Staff Study', *The Review*, 8(6):23-62.

Institute of Commonwealth Studies (ed.), (1975), *The Politics of Separatism*, Institute of Commonwealth Studies, London.

Iqbal, Mehrunnisa Hatim, (1972), 'India and the 1971 War with Pakistan', *Pakistan Horizon*, 25(1):21-31.

Islam, M. Rafiqual (1985), 'Secessionist Self-Determination: Some Lessons from Katanga, Biafra and Bangladesh', *Journal of Peace Research*, 22(3):211-21.

Jackson, Robert (1975), *South Asian Crisis, India - Pakistan - Bangladesh*, (Studies in International Security:17), The International Institute for Strategic Studies, London.

Jetly, Nancy (1988), 'India's Security Perspectives in South Asia in the Eighties', *Conflict*, 8(4):295-309.

Joshi, Manoj (1990), 'Commitment in Sri Lanka - and the Weakness of Decision Making', *The Hindu International Edition*, Article published on 19 May 1990.

Jupp, James (1978), *Sri Lanka: Third World Democracy*, Frank Cass, London.

Kabir, Mohammad Humayan (1985), 'Crisis Management: A Case Study of Tamil

Crisis in Sri Lanka', *Regional Studies* (Islamabad), 4(Winter):88-103.

Kailasapathy, K. (1979), 'Cultural and Linguistic Consciousness of the Tamil Community', in Social Scientists' Association (ed.), *Ethnicity and Social Change in Sri Lanka,* Social Scientists' Association, *Colombo* (161-74).

Kane, Jean Ellen (1980), 'Flemish and Walloon Nationalism: Devolution of a Previously Unitary State', in Uri Ra'anan & John P. Roche (eds), *Ethnic Resurgence in Modern Democratic State*, Pergamon Press, New York (122-71).

Kearney, Robert N. (1967), *Communalism and Language in the Politics of Ceylon*, Durham, Duke University Press, Durham.

Keesing's (1957-1982), *Keesing's Contemporary Archives*, Keesing's Publications, Bristol.

_____ (1983-1991), *Keesing's Record of World Events*, Longman, London.

Kemelfield, Graeme (1990), 'A Short History of the Bougainville Ceasefire Initiative', in (May & Spriggs 1990:62-72).

Khalilzad, Zalmay (1983) 'The Politics of Ethnicity in Southeast Asia: Political Development or Political Decay?', *Strategic Studies*, 1983:46-70.

Khergamvala, F.J. (1986), 'Of Neighbours and Friends', *The Hindu International*, Article published on 6 December 1986.

Kitromilides, Paschalis M. & Couloumbis, Theodore A. (1976), 'Ethnic Conflict in a Strategic Area: The Case of Cyprus', in Abdul Said & Luize R. Simmons (eds.), *Ethnicity in an International Context*, Transaction Books, New Brunswick.

Kitromilides, Paschalis M. (1990), 'Greek Irredentism in Asia Minor and Cyprus', *Middle Eastern Studies*, 26(1):3-17.

Knight, David B. (1982), 'Identity and Territory: Geographical Perspectives on Nationalism and Regionalism', *Annals of the Association of American Geographers*, 72(4):514-31.

_____ (1984), 'Geographic Perspective on Self-Determination', in Peter Taylor & John House (eds), *Political Geography: Recent Advances and Future Directions*, Croom Helm, London.

Kodikara, S.U. (1978), 'Contemporary Indo-Lanka Relations', *Sri Lanka Journal of Social Sciences,* 1(1):61-73.

_____ (1979), *Strategic Factors in Interstate Relations in South Asia*, The Australian National University, Canberra.

_____ (1982), *Foreign Policy of Sri Lanka, A Third World Perspective*, Chanakya Publications, Delhi.

_____ (1987), 'International Dimensions of Ethnic Conflict in Sri Lanka', *Bulletin of Peace Proposals*, 18(4):637-45.

_____ (1989), 'Continuing Crisis in Sri Lanka, the JVP, the Indian Troops and Tamil Politics', *Asian Survey*, 29(7):716-24.

Kourvetaris, George A. (1988), 'Greek and Turkish Interethnic Conflict and

Polarisation in Cyprus', *Journal of Military Sociology*, 16(2):185-99.

Krejci, Jaraslav & Velimsky, Vitezslav (1981), *Ethnic and Political Nations in Europe*, Croom Helm, London.

Kumar, Satish, (1975), 'The Evolution of Indian Policy Towards Bangladesh in 1971', *Asian Survey*, 15(6):488-98.

Kuper, Leo & Smith M.G. (1969), *Pluralism in Africa*, University of California Press, Berkeley.

Kuper, Leo (1969), 'Plural Societies: Perspectives and Problems', in (Kuper & Smith 1969:7-26).

Lawless, Robert (19776), 'The Indonesian Takeover of East Timor', *Asian Survey*, 15(10):948-64.

Leary, Verjinia (1981), *Ethnic Conflict and Violence in Sri Lanka*, International Commission of Jurists, Geneva.

Leemans, A. F. (1970), *Changing Patterns of Local Government*, International Union of Local Authority, The Hague.

Levy, Brian (1989), 'Foreign Aid in the Making of Economic Policy in Sri Lanka', *Policy Science*, 22:437-61.

Lijphart, Arend (1969), 'Consociational Democracy', *World Politics*, 21(2)207-25.

_____ (1977-a), 'Majority Rule Versus Democracy in Deeply Divided Societies', *Politikon*, 4(2):113-26.

_____ (1977-b) *Democracy in Plural Societies, A Comparative Exploration*, Yale University Press, New Haven.

_____ (1979), 'Consociation and Federation: Conceptual and Empirical Link', *Canadian Journal of Political Science*, 22(3):499-515.

_____ (1990), 'The Power-Sharing Approach', in (Montville 1990:491-509).

Lopez, George A. (1984), 'A Scheme for the Analysis of Government and Terrorist', in Michael Stohl & George A. Lopez (eds), *The State as Terrorist, the Dynamics of Governmental Violence*, (Studies in Human Rights No. 4), Aldwych Press, London, (59-82).

Lyon, Peter (1975), 'Separatism and Secession in the Malaysian Realm, 1948-65', in (Institute of Commonwealth Studies 1975:69-78).

Mackie, J.A.C. (1986), 'Does Indonesia Have Expansionist Designs on Papua New Guinea', in R. J. May (ed.), *Between Two Nations, The Indonesia-Papua New Guinea Border and West Papua Nationalism*, Robert Brown and the Associates (Aust.) Ptv. Ltd., Bathurst, (66-84).

Mackintosh, John P. (1962) 'Federalism in Nigeria', *Political Studies*, 10(3)223-47.

MacMahon, Arthur (1969), *Delegation and Autonomy*, The Indian Institute of Public Administration, Asia Publishing House, New Delhi.

MacQueen, Norman (1989), 'Papua New Guinea's Relations with Indonesia and Australia, Diplomacy on the Asia-Pacific Interface', *Asian Survey*, 29(5):530-41.

Maddick, Henry (1963), *Democracy, Decentralisation and Development*, Asia

Publishing House, Bombay.

Malarkey, James M. (1988), 'Notes on the Psychology of War in Lebanon', in Halim Baraket (ed.), *Toward a Viable Lebanon*, Croom Helm, London.

Manchanda, Rita (1986), 'Sri Lanka Crisis: Conflict and Intervention', *Strategic Analysis*, 10(15):571-90.

Manor, James (1983), 'Sri Lanka: Explaining the Disaster', *The World Today*, 39(11):450-59.

Marasinghe, M. L. (1988), 'Ethnic Politics and Constitutional Reform: The Indo-Sri Lankan Accord', *International and Comparative Law*, 37(3):551-87.

Markides, Kyriacos C. (1977), *The Rise and Fall of the Cyprus Republic*, Yale University Press, New Haven.

Marwah, Onkar (1979), 'India's Military Intervention in East Pakistan, 1971-72', *Modern Asian Studies*, 13(4):549-80.

Maxwell, Nevill (1980), *India, The Nagas and North-East*, (Report No.17), Minority Rights Group, London.

May, R. J. (1986), 'East of the Border: Iran Jaya and the Border in P.N.G's Domestic and Foreign Policy', in R. J. May (ed.), *Between Two Nations, The Indonesian-Papua New Guinea Border and West Papua Nationalism*, Robert Brown and Associates (Aust.), Bathurst, N.S.W., (85-159).

May, R. J. & Spriggs, Matthew (eds.), (1990), *The Bougainville Crisis*, Crawford House Press, Bathurst.

McCord, Arline and McCord, William (1979), 'Ethnic Autonomy: A Socio-Historical Synthesis', in (Hall 1979:426-36).

McDonald, Robert (1986), 'Cyprus: The Gulf Widens', *World Today*, 42(11):184-86.

————————— (1989), *The Problem of Cyprus*, (Adelphi Papers 234), International Institute for Strategic Studies, London.

McRae, Kenneth D. (1979), 'Comment: Federation, Consociation, Corporatism - An Addendum to Arend Lijphart', *Canadian Journal of Political Science*, 22(3):517-22.

————————— (1990), 'Theories of Power-Sharing and Conflict Management', in (Montville 1990:93-106).

McVey, Ruth (1975), 'Language, Religion and National Identity', in (Institute of Commonwealth Studies 1975:94-99).

————————— (1984), 'Separatism and the Paradoxes of the Nation-State in Perspective', in Lim Joo-Jock and Vani S. (eds), *Armed Separatism in Southeast Asia*, Institute of Southeast Asian Studies, Singapore, (3-29).

Melson, Robert & Wolpe, Howard (1970), 'Modernisation and the Politics of Communalism: A Theoretical Perspective', *The American Political Science Review*, 64(4):1112-130.

Meo, Leila (1977), 'The War in Lebanon', in (Suhrke & Noble 1977:93-126).

Miller, T. B. (1978), 'Weapons Prolification and the Security Problems in the South

Pacific Region', in Robert O'Neill (ed.), *Insecurity: The Spread of Weapons in the Indian and Pacific Region*, Australian National University Press, Canberra, (222-35).

Mitchell, C. R. (1970), 'Civil Strife and the Involvement of External Parties', *International Quarterly*, 14(2):166-94.

Modelski, George (1964), 'The International Relations of Internal War', in James N. Rosenau (ed.), *International Aspect of Civil Strife*, Princeton University Press, New Jersey, (14-44).

Montville, Josph (ed.), (1990), *Conflict and Peacemaking in Multiethnic Societies*, Lexington Books, Massachusetts.

Moore, Mick (1990), 'Economic Liberalization versus Political Pluralism in Sri Lanka', *Modern Asian Studies*, 24(2):341-83.

Morgenstern, Raimund (1992), 'Vanishing Hopes for Peace in Sri Lanka', *Tamil Times*, 11(6):10-15, 30.

Morris-Jones, W. H. (1972), 'Pakistan Post-Mortem and the Roots of Bangladesh', *Political Quarterly*, 43(2):187-200.

_____ (1975), 'Notes to Participants', in (Institute of Commonwealth Studies 1975:i-iii).

Mughan Anthony (1979), 'Modernisation and Regional Relative Deprivation: Towards a Theory of Ethnic Conflict', in L. J. Sharpe (ed.), *Decentralist Trends in Western Democracies*, SAGE Publications, London, (279-314).

Nagarajan, K. V. (1984), 'Troubled Paradise: Ethnic Conflict in Sri Lanka', *Conflict*, 6(4):333-53.

Nairn, Tom (1977), *The Breakup of Britain, Crisis and Neo-Nationalism*, Low and Brydone Printers Ltd., Thetford.

Nagel, Joane (1980), 'The Conditions of Ethnic Separatism: The Kurds in Turkey, Iran & Iraq', *Ethnicity*, 7(3):279-97.

Nanda, Ved P. (1972), 'Self-Determination in International Law, The Tragic Tale of Two Cities - Islamabad (West Pakistan) and Dacca (East Pakistan)', *American Journal of International Law*, 66(2):321-36.

Nasr, Salim (1990), 'Lebanon's War: Is the End in Sight ?', *Middle East Report*, (January-February):5-8.

Nedjatigal, Zaim (1981), The Cyprus Conflict - A Lawyer's view, A-Z Publications, Nicosia - Northern Cyprus.

Neuberger, Benjamin (1979), 'Federalism and Political Integration in Africa', in (Elazar 1979:171-88).

Nixon, Charles R. (1972), 'Self-Determination: The Nigeria/Biafra Case', *World Politics*, 24(4):473-97.

Nordlinger, Eric A. (1972), *Conflict Regulation in Divided Societies*, Centre for International Affairs, Harvard University, Cambridge, Mass.

Novicki, Margaret A. (1989), 'John Garang, A New Sudan, An Interview with John Garang, the Leader of the SPLA', *Africa Report*, 34(4):43-47.

Oberst, Robert (1988), 'Sri Lanka's Tamil Tigers', *Conflict*, 8(2-3):185-202.

Okole, Henry (1990), 'The Politics of the Panguna Landowner's Organisation', in (May & Spriggs 1990:16-24).

Owen, John E. (1972), 'The Background to Bangladesh', *IL POLITICO*, 37(1):172-81.

Parasher, S.C. (1987), 'Agreement and the Ethnic Crisis', *Foreign Affairs Report*, 36(7-10):109-61.

Patrika, Ananda Bazar (1987), 'Coercion without Tears, Need for India to Act', *Tamil Times*, 6(9):16.

Payne, James L. (1970), *The American Threat, The Fear of War as an Instrument of Foreign Policy*, Markham Publishing Company, Chicago.

Pfaffenberger, Bryan (1987), 'The Continuing Crisis in Sri Lanka', *Asian Survey*, 27(2):155-62.

Phadnis, Urmila (1986), 'Sri Lanka: Stress and Strains of a Small State', in B. S. Bajpai (ed.), *India and Its Neighbours*, Lancer International, New Delhi, (237-71).

Ponnambalam, Satchi (1983), *Sri Lanka and the Tamil Liberation Struggle*, Zed Books Ltd., London.

Premdas, Ralp R. (1976), 'Towards a Papua New Guinea Foreign Policy: Constraints and Choice', *Australian Outlook*, 30(2):263-79.

_____ (1977-a), 'Secession Politics in Papua New Guinea', *Pacific Affairs*, 5(1):64-85.

_____ (1977-b) 'Ethnonationalism, Copper and Secession in Bougainville', *Canadian Review of Studies in Nationalism*, (Fall):247-65.

_____ (1986), 'Papua New Guinea's Border Relations with Indonesia', *The Round Table*, 299(July):241-51.

Priyadarshini, A. (1987), 'India and the Ethnic Strife in Sri Lanka', *Journal of Political Studies*, 20(2):44-55.

Pugh, Michael (1987), 'South Pacific Security: Alarms and Excursions', *World Today*, 43(7):125-28.

Qureshi, Saleem M. M. (1973), 'Pakistan Nationalism Reconsidered', *Pacific Affairs*, 45(4):556-81.

Rahman, Mizanur (1975) 'Bangladesh', in (Institute of Commonwealth Studies 1975:37-48).

Rajan, M.S. (1972), 'Bangladesh and After', *Pacific Affairs*, 45(2):19-205.

Ram, Mohan (1989), *Sri Lanka, The Fractured Island*, Penguin Books, New Delhi.

Rao, P. Venkateshwar (1988), 'Ethnic Conflict in Sri Lanka, India's Role and Perspective', *Asian Survey*, 28(4):419-36.

_____ (1989), 'Foreign Involvement in Sri Lanka', *The Round Table*, 309:88-100.

Razvi, S. M. Mujtab (1989), 'India and the Security of Indian Ocean/South Asian States', *The Round Table*, 311:317-22.

Reddaway, John (1987), 'A Cyprus Settlement, Revelations in a Crystal Ball', *International Relations*, 9(1):23-30.

Richmond, Anthony H. (1987), 'Ethnic Nationalism: Social Science Paradigms', *International Social Science Journal*, 111(Feb.)03-18.

Rondinelli, Dennis A. & Cheema, Shabbir G., (1983), 'Implementing Decentralisation Policies, An Introduction', in Dennis A. Rondinelli & Shabbir G. Cheema (eds), *Decentralisation and Development, Policy Implementation in Developing Countries*, SAGE Publications, Beverly Hills, (9-34).

Rondinelli, Dennis A. (1984), 'Government Decentralisation in Comparative Perspectives, Theory and Practice in Developing Countries', *International Review of Administrative Science*, 47(2):133-45.

Rondinelli, Dennis A. et al. (1989), 'Analysing Decentralisation Policies in Developing Countries, A Political-Economy Framework', *Development and Change*, 20(1):57-87.

Ross, Lee Ann & Samaranayake, Tilak (1986), 'The Economic Impact of the Recent Disturbance in Sri Lanka', *Asian Survey*, 24(11):1240-255.

Rothchild, Donald S. (1970), 'Ethnicity and Conflict Resolution', *World Politics*, 22(4):599-616.

Rothchild, Donald S. & Olorunsola, Victor A. (1983), 'African Public Policies on Ethnic Autonomy and State Control', in Donald S. Rothchild & Victor Olorunsola (eds), *State Versus Ethnic Claims: Public Policy Dilemmas*, Westview Press, Boulder, (233-50).

Rudenco, G. et al. (1975), *The Revolutionary Movement of Our Time and Nationalism*, Progress Publishers, Moscow.

Ryan, Stephen (1984), *Ethnic Conflict and the International System: Foreign Involvement in the Cyprus Problem*, Unpublished Ph. D. Thesis, London School of Economics and Political Science.

—————————— (1990), 'Ethnic Conflict and the United Nations', *Ethnic and Racial Studies*, 13(1):25-49.

Saikal, Amin (1980), *The Rise and Fall of the Shah*, Princeton University Press, Princeton.

Saliba, Najib E. (1988), 'Syrian-Lebanese Relations', in Halim Barakat (ed.), *Toward a Viable Lebanon*, Croom Helm, London, (160-6).

Sawhny, Karan (1987), 'The Practice of Realpolitik: Sri Lanka's Ethnic Strife', *Contemporary Review*, 251(1460):131-5.

Schiff, Ze'ev (1988), 'The Political Background of the War in Lebanon', in Halim Barakat (ed.), *Toward a Viable Lebanon*, Croom Helm, London, (145-59).

Schrear, Christopher (1981), 'Autonomy in South Tyrol', in (Dinstein 1981:53-64).

Scott, M. Andrew (1964), 'Internal Violence as an Instrument of Cold Warfare', in James N. Rosenau (ed.), *Internal Aspects of Civil Strife*, Princeton University Press, Princeton, (154-69).

Scruton, Roger (1982), *A Dictionary of Political Thought*, The Macmillan Press

Ltd., London.

Seabright, Paul (1986), 'Effects of Conflict on Economy in Northern Sri Lanka', *Economic and Political Weekly*, 21(2):78-83.

Seth, S. P. (1985), 'Anzus in Crisis', *Asia Pacific Community*, 29(Summer):109-30.

Seton-Watson, Hugh (1975), 'Reflection on Europe's Experience of Separatism', in (Institute of Commonwealth Studies 1975:1-4).

Shackle, Christopher (1986), *The Sikhs*, (Report No.65), Minority Rights Group, London.

Shaked, Haim (1981), 'Anatomy of Autonomy: The Case of South Sudan', in (Dinstein 1981:151-70).

Sharma, S. R. (1978), *Bangladesh Crisis and Indian Foreign Policy*, Young Asia Publications, New Delhi.

Sherwood, Frank P. (1969), 'Devolution as a Problem of Organisation Strategy', in Robert P. Daland (ed.), *Comparative Urban Research*, SAGE Publications, Beverly Hills, (60-87).

Simon, Richard (1975), 'Introduction', in Richard Simon (ed.), Must Canada Fail, McGill-Queen's University Press, Montreal, (1-11).

Singer, Marshall R. (1986), 'Report on the Pressures and Opportunities for a Peaceful Solution to the Ethnic Conflict in Sri Lanka', *Journal of Developing Societies*, II:12-27.

_____ (1989), *The Tamil-Sinhalese Ethnic Conflict in Sri Lanka: A Case Study in Efforts to Negotiate a Settlement 1983-1988*, Graduate School of Public and International Affairs, University of Pittsburgh, Pittsburgh.

Sirryeh, Hussein (1988), *Lebanon: Dimensions of Conflict*, (Adelphi Papers 243), The Institute for Strategic Studies, London.

Sivaraja, A. (1987), 'Indo-Sri Lanka Relations and Sri Lanka's Ethnic Crisis: The Tamil Nadu Factor', (Seminar paper, serial no.114), Ceylon Studies Seminar, University of Peradeniya, Peradeniya, Sri Lanka.

Sivathambi, Karthigesu (1984), 'Background to the Round Table Conference [part 1], Evolution of the Tamil Question', *Lanka Guardian*, 6(18):12-14.

Smith, Anthony D. (1971), *Theories of Nationalism*, Duckworth, London.

_____ (1979), 'Towards a Theory of Ethnic Separatism', *Ethnic and Racial Studies*, 2(1):21-37.

_____ (1981), *The Ethnic Revival*, Cambridge University Press, Cambridge.

_____ (1982), 'Nationalism, Ethnic Separatism and the Intelligentsia', in Collin H. Williams (ed.), *National Separatism*, University of Wales Press, Cardiff, (17-41).

Smith, B. C. (1967), *Field Administration, An Aspect of Decentralisation*, Routledge & Kegan Paul, London.

_____ (1985), *Decentralisation, The Territorial Dimension of the State*, George Allen & Unwin, London.

Smith, M. G. (1969), 'Institutional and Political Conditions of Pluralism', in (Kuper & Smith 1969:27-65).

Smock, David R. & Smock, Audrey C. (1975), *The Politics of Cultural Pluralism*, Elsevier, New York.

Sohn, Louise B. (1981), 'Models of Autonomy within the United Nations Framework', in (Dinstein 1981:5-22).

Souter, David (1984), 'An Island Apart: A Review of the Cyprus Problem', *Third World Quarterly*, 6(3):657-74.

_____ (1987), 'The Cyprus Conundrum: the Challenge of the Intercommunal Talks', *Third World Quarterly*, 11(2):77-91.

Spriggs, Matthew (1990), 'Bougainville, December 1989 - January 1990: A Personal History', in (May & Spriggs 1990:25-30).

Spriggs, Matthew & May, Ron (1990), 'Postscript: August 1990' in (May & Spriggs 1990:113-18).

Sterling, R. W. (1979), 'Separatism in the International System', in (Hall 1979:413-25).

Stohl, Michael & Lopez, George A. (1984), 'Introduction', in Michael Stohl & George A. Lopez (eds), *The State as Terrorist, the Dynamics of Governmental Violence and Repression*, (Studies in Human Rights No.4), Aldwych Press, London.

Subramanyam, K. (1980), 'India and the Security of the Sub-Continent', *India Quarterly*, 36(3-4):296-306.

Suhrke, Astri & Noble, Leela Garner (eds), (1977), *Ethnic Conflict in International Relations*, Praeger Publishers, New York.

_____ (1977), 'Introduction', in (Suhrke & Noble 1977:1-20).

Tachau, Frank (1959), 'The Face of Turkish Nationalism', *Middle East Journal*, 13(3):262-72.

Tambiah, S. J. (1986), *Sri Lanka, Ethnic Fratricide and the Dismantling of Democracy*, The University of Chicago Press, Chicago.

Thompson, Herb (1991), 'The Economic Causes and Consequences of the Bougainville Crisis', *Resources Policy*, 17(1):69-85.

Thornton, Thomas Perry (1991), 'Regional Organisations in Conflict Management', *The ANNALS of American Academy of Political & Social Sciences*, 518(November):132-42.

Tiruchelvam, Neelan (1984), 'The Politics of Decentralisation and Devolution: Competing Conceptions of District Development Councils', in (Goldman & Wilson:196-209).

_____ (1987), 'G. P. the Architecture of the Accord', *Tamil Times*, 6(10):17-18.

Tiwari, Chitra K. (1989), *Security in South Asia and External Dimension*, University Press of America, London.

Tripathi, Deepak (1989), 'India's Maldives Mission and After', *The World*

Today,45(1):03-04.

Vaidik, V. P. (1986), *Ethnic Conflict in Sri Lanka, India's Options*, National Publishing House, New Delhi.

Verrier, June (1986), 'The Origins of the Border Problem and the Border Story to 1969', in R. J. May (ed.), *Between Two Nations, The Indonesia-Papua New Guinea Border and West Papua Nationalism*, Robert Brown and the Associates (Aust.) Ptv. Ltd., Bathurst, (18-48).

Viviani, Nancy (1976), 'Australians and the Timor Issue', *Australian Outlook*, 30(2):197-26.

Wall, James A. (1981), 'Mediation', *Journal of Conflict Resolution*, 25(1):157-80.

Wariavwalla, Bharat (1974), 'The Indo-Pakistan Agreement', *Survival*, 16(1):17-20.

Weiner, Myron (1965), 'Political Integration and Political Development', *The ANNALS of the American Academy of Political Sciences*, 358:52-64.

Weisman, Ethan (1990),'The Papua New Guinea Economy and the Bougainville Crisis', in (May & Spriggs 1990:45-54).

White, N. D. & McCoubrey, H. (1991), 'International Law and the Use of Force in Gulf', *International Relations*, 10(4):347-73.

Wilcox, Wayne (1973), *The Emergence of Bangladesh*, American Enterprise Institute for Public Policy Research, Washington, D.C.

Wilson, A. Jeyaratnam (1980), *The Gaullist System in Asia: The Constitution of Sri Lanka 1978*, The Macmillan Press Ltd., London.

_____ (1982), 'Racial Strife in Sri Lanka: The Role of an Intermediary', *Conflict Quarterly*, 11(4):53-64.

_____ (1988), *The Break-up of Sri Lanka, the Sinhalese-Tamil Conflict*, C. Hurst & Company, London.

_____ (1990), 'The Foreign Policies of India's Immediate Neighbours: A Reflective Interpretation', *Journal of Asian and African Studies*, 25(1-2):42-59.

Wood, John R. (1981), 'Secession: A Comparative Analytical Framework', *Canadian Journal of Political Science*, 14(1):106-34.

Wriggins, Howard (1960), *Ceylon: Dilemmas of a New Nation*, Princeton University Press, Princeton.

Young, Crawford (1976), *Politics of Cultural Pluralism*, University of Wisconsin Press, Madison.

Yun, Ma Shu (1990), 'Ethnonationalism, Ethnic Nationalism, and Mini-Nationalism, A Comparison of Connor, Smith and Snyder', *Ethnic and Racial Studies*, 13(4):527-41.

Zartman, I. William (1991), 'Preface', *The ANNALS of American Academy of Political & Social Sciences*, 518(November):8-10.

Index